ABDUL RIMDAP

CONFIDENCE IN DIPLOMACY

Defending Nigeria at
Home and Abroad

ABDUL RIMDAP

CONFIDENCE IN DIPLOMACY

Defending Nigeria at Home and Abroad

MEREO
Cirencester

Mereo Books

1A The Wool Market Dyer Street Cirencester Gloucestershire GL7 2PR
An imprint of Memoirs Publishing   www.mereobooks.com

CONFIDENCE IN DIPLOMACY: ISBN: 9781861516886

First published in Great Britain in 2018
by Mereo Books, an imprint of Memoirs Publishing

Copyright ©2018

Abdul Bin Rimdap has asserted his right under the Copyright Designs and Patents Act 1988 to be identified as the author of this work.

A CIP catalogue record for this book is available from the British Library.

This book is sold subject to the condition that it shall not by way of trade or otherwise be lent, resold, hired out or otherwise circulated without the publisher's prior consent in any form of binding or cover, other than that in which it is published and without a similar condition, including this condition being imposed on the subsequent purchaser.

The address for Memoirs Publishing Group Limited can be found at
www.memoirspublishing.com

The Memoirs Publishing Group Ltd Reg. No. 7834348

The Memoirs Publishing Group supports both The Forest Stewardship Council® (FSC®) and the PEFC® leading international forest-certification organisations. Our books carrying both the FSC label and the PEFC® and are printed on FSC®-certified paper. FSC® is the only forest-certification scheme supported by the leading environmental organisations including Greenpeace. Our paper procurement policy can be found at www.memoirspublishing.com/environment

Typeset in 12/18pt Century Schoolbook
by Wiltshire Associates Publisher Services Ltd. Printed and bound in Great Britain by Biddles Books

DEDICATION

For my beloved son, Ibrahim Nanpon Rimdap, who passed away suddenly on April 18, 2017. We love you, but Allah loves you more. Also for my colleagues with whom we navigated the Service together both at home and abroad who are no longer with us today. I love you all.

CONTENTS

List of acronyms
Introduction

CHAPTER 1: Joining the Foreign Service — 1

CHAPTER 2: Addis Ababa: New Flowers — 15
Nigerians in Ethiopia
Nigeria-Ethiopian Bilateral Relations
Developments at the ECA and the OAU
The Umaru Dikko Affair and the Addis Ababa Mission
Airlifts of Ethiopian Jews to Israel

CHAPTER 3: Brussels: Cock Fighting Arena of Europe — 44
Nigeria and the Lomé Conventions
ACP-EEC Joint Parliamentary Assembly
An Encounter with a Nigerian Businessman.
Record keeping at Headquarters in Lagos
Nigerians in Belgium

CHAPTER 4: Planning Nigerian Foreign Policy — 70
Nigeria and the Liberian Crisis
The Bakassi Peninsula Crisis between Nigeria and Cameroon
Southern Africa in Transition
The Closure of some Missions Abroad

CHAPTER 5: Geneva: Multilateral Diplomacy — 91
Eighth UN Conference on Trade and Development
The General Agreement on Tariffs and Trade
The Second World Conference on Human Rights
The Annulled Presidential Election of June 12
Ken Saro-Wiwa: Ogoni Bill of Rights at the UN
The Liberian Ceasefire Agreement in Geneva
Meeting with the South African Delegation
The African Group in Geneva
The UN Committee on the Rights to Development

CHAPTER 6: Diplomacy by a Pariah State — 137
Attempted Military Coup against General Sani Abacha
The Execution of Ken Saro-Wiwa and eight Others
Allegations of Human Rights Violations in Nigeria
Fourth World Conference on Women: Beijing China
Nigeria at the UN Human Rights Commission
The Death of General Sani Abacha

CHAPTER 7:	**Karachi: Consular Diplomacy**	177
	Duties of A Consular Post	
	Trade Faire of Military Armaments in Karachi	
	Agha Khan University Teaching Hospitals	
CHAPTER 8:	**Lusaka: Zambia Shall Be Free**	190
	Economic and Tourists Sites in Zambia	
	Diplomatic Problems with Departure from Zambia	
CHAPTER 9:	**Vienna: Sounds of Music**	203
	Organisation of Petroleum Exporting Countries	
	Nigeria and the International Atomic Energy Agency	
	Iran Nuclear Enrichment Programme	
	United Nations Industrial Development Organisation	
	Comprehensive Nuclear Test Ban Treaty Organisation	
	Committee on the Peaceful Uses of Outer Space	
	UN Convention against Corruption	
	The Nigerian Community in Austria	
CHAPTER 10:	**Incidents at the International Organisation Department, Abuja**	242
	Nigeria and the Organisation for Islamic Conference	
	Problem at the International Seabed Authority	
	Nigeria and the UN Counter Terrorism Committee	
	Benin-Nigeria-Togo Co-Prosperity Alliance Zone	
	Africa-South American Summit	
	Official Visit to the State of Israel	
	Reforms of the Ministry of Foreign Affairs	
CHAPTER 11:	**Nigeria's Quest for a Permanent Seat in the UN Security Council**	273
	The Ezulwini Consensus on UN Reforms	
	The Question of the Veto Power at the UNSC	
	Diplomatic Anecdotes with ambassadors in Abuja	
CHAPTER 12:	**Berlin: These Strange German Ways**	298
	German-African Forums	
	Renewable Energy Organisation	
	Collections of Benin Cultural Artifacts in Berlin	
	German President Köhler's Visit to Nigeria	
	President Yar'Adua's Visits to Germany and his Death	
	The Nigerian Community in Germany	
	Significance of Diplomatic Gifts	
	President Olusegun Obasanjo's visit to Berlin	
CHAPTER 13:	**An Overview of the Nigerian Foreign Service**	339
	Ratifications of Treaties, Conventions and Protocols	
	What is the Work of Diplomats?	
	Letters of commendation	355-357
	Bibliography	359
	INDEX	

LIST OF ACRONYMS

ACP	Africa, Caribbean, Pacific
ACP-EU	Africa, Caribbean, Pacific and European Union
ADC	Aide de Camp
AFRC	Armed Forces Ruling Council
ANC	Africa National Congress
ASAS	Africa South America Summit
AU	African Union
BASA	Bilateral Air Services Agreement
CAC	Corporate Affairs Commission
CAR	Central African Republic
CD	Conference on Disarmament
CEDAW	Convention on the Elimination of Discrimination against Women
CERD	Convention on Elimination of Racial Discrimination
CMAG	Commonwealth Ministerial Action Group
CHOGM	Commonwealth Heads of Government Meeting
CLO	Civil Liberty Organisation
COMESA	Common Market for Eastern and Southern Africa
COPAZ	Co-Prosperity Alliance Zone
COPUOS	Committee on the Peaceful Uses of Outer Space
CRC	Convention on the Rights of the Child
CTBT	Comprehensive Nuclear-Test-Ban Treaty
CTBTO	Comprehensive Nuclear-Test-Ban Treaty Organisation
DCM	Deputy Chief of Mission
DRC	Democratic Republic of Congo
CWC	Chemical Weapons Convention
ECA	Economic Commission for Africa
ECOMOG	Economic Monitoring Group
ECOSOC	Economic and Social Council
ECOWAS	Economic Community of West African States
EFCC	Economic and Financial Crime Commission
FEC	Federal Executive Council
FCSC	Federal Civil Service Commission

FUND	First United Nations Division
GATT	General Agreement on Tariffs and Trade
GNI	Gross National Income
GSTP	Generalised System of Trade Preferences
G-77	Group of Seventy-Seven
HMFA	Honourable Minister of Foreign Affairs
IAEA	International Atomic Energy Agency
ICCI	Islamic Chamber of Commerce and Industries
ICCPR	International Covenant on Civil and Political Rights
ICESCR	International Covenant on Economic, Social and Cultural Rights
ICJ	International Court of Justice
ICPC	Independent Corrupt Practices and other Allied Offences Commission
IECD	International Economic Co-operation Department
IGNU	Interim Government of National Unity
ING	Interim National Government
INPFL	Independent National Patriotic Front of Liberia
IOD	International Organisations Department
IPU	Inter-Parliamentary Union
ISBA	International Seabed Authority
ISS	Institute of Social Studies
JCA	Joint Consultative Assembly
LNTG	Liberian National Transitional Government
MAN	Manufacturers' Association of Nigeria
MDAs	Ministries, Departments and Agencies
MDGs	Millennium Development Goals
MFA	Ministry of Foreign Affairs
MICA	Ministry of Integration and Cooperation in Africa
MISTC	Military Internal Security Task Force
MOSOP	Movement for the Survival of the Ogoni People
NACCIMA	Nigerian Association of Commerce, Industries, Mines and Agriculture
NADECO	National Democratic Coalition
NAM	Non-Aligned Movement
NANCA	National Association of Nigerian Community in Austria
NASA	National Aeronautics and Space Administration
NASRDA	National Space Research and Development Agency

NATO	Northern Atlantic Treaty Organisation
NCG	Nigerian Community Germany
NEPAD	New Partnership for Africa's Development
NGOs	Non-Governmental Organisations
NIA	National Intelligent Agency
NIIA	Nigerian Institute for International Affairs
NIPSS	Nigerian Institute for Policy and Strategic Studies
NNPC	Nigerian National Petroleum Corporation
NNRA	Nigerian Nuclear Regulatory Authority
NPFL	National Patriotic Front of Liberia
NPT	Nuclear Proliferation Treaty
NTA	Nigerian Television Authority
NNWS	Non-Nuclear Weapons States
NUFIC	Netherlands University Foundation for International Cooperation
NYSC	National Youth Service Corps
OAU	Organisation of African Unity
ODA	Overseas Development Assistance
OIC	Organisation for Islamic Conference
OPEC	Organisation of Petroleum Exporting Countries
PAC	Presidential Advisory Council
PPC	Policy Planning Committee
PRC	Provisional Ruling Council
PRS	Policy, Research and Statistics
PTS	Provisional Technical Secretariat
SADC	Southern African Development Community
SADR	Sahrawi Arab Democratic Republic
SCOP	State Chief of Protocol
TAC	Technical Aid Corps
UAE	United Arab Emirates
UDI	Unilateral Declaration of Independence
ULIMO-K	United Liberation Movement for Democracy in Liberia
UNCED	United Nations Conference on Environment and Development
UNDP	United Nations Development Programme
UNCTAD	United Nations Conference on Trade and Development
UNECA	United Nations Economic Commission for Africa
UNEP	United Nations Environmental Programme

UNESCO	United Nations Educational, Scientific and Cultural Organisation
UNGA	United Nations General Assembly
UNHRC	United Nations Human Rights Council
UNICITRAL	United Nations Commission on International Trade Law
UNIDO	United Nations Industrial Development Organisation
UNFCCC	United Nations Framework Convention on Climate Change
UNODC	United Nations Office of Drugs and Crime
UNPO	Unrepresented Nations and Peoples Organisation
UNSC	United Nations Security Council
VOA	Voice of America
WEOG	Western Europe and Other Groups
WTO	World Trade Organisation
YEAA	Youth Earnestly Asked for Abacha

INTRODUCTION

―――∽∝∽―――

"Be polite; write diplomatically; even in a declaration of war one observes the rules of politeness".

Otto von Bismarck (1815-1898)

I never intended to join the Foreign Service after graduating from Ahmadu Bello University, Zaria in 1974 and after the compulsory National Youth Service Corps (NYSC) for all graduates under the age of thirty years. Our set of graduates was the second set of the NYSC scheme introduced by the Head of State, General Yakubu Gowon, after the Nigerian civil war, when I spent one year at Uli Boys' High School in the Ihiala Division of East Central State. Uli was an historical town in the Nigerian-Biafran civil war between 1967-70, as it served as an important airstrip for the Biafran war efforts. In fact, some of the tanks used for aviation fuel during the civil war were the ones used to store rainwater for the schools and the public for water supply in the town. It was the capture of this town and its airstrip by the Nigerian Army that ended the Biafran struggle in 1970.

To get to that position of being a participant in the NYSC was itself a long struggle in my life, because I went to school by accident; none of my senior brothers and sisters, numbering over twenty, did so. I was a village boy, herding cattle, sheep and goats, which were the symbol of wealth for those who owned them, including my father, who owned large herds of cattle. I did not grow up with my father but with my maternal uncles, for whom I was herding animals at Dorowa village in the present-day Langtang South Local Government Area of Plateau State. It was part of Lowland Division, comprising Langtang, Wase and Shendam Districts with headquarters at Shendam. I used to graze the animals near the school premises and took time to sneak over to watch the children learn the alphabet as well as numbers, and we rehearsed with those who went to school in the evenings.

It was while I was peeping through the windows that Mallam Stephen Kumzhi, the headmaster of the school, invited me to see him at home after school. He was attracted by an incident when I raised my hand from the window to correctly answer a question he posed to the class which they could not answer. He examined my eligibility to go to school by asking me to raise my hands over my head to see if my fingers could touch my opposite ears, which was the criterion for enrolment in school at that time. I passed that test, and was enrolled at the Dorowa Native Authority junior primary school in January 1958.

At the end of the third year I was invited to join the fourth class to take the competitive examinations to the senior primary school at Shendam, which was the only Native Authority senior primary school in the Lowland Division of Plateau Province. We were the pioneer students of that school at senior level as previously, students were going to the senior primary school at Pankshin. All other senior primary schools in the area were Christian missionary schools. One of my schoolmates was Jonah Domfa Wuyep, who later rose to become the Chief of the Nigerian Airforce.

The school at Shendam, which was also a native educational institution, introduced school fees at seven shillings per term, but it was not easy for me to pay. I had to trek for two days each both ways to get the money from my cattle-rearing father at Langtang. After Nigeria gained independence from the United Kingdom in 1960, Lowland Division was split into three Native Authorities, Shendam, Wase and Yergam, and Resettlement. As a result of this split I had to move to the Sudan United Missionary primary school at Langtang for one year before I went to the Teachers' Training College in Gindiri in 1965. Gindiri had three Christian Missionary colleges which were among the best in Northern Nigeria. Going to Gindiri was not my choice but that of my father, who forced me out of the Nigerian Military School at Zaria by claiming that teachers' college was better than what he called "hagu- dama" (that is "left-right, left-right"). But his decision was not well-conceived, because the former was free education while the latter was fee-paying, which he was not ready to shoulder. I muddled through, with lots of difficulties, nevertheless.

Most of the teachers at the College in Gindiri were European missionaries and were very sympathetic to the indigent students like me who had difficulty in paying their school fees. As a result, they arranged for us a scheme of washing up dishes and cleaning the kitchen after every meal to offset parts of our school fees instead of hiring outside workers to do it. That was how I was able to pay for my school fees, with some difficulty.

I met very stiff competition from three students from Kwara state, namely Daniel Dansoho Abutu, Solomon Ajiboye and Emmanuel Ocholi Attah, who were competing with me for the first position in the termly examinations. The competition between the four of us for first position in the class in term tests and examinations was fierce, and we graduated with distinction in all the subjects and were consequently admitted into the Ahmadu Bello University School of Basic Studies in 1970. Solomon Ajiboye and I later transferred to a degree course in Social Sciences, because we did the Cambridge University General Certificate Examinations (GCE) Advanced Level by correspondence.

Our fierce competition in class did not translate to our personal relationships, as it was Solomon who introduced me to this idea. We all rose to high positions in government, as Daniel became the President of the Federal Court of Appeal, while Emmanuel Ocholi Attah and Solomon Ajiboye became CEOs of merchant banks in Nigeria and I rose to become an ambassador or high commissioner in three important posts in the Foreign Service. From the information made available to me, the record we set in that college in 1969 has not yet been broken by any single set of students until today. It was due to the healthy competition between the four of us, and achieved the admiration of our teachers and the envy of our classmates.

These memoirs were written from recollections of most of the events narrated here and not from any well-kept diaries. In doing so I owe a debt of gratitude to many people without whom I could not have seen this book to fruition. I mention only a few of those who gave me their time to read the manuscript and made valuable contributions. Chief among them are Ambassador Enny Onobu, Dr Uchenna Cyril Gwam and Chris Newton of my publishers Mereo Books, who painstakingly edited and checked the text and offered valuable advice. Halimatu, my spouse, offered her valuable time while, Ishaq, Yusuf, Abdallah and Ramallan, my children, arranged the pictures and set up the whole text.

Whatever errors of fact or judgement remain in the book are solely my own responsibility.

Abdul Bin Rimdap

August 2018

CHAPTER 1

ENTRY INTO THE FOREIGN SERVICE

"A diplomat's life is made up of three ingredients: protocol, Geritol and alcohol"

Adlai E. Stevenson (1900-1965)

My first encounter with the Foreign Service was through a junior colleague, Frederick Durlong, son of Ambassador Ignatius Durlong, with whom I worked at the Ministry of Finance and Economic Planning department in the Plateau State Civil Service from 1975 to 1981. There was also an Indian, Dr. Nakra, the UNDP Economic Adviser to the Plateau State Government, who encouraged me to travel abroad on the scholarships provided by the Netherlands University Foundation for International Co-operation (NUFIC) as well as the United Nations Development Program (UNDP). The former sponsored me for the Postgraduate Diploma in Development Policy and Economic

Planning at the Institute for Social Studies (ISS) in The Hague and the latter for the postgraduate Master's Degree in International Economics at the University of Wales in Swansea.

While in The Hague and the University College Swansea, I came across students from many countries in Asia, Latin America, Africa, Middle East and Western Europe. One of them, the late Hillary Zinniel (later ambassador to Yugoslavia) from the Ghanaian foreign service, was my roommate, and he made me develop an interest in the foreign service. One good friend of mine and schoolmate in The Hague, who encouraged me in world affairs, was Kanayo Esinulo, who has today become a versatile journalist in Nigeria. But I was not totally convinced that I could make a career in the foreign service when I noticed that many indigents of Plateau State who held high positions in the foreign service were returning to the state in droves. They were Sulaiman Yero Wase, John Wash Pam and Adamu Adiwu, as well as HB Kolo from Niger State, all of whom left the foreign service and became permanent secretaries in the Plateau civil service, so there was no reason for me to leave the known to the unknown, especially with so many obstacles on the way.

On my return from the UK with a Masters' degree in Economics, I learned that the Plateau State government had made a move to encourage its citizens to join the Federal civil service in Lagos, but many of them declined and preferred to remain in the state. The decision to encourage transfer of officers to the Federal service was because Plateau State had very few of its citizens at the federal level, apart from the military and police services. I was encouraged by Dr. Jefferson S Mamven, the head of service, to leave. But as I indicated interest, there was resistance because I must fulfil my bond of scholarship before I left. Luckily for me, Plateau State was represented at the Federal Civil Service Commission in the person of Bagudu Mutlam Hirse (who later became Ambassador and Minister of State Foreign Affairs). Bagudu Hirse encouraged me to join the Foreign Service because there was a vacancy and at that time there were only a handful of Plateau State indigenes in the Service, namely Ezekiel Dimka, Binfa Selchum, M. Laminu Abubakar, Agwom G. Gotip, Joseph Chuwang Deme, Camillus Damulak, Ignatius Longjang, Mallam Ibrahim Garba Abbas and Danjuma Dombin. The first three became ambassadors in the Service. The next two died in the service, while the others were in the administrative and technical cadre of the Service.

It did not take more than six months after I made the move before my application for transfer was approved by the Federal Civil Service Commission (FCSC) and I left the Plateau State Civil Service without completing my two years of scholarship bond. But it was not a smooth ride from the state service to the federal service, as I faced two formidable problems. Firstly, there were insinuations that I would be victimized by the majority ethnic groups from the southern part of Nigeria namely, Yorubas and Igbos, especially since I come from one of the smallest ethnic groups in Nigeria, which is however relatively well represented in the military. The Taroh ethnic group of Langtang in Plateau state comprises about 450,000 people out of a population of over 170 million people in Nigeria, so it is really a tiny group. The members of this ethnic group are often highly educated and hold important positions, including the state Governor, Solomon Daushep Lar at that time. At one time it had five of its sons in the Armed Forces Ruling Council (AFRC), the Chief of Defence Staff, State Governors, Ministers, Chief of the Air Staff, Minister of External Affairs (Major-General Joseph Nanven Garba) and many directors at state level. They were referred to as the "Langtang Mafia" by the media, due to the role they played during the coups d'état of that year and in the recent past. Incidentally, and true to these perceptions, it was two of their sons, Major-Generals Joseph Nanven Garba and Joshua Dogonyaro, who made the radio announcements during the coups d'état of 1975 and 1983 which toppled General Yakubu Gowon and Major-General Muhammadu Buhari from power respectively.

The other problem I faced by moving from Jos was accommodation for me in Lagos, which was the most problematic. At the Jos end, the Plateau State Government allowed me free accommodation, while at the Lagos end the Ministry of External Affairs (MEA), through the kindness of Ambassador Blessing Akporode Clark, approved hotel accommodation for me for twelve months. I could not believe how kind he was, as he had just returned to headquarters from serving as Permanent Representative of Nigeria to the UN in New York. He was one of the five Directors-General in the MEA, which was equivalent to permanent secretaries in one ministry. Others were ambassadors George Dove-Edwin, Olujimi Jolaoso, Uthman Yolah and Ignatius C. Olisemeka. Ambassador Clark was the Director-General (Service Matters). I never met him before and I did not have the courage to visit him to express my appreciation for this kind gesture to me until he phoned me thirty years later, when I was the ambassador in Berlin. He phoned me seeking assistance for his nephew who was stranded in Germany and needed a passport, and I had that rare opportunity to tell him this story and convey my appreciation for his kindness to me, because other officers in my category did not have the same treatment as they were forced out of the hotel after three or six months, except those returning from being posted abroad.

I spent the twelve months at a hotel in Surulere in the suburb of mainland Lagos. It was an interesting area of the city that makes one love or hate Lagos due to the traffic. Our driver and most of the hotel workers were illegal immigrants from Ghana, for the obvious reason that they were readily available as cheap labour. That was before the "Ghana must go" episode of 1984 when illegal immigrants, mostly Ghanaians, were expelled from Nigeria with untold human rights violations, an act which was condemned by the international community.

I was deployed to the International Economic Cooperation Department (IECD), since I studied economics. The MEA had just been engulfed by fire at its headquarters on Marina Street the previous year and was relocated to temporary accommodation at the Nigeria Electricity Power Authority (NEPA) building on Awolowo Road, Ikoyi. I was already on a higher salary scale, as principal planning officer in my former job in Plateau state, than the peers with whom I graduated in 1974. The only classmates of mine who joined the Foreign Service directly from our University were Akatu "Washington" Ella, Fate Abubakar and Suleiman Dahiru. Enny Onobu was also our colleague; he graduated a year earlier but stayed back at the university after his NYSC to obtain a Master's Degree before starting his foreign service career with us.

The Economic Department was headed by a highly-experienced director and a deputy director in the persons of ambassadors Ade-Adekuoye and Olufemi Ani, both Yoruba, and I was warned they would victimize me in the Service. But that was not the case. On the contrary, both gave me the kind of training I would never get if I had remained in Plateau State. I met some young officers, including Uchenna Cyril Gwam and Olabode Adekeye, with whom I later worked together at our missions abroad.

I expected a kind of training in the field of diplomacy and international relations such as protocol, mode of dressing, etiquette, use of language, negotiation and public speaking before I settled down in the department, but that did not happen. However, Ambassador Ade-Adekuoye was a teacher *par excellence*, as he devoted much of his time to putting me through the art of diplomacy. Most of the economic theories were put to practical use in the Department in most issues, whether bilateral or multilateral diplomacy. There was always reference to the Keynesian theory of supply and demand on topical issues referred to us in the department. He told me that I should learn diplomacy by doing it or training on the job, since the chances of going for training in an institution outside the Ministry were remote. Moreover, I was already a middle-level officer, so there was no point in worrying myself about formal training. But he was wrong, as the effect of lack of formal training in other areas of the job, or deployment to other departments before my first posting abroad, manifested in later years in the Service.

As mentioned by Femi George in his book "From Rookie to Mandarin: The Memoirs of a Second-Generation Diplomat" and by Adlai E. Stevenson, an important aspect of diplomacy is protocol, without which it is not complete. In his book "Ever the Diplomat" Ambassador Sherard Cowper-Coles of the UK Foreign Service enumerated a number of ingredients to successful diplomatic entertainment: "guests should enjoy the function; guests are among the people they want to be with; mixing people up intelligently; couples should never be seated together or even on the same table; use of round tables is better than single long ones; good food and good wine". But I missed this training in my entire diplomatic career with near mishaps as I grew up in the service, and I had to muddle through them, as will be seen in subsequent chapters.

Ambassador Adekuoye also taught me one thing that lived with me throughout my Service years, and that was that I should never meddle with government resources under my custody. He warned that that would be the first offence that would tarnish my name and they would send me packing out of the Foreign Service.

My main schedule of duties was on Nigerian economy, aid to African and Caribbean countries, issues connected to the oil and gas industries, the Nigerian National Petroleum Corporation (NNPC), technical assistance to and from Nigeria and coordination with relevant economic ministries and departments such as National Planning, Commerce and Industries, Finance and the Central Bank as well as the Federal Office of Statistics. My desk was inundated with requests for technical assistance from many African countries. Two such requests are worth mentioning. The first was from Equatorial Guinea and was hand-delivered by a delegation from that country accompanied by the Ambassador, Navy Captain Festus Porbeni. They sent a long list of items they wanted Nigeria to provide for them, which included vehicles and spare parts, security, road construction and maintenance, feeding school children, clothing, milk, shelter and toilet paper etc. It was a laughable request, because some of these items were not freely available to Nigerian citizens and I wondered how we could provide them to our poor neighbour at our southern border.

My boss directed me to see my colleagues in the Inter African Affairs Division as well as the East and Central African Affairs to discuss the best options to recommend. While we saw no reasons why Nigeria should splash out cash to Equatorial Guinea to meet her requests, due to the strategic security considerations it was decided that Nigeria should provide Equatorial Guinea with all her requests in one form or the other. The main argument was that the apartheid South Africa was using Malabo as a base for their aircraft, with security implications for Nigeria and other African countries. It was therefore a matter of necessity to woo Equatorial Guinea away from South Africa to lean towards Nigeria.

The second request for assistance was from the Central African Republic (CAR). Ambassador Gabriel Falase arrived home for consultations with a long list of requests for technical and financial assistance from his host government. The list included, among others, the supply of refined petroleum, gas, Peugeot cars and easing of border transportation from Maiduguri to Bangui, the capital of CAR. As with the request from Equatorial Guinea, the question of strategic security overrode any other considerations. We recommended that we should buy the cars from the Peugeot Automobile Assembly plant of Nigerian (PAN) in Kaduna and send them to them instead of giving them the money to buy from France.

I left the Department on being posted abroad before Professor Bolaji Akinyemi was appointed foreign minister, and he rightly dispensed with these kinds of requests by the establishment of the Technical Aid Corps volunteer scheme (TAC). I commend him for this initiative, which fulfilled one of our cardinal objectives, technical assistance to needy countries in Africa, the Caribbean and the Pacific. It is an irony that Equatorial Guinea, which was one of the poorest countries in our backyard, is today one of the wealthiest countries in Africa, with the discovery of oil, which they could not manage well. A book by Robert Klitgaard entitled "Tropical Gangsters" depicting the development of that country before the discovery of oil and its inability to manage the resources is a good read.

My desk was also instrumental to one high level international appointment, that of Yusuf Seyyid Abdulai as the Director General of the Organisation of Petroleum Exporting Countries (OPEC) Fund for Technical Cooperation. He was the Director General of the Federal Mortgage Bank, and had just returned from the World Bank. He was an intelligent, articulate and hard-working man with incredible credentials and experience. My job was to send a "note verbale" accompanied by his credentials to all OPEC member countries through their missions in Lagos and forward some to our missions in those countries soliciting for their support. The reactions were positive and Dr Abdulai was elected Director General of the OPEC Fund in 1982.

Soon after that appointment, I travelled to Vienna for an OPEC investment meeting. Jonathan Kabo Umar, Nigeria's ambassador in Vienna, hosted us and it was a happy moment for me to meet Dr Abdulai. He was still the Director General when I assumed duties as Nigeria's ambassador to Austria and Permanent Representative of Nigeria to UN offices in Vienna twenty year later. He is a man of high quality, style and taste well suited for the organisation and he assisted me greatly to settle down in Vienna. Ambassador Umar allowed me to stay with him at the Residence, a splendid building located in the highbrow 19 District of Vienna at Krapfenwaldgasse. It is surrounded by vineyards and drinking places, and famous with tourists and visitors to Vienna. I took residence in the same building as Nigeria's ambassador and always saw the small room in the reception hall where I stayed twenty years earlier with nostalgia.

I spent only one year at the Ministry of External Affairs headquarters and in the same International Economic-Cooperation department without moving to any other desks and was embedded with work, some of which took me outside the MEA. I went on a one-month annual leave and upon return I found a posting order sending me to Conakry, Republic of Guinea, with the directive to leave immediately. I was surprised with that posting because I expected some form of training in the art of diplomacy, including French, since that is the official language of the Republic of Guinea.

However, I thought that posting was to enable me to learn the French language, which I started at the Ahmadu Bello University's School of Basic Studies, but I opted out in favour of mathematics, which I found much easier than the French language. I was told that it was a regular posting since I had entered the Service as a middle-level officer and my one year at headquarters qualified me to serve abroad. I was posted to replace a colleague who was cross-posted to Caracas, Venezuela. But Ambassador Ade-Adekuoye, my boss, was not happy with the posting and told me that he was going to stop it and would recommend that I went to a multilateral post to man the economic desk and write economic reports. He said that posting me to Conakry was a waste of manpower and skill. He referred me to Pius I. Ayewoh, the Deputy Director (Administration), who told me that there was no vacancy at any multilateral post but advised that I should proceed to Conakry with the assurance that once a vacancy was opened at a multilateral post I would be cross posted. Pius Ayewoh even offered me Tokyo, Japan, with huge economic opportunities that offered me lots of work on the economic desk, but I was not very keen on going too far from Nigeria and besides that I would not be able to learn any foreign language other than Japanese, which was not a UN language. I did not mind going to Conakry, as I would learn the French language, and moreover the long stay in the hotel in Lagos with my wife and three children had become unbearable. But as I prepared to leave, my colleague in Conakry, Mr Oworu, whom I was to replace, seemed to have enjoyed his posting and used his close connections with the Guinean President, Ahmed Sekou Touré, to lobby for his continued stay in that country. President Sekou Touré called President Shehu Shagari to stop our movements. The officer was known to be more accessible to the host president than Ambassador Musa Bello. It infuriated the Ambassador and the MEA that a low-level officer would be more accessible to the President of a foreign country than the accredited head of Mission. Consequently, I was directed to still proceed to Conakry and strengthen the mission, and was accompanied by Ahmed Dauro Manzo, who was going on a one-year training attachment.

The departure of officers to postings abroad was usually a happy moment due to the harsh realities of Lagos life and traffic, and in my own case the long stay in a hotel was an added problem. But Conakry had its own difficulties, which were even worse than Lagos. We had to transport virtually everything we would need from Lagos to Conakry, including food. The idea of leaving my wife and children in Lagos was ruled out due to lack of accommodation, so we had to leave together.

We were booked to travel on the twice-weekly Nigerian Airways flights. Then, after checking in and waiting to board the flight, a protocol officer from the MEA told me that my posting to Conakry was cancelled and that I should return to the ministry. This action of stopping officers at the airport from proceeding to postings abroad became common in the service in later years, for different reasons from mine. I later learned that my colleague in Conakry objected to the idea of sharing his schedules of duties with another officer of his rank, even though we had never met. He lodged a complaint with President Sekou Touré, who told President Shehu Shagari to cancel my posting. That development was strange to me, because we were so junior in the service, yet heads of state were deciding our movements on a minor issue of posting. This incident later led to the retirement of my colleague from the Service during the mass purge of officers in 1984.

I returned and settled down at my desk in the Economic department, and then, towards the end of November 1983, a vacancy was made available in Addis Ababa, Ethiopia through the demise of an officer who was posted there, and it was one of those missions being sought out for me.

During my year at MEA, without any formal diplomatic training, I nevertheless interacted very well with Nigerian officials relating to my desk, particularly NNPC officials. Chief among them were Ogbuefi Nwokedi and Aret Adams (now late) who later rose to high positions in the oil and gas sectors in the Corporation. The former was the Director of Media and Publicity of the NNPC and the latter the Group Managing Director of the Corporation. I was also involved in verifying status reports on companies doing business in Nigeria and abroad through the assistance of relevant home ministries and departments, as well as liaison with missions abroad. There were a few cases of advanced free fraud scams (now known as 419). I recall one status request made by a Nigerian in the Cayman Islands. My boss asked me to locate the place on a world map and wondered what kind of business the Nigerian was doing over there. I never forgot that incident, and in subsequent years the Cayman Islands became a household name to me.

Two weeks before I left Lagos for Addis Ababa, I was advised to read the various economic and political reports written by my colleagues to familiarize myself with the kind of work expected of me when I arrived in post. I also read the Ambassador's dispatches as well as the Annual Reports and Post Reports, which give detailed information about the country, its history, climate, government among other important issues of interest to Nigeria. There was also the issue of the "Station Charter" which gives detail of the issues one should pursue at each post for the benefit of Nigeria, but that was limited to the Heads of Mission. In any case I had no idea of this until later, when I served in the Policy Planning Department on my return from the posting.

Of the three reports mentioned above, the one that is most misunderstood is the Ambassador's dispatches to his/her foreign minister in the sending state. The traditional diplomatic dispatches are usually confined to one subject matter without courtesy phrases, and addressed as "you". In most cases paragraphs are numbered and file reference or references are given. The recipients of copies are listed in the last paragraph. The dispatch opens with "Sir or Madam", and in many cases, it usually ends with:

I am,
Sir or Madam,
With truth and respect,
Your obedient Servant,
(signed).

CHAPTER 2

ADDIS ABABA: NEW FLOWERS

"One of the first rules of diplomacy is that you shouldn't insult your own country abroad."

Lord Paddy Ashdown

"A diplomat is a person who can tell you to go to hell in such a way that you actually look forward to the trip."

Caskie Stinnett

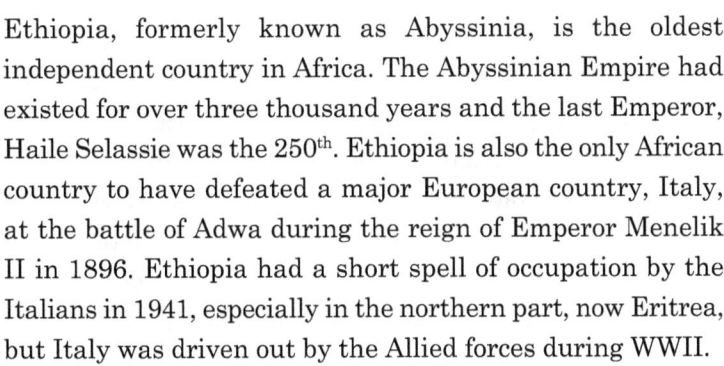

Ethiopia, formerly known as Abyssinia, is the oldest independent country in Africa. The Abyssinian Empire had existed for over three thousand years and the last Emperor, Haile Selassie was the 250th. Ethiopia is also the only African country to have defeated a major European country, Italy, at the battle of Adwa during the reign of Emperor Menelik II in 1896. Ethiopia had a short spell of occupation by the Italians in 1941, especially in the northern part, now Eritrea, but Italy was driven out by the Allied forces during WWII.

The history of modern Ethiopia was dominated by the reign of Emperor Haile Selassie from 1930-1974. Colonel Mengistu Haile Mariam, who ruled the country from 1977-1991, brutally executed the military juntas led by General Tafari Benti that had ruled the country after the execution of Haile Selassie in 1974. Brigadier-General Tafari Benti was the Chairman of the Provisional Military Administrative Council, known as the Derg. After coming into power, Mengistu Haile Mariam embraced the Warsaw Pact countries, USSR and Cuba and maintained a large army, second only to Egypt in Africa. Three major ethnic groups dominated the country, the Oromos, Amharic and Tigrinya. Although Amharic was not the most populous ethnic group, it dominated the landscape politically and economically and imposed its language as the official language in the country. There was resistance from the majority Oromos, which form over 40% of the population, in the south of the country and the less populous Tigrinyans in the north. The two groups founded the Oromo Liberation Front and the Eritrean People's Liberation Front respectively and waged a deadly war in the north and the south of the country against the central government in Addis Ababa. It was widely believed that under the communist government of Mengistu, Ethiopia received the lowest per capita development aid in the world.

We arrived in Addis Ababa in late November 1983 and K.W. Benibo, the Administrative Attaché (now late), received us and lodged us at the Wabishabeele Hotel, one of the very few hotels available to foreigners. Addis Ababa means "new flowers" in the Amharic language. The Addis Ababa Mission had four senior officers, namely Ambassador

Ampin Jimmy Blankson, Godwin Okwuaka, Charles Ononye and me. Olabode Adekeye was on training attachment and Austin Esedebe was the Finance Attaché. There were also two administrative and technical staff and many locally recruited staff.

My schedule was already assigned before I arrived; it was economic desk dealing with economic relations between Nigeria and the Democratic People's Republic of Ethiopia. The other main duty was to cover UN Economic Commission for Africa (UNECA) meetings and conferences.

The Addis Ababa post had lots of challenges, such as lack of public transportation, accommodation and harsh conditions of living. There were shortages of most essential commodities and most diplomats were making orders through catalogues. Since Ethiopia was classified as a hardship post, we had the privilege of holidaying in Kenya at government expense, and used the opportunity to import essential commodities. Public transportation served designated routes, so we might have to change taxis twice or more before going to the office or home. Since most of us arrived at the mission from headquarters and were on our first overseas posting, we faced the same problem of lack of personal cars. The mission arranged a vehicle to transport us to and from the Chancery, but those of us covering meetings at the UNECA and OAU, located in different directions, posed problems of coordination of movement. The other main challenge was accommodation, which was strictly controlled and allocated by the Ethiopian Housing and Rehabilitation Commission. Because I arrived at an odd period and took over from an officer junior to me in rank, I was allocated the only house available to the Embassy of

Nigeria. The house was located opposite the "Kebele" office with only one toilet, even though I had three children. Unsuitable as it was, its location made me learn more about the Ethiopian people and their socialist system. I could watch people lining up for weekly food rations and they also monitored those coming in and going out of my house, so it was a double-edged sword for me.

Many Ethiopians, including my classmate at the Institute of Social Studies (ISS) at The Hague, could not visit me at home for fear of being arrested for interacting with "capitalist" foreigners. But the locals were not deterred, as they thronged in and out without any fear of arrest in search of hot drinks, black coffee and cigarette, which were the most valuable items for them. As they smoked or drank these valuable items they would behave as if they were having both their first and last cigarette or hot drink and were determined to make a show out of them for weeks.

One incident that reverberates in my mind about my service in Addis was when I gave money to a visiting delegation for the ECA conference to buy for me a pair of shoes at the so-called diplomatic shop at the ECA, but he bought me an oversized pair and left before I could try them. Since the shop was not meant for residents including diplomats, there was no way I could return them for refund or replacement, so I decided to wear more than two pairs of socks to fill the gap. Ethiopian tea and coffee were of high quality but were not available for local consumption but exported.

The Nigerian Embassy was located in a large courtyard, where the ambassador's residence was also located. That was the only property owned by Nigeria, as there was a general restriction by the socialist Ethiopia on foreign missions buying houses or land. The land allocated to us for building the Chancery and Residence was one of the biggest areas, like those of the US, UK, Germany, Italy, Soviet Union and Cuba, but our buildings were smaller than their own.

I had barely spent two months there when there was mass purge of officers of the Ministry of External Affairs (MEA) following the coup d'état of 31 December 1983 by General Muhammadu Buhari that ousted President Shehu Shagari. One of the most versatile and hardworking members of the mission Godwin Okwuaka, the Head of Chancery was affected and was recalled to Lagos. His schedules of duties were transferred to me and overburdened me with work. After that purge there were only two Foreign Service officers at the big mission, Charles Ononye and me, because the third officer, Olabode Adekeye, was on training attachment and was being moved from one desk to the other as part of the training exercise.

Nigerians in Ethiopia

There were two categories of Nigerians in Ethiopia, namely those classified as unskilled and illegal immigrants, and skilled workers at the two regional organisations, namely the Economic Commission of Africa (ECA) and the Organisation for African Unity (OAU). The other category of Nigerians had unique challenges due to their activities, which we managed without much difficulty with the host country. In fact, most of them had been integrated into Ethiopian society and were hardly noticeable as they no longer spoke any of the Nigerian languages. However, we maintained a long list of people with roots in Nigeria which was kept at the mission and meant to prevent forced conscription by the Ethiopian government for the civil wars in the country. They were mostly those Nigerians who went to Makkah by road and later settled in Ethiopia and lost their Nigerian identity but continued to claim it when the need arose. They were like those people of Nigerian origin in the Sudan, estimated to be millions in number. Other Nigerians were involved in the Sudanese civil wars and at times appeared in the embassy seeking assistance. I had an interesting discussion with one who was fighting on the side of John Garang against the Arab Sudanese in Khartoum. He claimed to have been recruited from Nigeria into the SPLA army at a price, so he was a mercenary, but he refused to be so classified.

One morning A.K.W. Benibo rushed into my office screaming, with a file titled "STOP LIST", and asked me to remove a document to indicate that the mission did not receive the message. His fear was that the document would implicate him for hastily rendering assistance to a known scam kingpin, which was against a headquarters directive for missions not to do so. The man was on a stop list, but without a proper check the Administration Attaché had issued him a letter for arranging a sham marriage with an Ethiopian woman. The person in question had duped Nigerians in two of our missions in Asia and the Caribbean. Unknown to Benibo he had issued him the letter, and by so doing had violated headquarters directives, which was a great offence. In the euphoria of the retirement of officers in the MEA, he believed that if urgent action was not taken to stop the man his job would be on the line.

I decided to woo the man back into the Embassy with the letter, saying I needed to put the seal of the mission on it or it would be invalid. The man reluctantly agreed. As soon as he entered my office, Benibo locked the door and grabbed the letter from him. The man left fuming with anger that we had refused to render common assistance to him, and saying the Nigerian embassy had deprived him of the marriage he was arranging. The man was dropping names of highly influential Nigerians, saying he would call them to deal with us, but we were not deterred with that threat since we had directives from headquarters. We learned that before he left Addis Ababa he took away all the musical instruments belonging to his host at the ECA, a fellow Nigerian from his state of Cross Rivers, and sold them off cheaply. That was my first encounter with scam, fraud and deceit by a few Nigerians, which metamorphosed into big business with damaging effects to the image of our country. In later years I was confronted by large-scale scams which Nigerian diplomats had to manage and correct with much difficulty. There were also several cases of non-Nigerians arriving with Nigerian passports travelling to Saudi Arabia en route to Addis Ababa and running into trouble requiring our assistance, but they would deny being Nigerians even though they were holding our passports. A case in point was that of a Chadian pilgrim holding a Nigerian passport on her way to Makkah through Addis Ababa. The child died on board the Ethiopian Airline plane, and we were contacted to handle the problem and pay possible compensation to the family. Benibo, the Administration Attaché and I went to see them at the morgue, where we found that they were not Nigerians but Chadians holding Nigerian passports.

There was a similar case in my next post where a Ghanaian holding Nigerian passport died in Brussels and the family refused to avail themselves of our assistance. They avoided being called Nigerians even though they were holding our passports. These incidences were rampant and made us question whether the possession of a passport obtained illegally confers nationality to the owner. We believe it was an issue which had not been thought through by whoever was behind the illegal documents in the face of international law and jurisprudence. But the fact remains that a document obtained illegally renders itself null and void in the court of law. That was why we turned down most of those who obtained Nigerian passports fraudulently. But these experiences were drops in the ocean in my later years in the service as I was confronted with much more difficult situations that will unfold in subsequent chapters in this book. What an irony of life that Nigerian nationals, in subsequent years, were destroying their passports and even denying their nationality and seeking for asylum due to corruption and bad governance by their leaders.

Nigerian-Ethiopian Bilateral Relations

My work as the Economic desk officer involved monitoring and reporting economic development and cooperation between Nigeria and Ethiopia. But I did not find any items of commercial interest to Nigeria in Ethiopia or from Nigeria to Ethiopia. Apart from solid minerals, oil, handcrafted items like carpets, hides and skins, and coffee and tea, which were not produced in sufficient quantity for both domestic use and export, there was nothing of commercial value between our two countries. Nigerian petroleum products were not exported to that country since they got most of their supplies from North Africa or the Middle East. There was very little commercial or cultural activity between our two countries apart from the aviation sector. Most of the Ethiopian products were exported to the Soviet Union to pay for that country's support and technical assistance and for the armament to wage the deadly war in the north and south of the country.

I was involved in a co-operation and visit arrangement between the Nigerian universities and the University of Asmara, which was still part of Ethiopia. Some university professors were to visit Asmara and I was to accompany them, but unknown to me I needed a special pass to travel from Addis to Asmara, even within the same country, due to the travel restriction beyond 50 kilometres from the capital. After stopping over at Addis Ababa to Asmara the professors could not continue their journey because they did not have the required passes, so their visit ended in Addis Ababa.

There was also a lack of direct telephone contact between Nigeria and Addis Ababa, and any time I had cause to call Nigeria, I used to telephone my nephew, Professor Decent Sheni, in Canada and relay my messages to him and he would in turn call Nigeria and relay it to them. But for official mail, we had the weekly diplomatic bags courier who delivered and received them, in addition to the normal telexes and telegrams as the major means of communication with Lagos. The diplomatic bag days were always the best days for the Embassy as they brought good news from Headquarters, including personal mail from friends as well as daily newspapers, which were the only means of following developments at home.

Despite the deteriorating standards of living in Ethiopia, local food items, mostly *"njara"* and animal products such as meat and milk, were very cheap and affordable. We always bought live animals, instead of buying the meat in kilos. Ethiopia was also a major source of live animals, sheep and goats exported to Libya and Saudi Arabia for *hajj* pilgrimages. In addition to the cheap local food items, I admired three other things in that country that we lacked in Nigeria, namely an efficient telephone system, constant electricity and an efficient national airline. The Ethiopian Airline, which was founded in December 1946, was one of the best in Africa. Although it was state run, it operated with the aim of making profits. It was the only area where we made a bilateral agreement (BASA), between Nigerian Airways, the Nigerian Air Force and the Ethiopian Airline to train and service our planes at their hangar at Bole airport. Nigeria Air Force engineers, air traffic controllers and ground staff received regular training there. BASA favoured Ethiopia as their flights to Lagos were full, but the Nigerian airways was making losses at times, flying empty with our diplomatic bag courier and a few officials attending ECA or OAU meetings.

Ambassador Ampin Jim Blankson, now deceased, was recalled to headquarters on completion of his duties four months after my arrival in post without an immediate replacement. As such the mantle of leadership at the mission fell upon me as Chargé d'Affaires ad interim (ai). I had a much more difficult task on my hands, as I then had to combine the work of the two most senior officers of the embassy, the Ambassador's representational duties and that of the head of Chancery and my own as the Economic Desk officer. Thus, the mission was further depleted, and without an ambassador it became unbearable to cope with the kind of duties in such a mission.

One morning, I accompanied my boss, Ambassador Blankson, to bid farewell to Chairman Mengistu (Ethiopians call their people by their first name) before he left Addis Ababa in April 1984. Instead of wearing Nigerian national dress or at least a dark suit, I wore a cream-coloured suit which I had imported through a Hong Kong tailor for the occasion. Mr Benibo came to pick and dropped me at Mengistu's office and was full of praise for my beautiful suit and tie to match. I sat in the anteroom of Chairman Mengistu waiting for the Ambassador, who arrived in full "baban-riga" and cap to match the Nigerian attire. He shouted at me "Abdul, why are you wearing a suit for this important occasion?" Before I could explain that it was the best and just imported from Hong Kong, he retorted, "go and change your useless made in Bukuru suit, or else you cannot accompany me," and he added "more so a white one for that matter". So I asked him to allow his driver to take me home to change, since my house was not far from that place. I was surprised that he obliged me with the use of the official car and driver, as I had never dreamed of being driven in it and I did so in four embassies in later years, if I include my stint in Karachi as the Consul-General.

Chairman Mengistu received Ambassador Blankson very warmly and he appeared to be in firm control of the

Derg, the ruling junta. He talked of African solidarity and cooperation in tackling humanitarian problems, which was a major problem in Ethiopia at that time due to the civil wars in both the north and south of the country. He presented a gift to the ambassador and said it was from the Ethiopian people.

When we got back to the Chancery, the Ambassador started lecturing me on protocol, including mode of dressing for official diplomatic engagements or functions. He said that unless otherwise stated on the invitation card, one must dress formally. In most cases this is stated on invitation cards, and he produced a few examples to show me. Others stated "smart casual" national dress as was the case with Nigerian national dress, with a cap to match. He said if I had put on a tuxedo or dark suit, he could have tolerated it, but a white or cream suit was out of order. He went on to give me a lecture on protocol terminology such as "dress code", "decorum", "etiquette", "order of precedence", "seating arrangements" and various forms of reception, food, wine and drink and the different glasses. He went further, to lecture me on the superiority of headquarters to those of embassies abroad. He pointed out that any instructions issued from headquarters, even by the most junior officers, were directives to be obeyed by missions without question. He said that such instructions were taken as having emanated from the minister or the President of the country, even if they had no prior knowledge of them. He summed up by saying that all officers at headquarters were regarded as senior to those at post, and as such we must obey their directives unless there was a local objection. In later years, due to errors and unclear directives contained in some such instructions and telegrams, it was decided that junior officers should not send and sign out telegrams to senior officers in post. But the underlying principle that headquarters was the boss was never lost, and has continued to date in our service.

The Ambassador concluded by telling me that I was lucky because he had a soft spot for me, as all the others who had served as his number two had been retired from the Service in the recent exercise. I teased him by saying that he had forgotten to lecture me on cigarettes and cigars, as I had noticed that he and most of his peers made it a duty to hold one even if they were not really smoking it. He smiled and sent me off from his smoky office. That was the only moment I had the chance to know the better side of Ambassador Ampin Jim Blankson.

Addis Ababa was my first posting abroad and I expected the Ambassador to put us through the gamut of diplomacy, but he did not, although he attempted to do so belatedly with protocol issues. Instead he was unreachable and intimidating and did not allow us to learn and interact freely with others around us, even at the ECA and the OAU. He instructed me never to make statements or interventions at the ECA without his prior knowledge, even within the meetings of counsellors. I was unhappy with my work under such pressure and kept mute at all meetings even though I could have made meaningful contributions to the debates. At a reception organised for Professor Ibrahim Gambari, the Ambassador literally locked us up in his kitchen, telling us never to come out. But when the Minister could not see me at the reception to do an errand for him, his Special Assistant, Dr. Orobola Fasehun, who was the same rank with me, came into the kitchen fuming with anger and asked "Abdul, what are you doing in the kitchen? The Foreign Minister is looking for you".

A similar thing happened at the Addis Ababa Hilton hotel, where the Ambassador could not believe it when he saw me coming out of the Minister's inner bedroom suite counting money to go out to town to buy Ethiopian dresses for him as well as give alms to the poor at the mosque. Despite all this the Ambassador was a pleasant fellow, but he kept us at bay without any motivation to learn as I did with those before and after him at headquarters and at subsequent posts.

I have mentioned this to bring home some of the mean and nasty treatment of the Nigerian Foreign Service which some senior officers exhibited to their juniors for no reason other than to show them who was boss. That type of behaviour was not helped by the fact that there were no regular staff meetings; we never had one throughout my posting in Addis Ababa. In later years, worried by the lack of interaction among officers in most of our missions' headquarters, it directed that there should be periodic staff meetings and their reports should be rendered to them for information and necessary action. That was a welcome development and was very useful, especially in multilateral posts like New York, Geneva, Addis Ababa, Brussels and Vienna. The objective was to foster the spirit of camaraderie among officers for the good of the Service. These regular staff meetings were to enable officers to know what others were doing and to help them take decisions on diverse issues including administrative, consular and protocol matters as well as resolutions and decisions to be taken that did not require headquarters directives.

Before the Ambassador left the Mission, the agrement for his successor, Ambassador Ejoh Abuah, had been given by the Ethiopian government. As such it was expected that the new Ambassador would arrive in post without delay, especially with the forthcoming OAU Summit to be held in Addis Ababa. Since the Ambassador could not make farewell visits to some important departments of the host Foreign Ministry, including the director of Africa, he told me to deliver personal apologies to them. That gave me the opportunity to get close to the Foreign Minister, Goshu Wolde.

Mengitsu was the chairman of the OAU, so there were many opportunities to interact with the Foreign Minister and other officials of the Ethiopian government, which kept me busy. I frequented the office of the Foreign Minister more than ever and got to know him well. Goshu Wolde was a Colonel in the Ethiopian Army, and he was highly intelligent and commanded respect among diplomats in the country. Heading the mission as the Chargé d'Affaires ad interim, I met him often and delivered messages directly to him from headquarters. There were lots of occasions that brought us together at the ECA and OAU and at the bilateral meeting with the Nigerian Foreign Minister, Prof. Ibrahim Agboola Gambari. I believed that it was due to the charisma and personality of Goshu Wolde that Mengitsu had credibility and lasted for so long as chairman of the Derg and President of Ethiopia.

The country was under daily curfew from 2200 hours to 0500 hours, which was later relaxed to start from 24 hours to 0500 due to complaints from the ECA and the OAU secretariats where negotiations sometimes went through into the early morning. One such occasion was when the UN negotiations ended by 1:30 am and we were issued special passes to go home. One of my colleagues, Enny Onobu (later Ambassador) arrived from our Permanent Mission to the United Nations in New York for an ECA meeting and was amazed at the poor working environment of Ethiopia. He felt great pity for me and often mentioned it when we met. But as fate would have it, he experienced worse conditions when he later served as Nigerian ambassador in Liberia from 2003-2007 after that country's civil war, and it was now my turn to pity him for such hardship posts as I was then ambassador in Vienna before taking over from him as the director of First United Nations division at headquarters in September 2003.

Despite the harsh working conditions in Ethiopia, Addis Ababa was a lively city with beautiful flowers everywhere, the flowers having given it its name in the Amharic language. There were high-level visitors from Nigeria for either the ECA or OAU meetings. Prof Gambari, as Foreign Minister, tops the list of frequent visitors to Addis Ababa. Through him, I visited the Addis Ababa main market to give alms to the poor and bought Ethiopian clothing for his family.

It was during such visits that I observed that some of the items donated for humanitarian assistance by international community were diverted for sale in the market. It was an open secret, as most diplomats and donor countries were aware of such diversion of relief materials by the military junta for personal gains at the expense of those who needed them most. That was why the donor community often calls for the disbursement of relief material through NGOs and not by governments.

The Nigerian Minister of Labour, Major-General Solomon Omojokun, arrived for the African Ministers of Labour Conference and we hosted him and his delegation at my home. Despite the shortcomings the minister went back to Lagos with high appreciation and sent me a well-designed commendation letter which I cherished very much. That letter of commendation encouraged me to do more for my country and for the people that crossed my path from all walks of life. I never knew the value of such letters until much later. I recommend it as a motivating factor to appreciate young diplomats when they try their best rather than otherwise.

Developments at the ECA and the OAU

Seating arrangements at ECA and OAU Conferences saw Nigerians seated between Niger on one side and Mozambique on the other side. At one OAU Summit, the Nigerian delegation, which was always large, spilled over to the back seat allocated to our neighbours mentioned above. I found myself in the back seat allocated to Mozambique and the Foreign Minister of Mozambique, Joaquim Chissano, grabbed the kola nut I was chewing and jokingly told me that it was the price to pay for Nigeria's craving to spill over into other African countries including even seating arrangements. President Samora Machel was on the front seat, while Chissano sat behind with me. When I remarked that I would not sit there again on the second day of the three-day meeting he told me that the following day he would be sitting on the front seat, as his president would have left for Maputo. He said that African leaders never wanted to stay away from their capitals for more than a day due to the fear of being toppled by a military coup.

When Chissano became the President of Mozambique after the demise of President Samora Machel, I met him at New York during the annual session of the United Nations General Assembly (UNGA). I recalled what he told me in Addis Ababa and he laughed over it and jokingly said that things had changed in Africa since the 1970s and 1980s as military coups were condemned and leadership through that process was not welcomed and the affected country would be expelled from the continental organisation. Chissano told me that the African Union (AU) expunged from its Charter the issue of "non-interference in the internal affairs of member countries". According to him, that was the stabilizing factor for democracy to flourish in Africa. I met him several times at the UN corridor in New York after he had stepped down as the President of Mozambique, offering commendable services to humankind under UN auspices. The issue of non-intervention in the internal affairs of member countries was revisited later during the transformation of the OAU into the AU as well as the Canadian idea of "responsibility to protect" introduced by the Canadian delegation at the UN during the debates on the reform of the Organisation in 2005. Both actions have been commendable and instrumental in restoring sanity and the protection of lives and property in Africa.

There were over ten Nigerians working at the United Economic Commission for Africa (ECA) and the OAU. Both organisations were headed by eminent Nigerians, namely

Professor Adebayo Adedeji and Ambassador Peter Onu respectively. Ambassador Peter Onu was the Acting Secretary-General for two years, from 1983 to 1985, due to the stalemate at the election of a new Secretary General to succeed Edem Kodjo from Togo. Peter Onu was on secondment from the Research Department (now NIA) of the Nigerian Foreign Service. During the two-year period, he performed creditably, earning the admiration of many member countries who wanted him to be confirmed as substantive Secretary-General.

Under his leadership the OAU faced a major crisis, due to the admission of Western Sahara as a full member of the organisation. In reaction, Morocco pulled out of the OAU with its valuable financial contributions to the organisation, due to the invitation to a Western Sahara delegation to attend the OAU Summit in 1984. Morocco laid claim to the former Spanish colony as part of its territory and argued that with the exit of Spain, without granting the territory independence, it should be returned to them.

Although the Sahrawi Arab Democratic Republic (Western Sahara) was admitted to the OAU in 1982, it did not feature at the OAU Summits until 1984, which was opposed by Morocco. The other contentious issue was the severance of diplomatic relations with the State of Israel. as many African countries were restoring diplomatic relations with the Jewish state in reaction to the unilateral decision by President Anwar Sadat to restore diplomatic relations with Israel without consulting them. Some of those countries that restored relations with Israel argued that they had severed relations with Israel at the instance of Egypt after the Arab Israeli war of 1973, the Yom Kippur

War, but Egypt did not consult them when she restored relations with Israel and thought that a continued thaw in relations with the Jewish state was no longer necessary.

Ambassador Peter Onu, through skilful diplomacy, was able to handle the situation creditably and many delegations even campaigned for him and requested Nigeria to present his candidacy as substantive Secretary-General of the OAU. In a meeting with Ambassador Onu at his office, he informed me that it was not possible for him to stand as a candidate. This was due to an unwritten agreement among the major contributors to the OAU budget not to present their nationals as candidates for the post of Secretary-General. I was surprised at that information and told him it was contrary to the situation in the World Bank and the International Monetary Fund (IMF), where the major powers often fielded and elected their candidates to head the organisations. He told me that those organisations were non-political and purely economic.

At a meeting of African ambassadors at the Malawian Embassy, the main topic was who would be the next Secretary-General of the OAU. Ambassador Tichaona Jokonya of Zimbabwe, whom I later met in two other posts, Geneva and New York, informed me that they believed that Ambassador Peter Onu was the most suitable candidate to take the mantle of leadership at the OAU and they would be glad if Nigeria could field his candidacy as the next OAU Secretary-General. After the meeting we contacted Lagos for instructions with a recommendation to present the candidature of Ambassador Peter Onu as the next OAU Secretary-General to succeed Edem Kodjo, whose tenure expired in 1983, but Lagos informed us that Nigeria had no candidate for that post and that Ambassador Onu should continue as Deputy Secretary-General of the OAU. We were directed that it was in conformity with the decision of the major contributors to the OAU budget that they should not sponsor their nationals to the top post. It was the same reason advanced for the ECOWAS, as Nigeria has never aspired to be the Secretary General. I wondered why the Arab League, based in Cairo, is always headed by an Egyptian.

As I grew in experience in the Service I got to understand the import of such decisions. The major contributors to the OAU budget were Libya, Egypt, Algeria, Nigeria and Morocco, before the latter pulled out. Since the OAU was established in May 1963, none of these countries had ever presented their nationals as candidates for the OAU top job and its successor organisation the African Union. It was a decision similar to the United Nations, where the major contributors have never presented candidates in order to give a chance to smaller countries to vie for its top job. It might also be absurd for an Arab member country to lead the organisation and at the same time head that of the Arab League based in Cairo. This unwritten agreement was decided by the founding fathers of the OAU in 1963; similar to the UN Secretary-General, with a view to encouraging smaller African countries to play an active part in that organisation. That was why Nigeria has not reneged on this understanding by not vying for that post, and why instead we supported the election of Ide Oumarou of Niger in 1985. This unwritten understanding manifested with the African Union Commission President in the re-election of Jean Ping and the South African candidate Ms. Nkosazana Dlamini-Zuma. Nigeria supported the re-election of Jean Ping from Gabon as against the South African candidate as a matter of principle. Nigeria rallied round ECOWAS countries to support the Gabonese candidate as against the South African candidate, because South Africa is among the major contributors to the coffers of the AU so she was not supposed to contest for the leadership of the organisation. With the election of the South African candidate, a major contributor to the AU, the unwritten understanding was jettisoned, and nothing could stop any of the major contributors, including the Arab countries of North Africa, from heading the AU.

I was getting agitated by the absence of an Ambassador to relieve me with the myriad of problems of the Mission, such as the continued meetings and conferences at the ECA and OAU and constant summoning to the host Foreign Ministry for mundane matters, one of which was to remove the "sign boards" of the Embassy, and another about the list and salaries of Ethiopian local staff under our employment. There was also anxiety about the new ambassador, in the person of Ambassador Ejoh Abuah. After obtaining agrément for Ethiopia, he was withdrawn and posted to Brazzaville, Republic of Congo. The reason given for the change was the altitude of Addis Ababa, which was unhealthy for the Ambassador, who was said to be asthmatic, and we had to inform our host country discreetly. I was also feeling a similar situation with my spouse, who was always suffering from shortage of breath and constantly visited the only decent clinic that could attend to foreigners. On one occasion my wife fainted, and she was rushed to the clinic without the Mission reaching me, because I was attending a meeting with Ambassador Camara of Senegal who was the Dean of the Diplomatic Corps and had spent over 17 years in Addis Ababa. The Deputy Dean was the ambassador of Liberia and he had clocked up 15 years. To my surprise, I met similar situations in my subsequent postings to Brussels and Geneva, where the ambassadors of Senegal were the Dean of the Diplomatic Corps after being there for the same number of years.

The Umaru Dikko affair and the Addis Ababa Mission

After the withdrawal of the nomination of Ambassador Ejoh Abuah, it took headquarters over four months to send a request for his replacement. This was when Major-General Anthony Haladu Hananiya, posted as High Commissioner to the Court of St. James, London, was recalled to Lagos due to an incident involving Alhaji Umaru Dikko. For those unfamiliar with this case, it is worth mentioning briefly. The Government of Alhaji Shehu Shagari was toppled by the military junta led by Major-General Muhammadu Buhari in December 1983 and most of the ministers were arrested and detained. Alhaji Umaru Dikko, then minister of Transport, fled to London. He was one of the key ministers sought after by the military government on allegations of corruption. The military government alleged that most of those who took part in the Shagari administration were guilty before they could prove their innocence in the court of law, which was a violation of Nigeria's constitution. Alhaji Umaru Dikko was abducted in London. He was put in a crate and an attempt was made to fly him to Nigeria disguised as a 'diplomatic bag', but he was stopped by the

UK security agents at Stansted airport. That incident led to a diplomatic crisis between Nigeria and the United Kingdom, because the UK demanded a waiver of diplomatic immunity of some officers at the Nigerian High Commission so that they could be interrogated and tried in court. Nigeria refused to lift their diplomatic immunity. In protest at the treatment of the officials, Nigeria protested by recalling its High Commissioner, Anthony Hananiya, for consultations. In response, the United Kingdom decided that the High Commissioner was no longer welcome back in London. The UK further expelled two officers from the Nigerian High Commission and tried those without diplomatic immunity and jailed them with long prison sentences. In reaction to this Nigeria requested the UK to recall its High Commissioner from Nigeria. The fallout from this incident was the suspension of diplomatic relations between Nigeria and the UK for two years; it was restored in 1988. That was why General Hananiya was posted to Ethiopia as Ambassador after I had left Addis Ababa for Brussels.

The Foreign Service was full of rumours, and one such rumour I heard was that I was being cross-posted to another mission. I was not bothered, since I was enjoying my posting in Addis Ababa. With the mantle of leadership of the Mission I had the opportunity to meet highly-placed diplomats, ambassadors, chargés d'affaires and some Ethiopian officials at the Foreign Ministry. The US chargé d'affaires introduced me to many other chargés d'affaires, mostly from the developed countries, as their ambassadors were recalled without replacement due to the policy of the country. Due to the restriction of travel beyond 50 kilometres radius of Addis Ababa, I was not aware of the ravaging war against the Mengistu regime in the north and south of the country.

Also, unknown to me and to most diplomats was the fact that there was serious drought and famine in the country, from which thousands of people were dying. The famine was exacerbated by the forced resettlement of the people by the regime and the wars. One evening, David A. Korn, the US chargé d'affaires, invited me to dinner at his residence. He gave me a full report on the situation ravaging the country, which from his body language they tacitly supported. He told me that they had only four diplomats in their large Embassy, with over 50 local staff and more than 30 houses unoccupied. That was because the United States had been forced to reduce its officers after their ambassador was recalled in July 1980, at the request of the Ethiopian government, and since then their Embassy had been headed by chargé d'affaires. He was optimistic that the US would one day return to its strong position in Ethiopia, and that was why they kept their houses.

As he was leading me to the gate he showed me a Soviet-installed gadget directly overlooking his residence and said it was spying equipment monitoring whoever entered or left the premises. It did not bother them, as they used secure and more sophisticated devices to counter it.

As I left the American, since my own house was directly opposite the Kebele headquarters, I tried to check if a similar device was also installed around my own house. Since I did not see any such device I felt a sense of relief. But the Ethiopian visitors who thronged into my house for coffee and hot drinks told me that all diplomatic premises were under strict surveillance and mine was no exception, although Nigeria was not part of the rivalry between the East and the West or the Cold War.

After waiting for the agrément for a new ambassador or an officer of my grade to relieve me of the tension of Addis Ababa, I was forced to raise the matter with Professor Ibrahim Gambari, during one of his visits to Addis Ababa. He then told me that he had approved a new posting before he had left and confirmed to me that I was being cross-posted to Brussels and pending the arrival of a new ambassador, a senior officer, I B Mohammed from Madrid, had been cross-posted to take charge of the Mission. Departure formality from Ethiopia was cumbersome if one was leaving with an Ethiopian as spouse or house help. Because of the cheap labour and the urge by Ethiopians to leave the country due to the oppressive and harsh living conditions under the regime, I decided to take my housemaid (*marmite*) to Brussels, but I needed an exit visa for her to do so, which was not approved until almost six months after I departed. The export of exotic Ethiopian carpets and rugs was banned, but I needed them badly and I literally smuggled two out of the country using unconventional method to get them air-freighted to Brussels under diplomatic cover. I cherished the two hand-woven carpets for many years, because they were as beautiful as the Ethiopian themselves. I also needed to dispose of the new Volvo car of which I had just taken delivery from Sweden, but only a diplomat could buy it from me and I could not take it to Belgium because it would not be registered due to the African specification. I decided to send it to Nigeria.

A few points worth pointing out regarding the movement of diplomatic cargo across borders were clearly demonstrated by the Umaru Dikko affair in London. The claim that the wooden crates were diplomatic bags could not be substantiated, because they failed the test as required by Article 27(4) of the Vienna Convention on Diplomatic Relations and Immunities of 1961. The crates were not marked with the words "Diplomatic Bags" and they were not accompanied by an accredited diplomatic courier or had relevant documentation to qualify as diplomatic bags. As such the crates were subjected to inspection as required by Article 36(2) of the same Convention in the presence of an official of the sending state. It was the same provisions that covered the movement of my two exotic carpets which, although they were banned items for exports, we declared as "personal effects". They were airlifted to Brussels and could not be subjected to inspection by the Ethiopian authorities. My action was a flagrant violation of the laws of my host country, but I saw no reason why they would ban some of their best export items, which would earn them foreign exchange. Other items on export prohibition were tea and coffee, except to the Warsaw Pact countries.

Airlifts of Ethiopian Jews to Israel

One issue which started just before my departure from Ethiopia was the secret airlifts of Falasha (or Beta) Jews from Ethiopia to Israel under an agreement between Israel and the Ethiopian Government in exchange for arms to execute the civil wars in the country. Due to the suppression of independent news media, it came to us as a rumour. Even the BBC, the Voice of America (VOA) and other Western news media were jammed and hardly audible except with satellite radio. Both Israel and Ethiopia denied the exercise, but insider sources through the US Embassy confirmed to me that it was taking place through Sudan. Through this method, over eight thousand Ethiopian Falasha Jews were airlifted to Israel, apparently with the aim of swelling the Israeli population in their quest to outbalance the Arabs. The airlift was code named "Operation Moses". The airlifts were done openly in November 1984 and ended in January 1985, but because the news leaked out the operation ended abruptly as Arab countries pressured Sudan to prevent its territory from being used for this secret operation. Because of this many Falasha were left stranded in Ethiopia after some of their families had been airlifted to Israel. Several years later, in 1991, "Operation Solomon" was launched, in which over fourteen thousand of them were airlifted from Ethiopia to Israel and united with those left separated by "Operation Moses".

At the same time as these secret airlifts of the Falasha to Israel, a BBC reporter, Michael Buerk, aired a report of the famine in October 1984, showing that hundreds of Ethiopians were dying, mainly because of the drought and the war in the country. I could not believe this as I watched the images when I arrived in Brussels, because there were no signs of the famine and the war in Addis Ababa or any sign of the sufferings of the people in the hinterland. These images led to Bob Geldof launching a concert to raise funds for the Ethiopian famine, with the song 'Do they know it's Christmas?"

I waited for Ishmael B. Mohammed (later ambassador)

who was cross-posted from Madrid, but his arrival was delayed for reasons unknown to me, and I could not wait much longer due to the OAU Summit, which required adequate preparations, and I feared that headquarters might change their decision and keep me there much longer than necessary. I decided to leave the Mission to Charles Ononye without any news about I B Mohammed, but suddenly we met at Bole Airport. I did not know that he would be my boss when we returned to headquarters in 1987, because the telegram conveying his arrival was not received at the mission on time. That kind of problem with non-receipt of letters and telegrams had put some of our missions in trouble if they involved high government officials, especially those in Africa with poor communication facilities.

My one-year posting in Addis Ababa was eventful, and I learned a lot about the art of diplomacy, particularly multilateral or conference diplomacy. Ethiopians are hospitable and friendly people and very proud of their history, particularly their victory against the Italians at Adwa on March 2, 1896 or Yekatit 23, 1889 on the Ethiopian calendar. Surprisingly, they never refer to themselves as Africans, but Ethiopians. Like Somalis, their warring neighbours, they regard themselves as superior to the other African races and they show it openly despite their poverty. They demonstrate their ignorance as a people suffering from delusions of adequacy and false superiority complex or delusion of grandeur in their relations to the other African countries south of the Sahara.

CHAPTER 3

BRUSSELS: THE COCKFIGHTING ARENA OF EUROPE

"Why do diplomats never discuss anything except houses, furniture, motorcars, good wine, money and receptions?"

Harold Macmillan, 1894-1986

Belgium was a melting pot of wars between other European powers fought or campaigned on its territory, which gave it the nickname 'Cockfighting Arena of Europe.' The territory now called Belgium was part of France under Napoleonic rule, but when the British General Wellington stopped Napoleon's imperial ambition to conquer the whole of Europe at the battle of Waterloo on 18 June 1815, the territory came under the rule of the United Kingdom of the Netherlands. The country was fashioned by the four victorious Axis powers, namely Austria, Prussia, Russia and Great Britain, at the Congress of Vienna, which was held in Vienna from September 1814 to June 1815 by merging the

Northern and Southern Netherlands into one country, with King William as the first ruler. But the King was protestant, while most of the population in the newly-created country was Catholic. This led to a crisis of confidence until independence was achieved under King Leopold I on October 4, 1830. His son King Leopold II succeeded him and represented Belgium at the Berlin Conference on the partition of Africa in 1884.

The King sponsored Henry Morton Stanley's expedition to Central Africa in search of colonies and colonized the Congo as a personal estate until it was handed over to Belgium in 1908. The allied powers created Belgium as a buffer zone and as a monarchy rather than a republic. The most contentious issue was the language question, because of which the capital city and its streets are named in both French and Flemish (Bruxels or Brussels). During the First and Second World Wars in 1914 and 1939, Belgium was neutral, but its strategic location made it a prime target for German invasion. Belgium played a key role in European integration and the de facto capital of Europe is also the headquarters of NATO. The country is divided into three regions: Brussels (bilingual French/Dutch), Wallonia (French) and Flanders (Dutch).

We arrived in Brussels in October and were received by Moses Ologun, the Administration Attaché, and taken to a service apartment. As we were disembarking from the van that brought us, Yusuf, my third son, almost lost his life as he ran across the road without looking and an oncoming vehicle crashed into a ditch to avoid him. In Addis Ababa there were no vehicles on our street and even if there were, the Ethiopians often crossed the road without looking right or left. It is the driver that is responsible for avoiding pedestrians.

The Nigerian Embassy had no ambassador, as Ambassador Peter Afolabi had left before I arrived and his successor Ambassador Joshua Iroha was yet to arrive at the mission (both are now deceased). The purge of 1984 also affected Anthony Dibie, the Head of Chancery in the mission, and Adegboyega Boyede (later Ambassador) was the chargé d'affaires a.i. There were 15 home-based officers and staff and many locally-recruited staff in Brussels with man-made problems to solve. Some of the attachés from the Ministry of Commerce and Industry, Customs and Information were very senior officers in their ministries, even more senior than the rank of the Ambassador in the mission. Kevin Efretei (now late), the number two officer, was also yet to arrive from Ankara, Turkey, where he was winding down the closure of the mission as part of the austerity measures by the Muhammadu Buhari's administration of 1984. The closure and reopening of missions was frequent throughout my diplomatic career and never achieved the desired result of saving financial resources. In fact, more resources were wasted in the process.

Since I was arriving from a mission where I had been faced with so many problems, for me to take control of another with far greater problems of man-management than the actual work and in a strange terrain, I decided to play safe. I also observed that the incumbent chargé d'affaires was unwilling (rightly of course) to relinquish the position to me because the departed Ambassador had forwarded his name as the officer in charge until the arrival of his successor. I wondered if that harmony could have continued if it took a longer time for the Ambassador to arrive. It turned out to be the wisest decision for me to allow him to take charge, because the mission was in chaos, as it was divided along ethnic lines. Some of the attachés, like information and trade, created parallel missions which were independent from the Embassy with serious financial problems, but they were later forced to close and returned to the mission. That also coincided with the time the Chancery moved from its former location at Montgomery Square to Avenue de Tervuren.

Our accommodation was at an excellent villa located at Sneppen Laan in Tervuren, the Flemish part of Belgium. I understand a little of this language, which I learned when I was attending post-graduate studies at the Institute of Social Studies (ISS) at The Hague, but I was interested in learning the French language, which is one of the official languages of the UN. I learned French with much interest and picked it up well, particularly reading and conversation, which I found very useful in my later years in the Service.

Ambassador Iroha and Kevin arrived in Brussels at almost the same time to take over the Mission, to my greatest relief. Both were among the best officers I had ever known as they were very intelligent, resourceful, tactful and hardworking and ready to teach others. They also had excellent spouses, Dorothy (Dora) for the ambassador and Arit for Efretei. I was assigned the duties of Head of Chancery responsible, for many issues, such as the control of the finances and expenditure of the mission, arrival and departure of officers, vehicles and transportation, overall upkeep of the chancery, staff quarters, local staff matters, schools for officers' children, payment of bills and many contentious issues, crisis management and liaison with the host Foreign Ministry. With such many staff I was glued to my desk and was never involved in dealing with the economic or political developments in the country. Sensing my displeasure with my schedule the ambassador assigned to me the Joint Parliamentary Assembly (one of the Organs of the ACP-EEC), which I loved very much.

My secretary, Ms Zarafa, was an Ethiopian, so I was still being surrounded and kept abreast with developments in Addis Ababa. The most topical news in Ethiopia was the famine of 1984, which caused the deaths of thousands of people. I could not believe that Ethiopia was experiencing famine in the north and south of the country while it was not noticeable in the capital. The only complaint was from my children, who always asked me to take them back to Nigeria as there were many deaths seen on their way to and from school, which lay in a different direction from my route to the Chancery. The second most topical news was the airlift of Falasha Jews from Ethiopia through Sudan to Israel, which abruptly ended in January 1985. Most Ethiopian non-Jews were not in support, as those within and outside the country condemned their government for that action and so did the Arab world for the attempt by Israel to unbalance the population equation of the Jewish state in their favour.

My last contact with development in my former Mission was the news of the visit to Brussels of the Ethiopian Foreign Minister, Goshu Wolde. I requested a meeting and he told me that he was on his way to Canada on asylum because he had been forced to defect as he could no longer defend the falsehood of the Mengistu regime. He told me of the wars both in the north and the south of the country, as well as the devastating famine that had killed thousands of people. He said that the famine had been compounded by the forced movement of people from their lands to new areas against their will. He also told me that Ethiopia was also paying the USSR and other Warsaw pact countries for their support to the regime at great cost to the Ethiopian people. Because of these problems and fear for his life, he had decided to defect and leave the country.

The most contentious duties for me as the Head of Chancery were settlement of children's school fees and utility bills, which had been a big burden on officers due to the new austerity measures by the new military administration. Since officers and staff occupied large villas, their share of utility bills was very high (an increase from 2½% to 45% or even 55%), and many, including me, could not bear it. The other contentious problem was the ceiling for the supplement for children's school fees, which if strictly applied would make it impossible for many of us to send our children to school. It was an impossible task for me, so I approached Kevin to proffer a solution and he said we should meet the Ambassador to decide. Ambassador Iroha, a non-carrier appointee, was a nice-looking man, full of life, chain smoking exotic Cuban cigars and cigarettes in between. He was heaven-sent for the mission. The lifestyle he exhibited was like that of my former boss in Addis Ababa, to confirm my notion that flamboyance was an integral part of diplomacy, but I detested the smoking and hot drinks aspect of it. Ambassador Iroha took our problems lightly and directed that since Belgium was not an English-speaking country we should ignore the ceiling on educational supplements. He also directed that we should include bus transportation of our children as part of the educational supplement to solve the intractable problems of transporting children to schools in different parts of the city.

Another novelty introduced by Ambassador Iroha was the directive for all officers and members of their families to take health insurance, to reduce the high bills on medical expenses. As a result, medical bills plummeted drastically, which was emulated by many missions through a directive from headquarters.

With these decisions, my duties were lightened, and I decided to add protocol duties to my job by assisting Ms Jumoke J Opaleye (later Opaleye-Majekodunmi) and found myself always at Zaventem Airport to receive or see off guests, who often arrived or departed at very odd hours of the night. I also found time to attend to my other assignment, the ACP-EEC Joint Parliamentary Assembly, which was the most enjoyable aspect of my duties at our Embassy in Brussels. I also had time to coach students on football and baseball at the American International School, which my children were attending.

Nigeria and the Lomé Conventions

I got to Brussels during the Lomé II convention, while the Lomé III was being negotiated and concluded in 1985, giving prominence to the trade provisions in 1986 which were to expire in 1990. It should be recalled that on June 6, 1975 about 37 African, six Caribbean and three Pacific groups of countries had signed the George Town agreement establishing the ACP, thus comprising 46 countries. The main objective of the ACP was to forge economic and trade cooperation between itself and the European Economic Community (EEC). The ACP was conceived by the founding member countries as the mechanism for cooperation in international trade. It was the most comprehensive North-South dialogue.

The most important interest of the EEC was in securing raw materials from ACP member countries in exchange for preferential treatment of their goods and services being sold into the European member countries. The first ACP Conference was held in Lomé, Republic of Togo, in 1976. The framework of cooperation between the EEC and their former colonies was very limited and was never sustainable by the provisions of the World Trade Organisation (WTO) when it came into effect in 1994. The Conference and the Convention agreed to provide the ACP preferential treatments and stabilisation of export prices for agricultural and mineral products - Stabex and Stamin - that would enter the EEC free of duties. The preferential access was based on quotas for sugar and animal products and was later extended to cover bananas. The EEC provided up to 3 billion European currency units of aid and investment in the ACP group of countries.

By the time I left Brussels in 1987 there were over 60 ACP countries which were signatories to the Lomé Convention, while the level of development aid and technical assistance, including investments from the EEC, was over 10 billion European currency units. The emergence of the single European market (the EU) at the end of 1992 affected the ACP preferential access to the EU markets, particularly bananas from the Caribbean countries. These preferential accesses to agricultural produce from the ACP into the EU were direct violations of the provisions of the WTO when it came into effect in 1994. The US petitioned the WTO dispute settlement procedure and it was ruled against the ACP-EU arrangements or agreements. The experiences gained at the Brussels mission on the trade-related concessions granted to the ACP countries became a big asset to my understanding of the issues under negotiations in my next posting to Geneva during the Uruguay Round of multilateral trade negotiations that culminated into the establishment of the World Trade Organisation (WTO).

The ACP-EEC Joint Parliamentary Assembly

I had the privilege of accompanying the Ambassador to the ACP-EEC Joint Consultative Assembly in Bujumbura, Burundi in February 1985 as well as the second session in Inverness, Scotland in September 1985. I also accompanied him to the one held in Mbabane, Swaziland in January 1986. The meeting in Bujumbura was the last meeting under the name of Joint Consultative Assembly (JCA). During that meeting, the Assembly changed its name to Joint Parliamentary Assembly, which was later enshrined in the successor to Lomé Conventions, the Cotonou Agreement.

We flew directly from Brussels to Bujumbura through Kigali, but as we were leaving the freezing cold weather of Europe for the hottest tropical climate it was quite challenging to us. More so because we were left loitering on the Kigali Airport tarmac without anything to drink or eat. The airport was under construction and only one runway was used for take-off and landing.

After over two hours of waiting on the tarmac an old and dilapidated plane picked us up to take us to Bujumbura. It looked like a military aircraft and was devoid of any item of luxury or security. The Ambassador, who was sitting with me in a classless cabin, whispered to me, "maybe this is our journey of no return in this African jungle". Some passengers were even standing up, as in city buses. I believe it was a C130 used for military cargoes.

As we landed in Bujumbura airport we were amazed by its large size and saw that all luxury items were readily available, unlike in Kigali. As we checked into the French-owned hotel, I mistakenly asked if the workers were from Ethiopia, because they had the same complexion and were slim with pointed noses, beautiful, tall and hospitable.

Apart from the meeting itself I decided to venture into the local market place and to tour the city of Bujumbura. I came across Nigerian traders selling all sorts of items such as kola nuts, precious stones, second-hand cloth and clothing. They were mostly Igbos and a few Hausas, and they informed me that business was good. I also observed that small businesses like tailoring, hairdressing and provisional stores were owned by French nationals. I did not bother to ask the Nigerians if they were legal or illegal immigrants and how they got there, as I believed they were the latter.

The second ACP-EEC meeting, to which I accompanied Ambassador Iroha, the first under the new name, was held in Inverness, Scotland in September 1985, even though

Nigeria was not yet a democracy. The Inverness meeting was opened by Princess Anne, the only daughter of Queen Elizabeth II and Prince Philip. She was in Scotland for an equestrian competition and delegates were invited to watch the event. She was also known to be a keen sailor and she mingled freely with delegates. I admired her for her openness, despite the tight security around her after her attempted kidnap in 1973.

The third meeting, which was the second under the change of name, was held in Mbabane, Swaziland in January 1986 and I accompanied the Ambassador. Flying into Swaziland created some problems to us as the easiest connection was through Johannesburg in apartheid-ridden South Africa. We were worried about transiting into South African territory without our passports being stamped by the apartheid regime. We feared that it would create problems for us, as the South Africans might use it to embarrass us, which would be severely sanctioned by our government. Accordingly, we had to go through Nairobi, from where we connected to Mbabane with a small but efficient aircraft. It turned out that the aircraft was owned by a South African and my boss told me that if we could not beat the South African system we were promoting their businesses, adding that it was an "act of necessity".

That was just the beginning, as we were astonished to find that the hotel we lodged in was owned by South Africa, including the TV station, radio, shops, food and transportation. The Ghanaian parliamentarians, who arrived for the same meeting from Accra, told us that they had come by road from Johannesburg, but their passports were not stamped since they were not valid for South Africa.

Our fear was due to the ban of any contacts with the apartheid country. Any visitor to that country was barred from entering Nigeria; if we violated that sanction, it would be taken seriously against us.

One of the main reasons for changing the name of the ACP-EEC Joint Consultative Assembly to Joint Parliamentary Assembly was that the European members were all elected members of the European Parliament, but their ACP counterparts, including Nigeria, were government officials or diplomats based in Brussels. Only a few ACP delegates were elected members of parliament. The Europeans wanted discussions on political issues such as democracy, human rights, the role of civil society, NGOs and good governance, but their ACP counterparts wanted to deal with economic, trade, investment, aid, technical assistance and development issues. The change of name was aimed at encouraging democracy, promotion and the protection of human rights and the rule of law.

The Joint Parliamentary Assembly was established to bring together elected representatives of equal number from the ACP and EEC (now EU) countries who were signatories to the Lomé Convention. It meets twice in a year alternatively between ACP and EU countries. In all the meetings I attended there were decisions and resolutions on topical political issues at the time such as Western Sahara, the situation in apartheid South Africa, subsidized EU agricultural products, conflict prevention, abolition of the death penalty, human rights questions, environment, sugar, bananas, tuna, rum, technical assistance, aid, trade relations, fake drugs and health among others. The Assembly elected two co-presidents and an equal number of vice-presidents, which constituted the Bureau.

As in Burundi, I ventured into the countryside and the local market in Swaziland, but I never met any Nigerians due to the travel ban between Nigeria and apartheid South Africa, since one cannot travel into Swaziland without passing through South Africa. However, I was told that one Nigerian from a famous Lagos family by the name of Antonio Oladeinde Fernandez (now deceased) had extensive businesses in Swaziland, Mozambique and Central African Republic. He was at one time the Deputy Minister of Finance of Swaziland, but he did not live in the country at the time of our visit.

I went on a safari tour and found the tourism facilities to be of a high standard, comparing favourably to those of Kenya and Burundi but owned and organized by a South African tour operator. We found that even the tourist sites were owned and maintained by South African whites. So if we could not beat the South African apartheid system, then we would have to either join them or leave them.

I revisited Mbabane again in February 2005 for an African Union (AU) ministerial meeting on the UN reform at Ezulwini. There had been major changes, as we even travelled back by road to Johannesburg with Ambassador Oluyemi Adeniji. There were many Nigerians living in the country, mostly Technical Aid Corps (TAC) volunteers who stayed back and took to teaching and medical practice.

As we drove into South Africa we saw large farms owned mostly by white South Africans. We observed that the white settlements were well organized and neat with better facilities, roads, schools and sporting facilities compared to the settlements belonging to the black population. That was an indication that the dismantling of apartheid was yet to transform the socio-economic development of most South Africans.

An Encounter with a Nigerian Businessman

As we were preparing to travel to Bujumbura for the Joint Consultative Assembly meeting, I received a call from reception that one Alhaji Bashir had arrived to see me. I wondered who he was, as there was no prior request for a meeting with me. The only foreign service officer with that last name was Ambassador Abbah Ibrahim Bashir, Honourable Consul General in Buea, Cameroon. I thought it was him, so I invited him to come in. But when the man came into my office he started by condemning the quality of the furniture in my office, including the crockery he was drinking tea from. Since I had never met him before, I started by introducing myself and expected him to tell me who he was, but he simply told me where he was from and the countries he was travelling to. He was full of himself and said he had just landed from the US by Concorde aircraft at Zaventem Airport with a group of businessmen and women, and he needed to stay in our guest house if we had one. I was curious, because Concorde could not have landed at that airport directly from the US; it would have gone first to the UK and not to Brussels. I knew that something was amiss. When I told him that we did not have a guest house to accommodate visitors, he stood up and started shouting and condemning the Embassy for not having such a basic facility. He wondered how we accommodated our visitors without a guest house. Then he asked for a car to drop him off, which I did. But I did not know that there were more problems to come.

The following day calls were made from a hotel in downtown Brussels telling me of unpaid bills by Nigerians who booked rooms and issued fake credit cards. They would check out late in the night and leave a girl behind as evidence that they were just going out to a late party or a disco. The girl was from a well-known family in Nigeria and was crying on the phone that the hotel refused to allow her to eat or drink anything. I rushed to the scene to rescue the situation. The lady was totally confused and told me a long story of how the man had persuaded her to travel with him to Brazil, Mexico and two other countries in the Caribbean, and saying that all her belongings, including tickets, were with Alhaji Mohammed Bashir. But as they got to Brussels she noticed that Alhaji had run out of funds and decided to use her resources, and that was why he had left them at the hotel to go to the Nigerian Embassy. He had never returned. She was surprised that her travelling partners had also left, leaving her stranded in the hotel. Even her travelling documents were not with her, and the hotel refused her dining facilities. She did not have any warm clothing in the freezing winter and was desperate for help.

I gave her my jacket and took her to the mission and arranged breakfast for her. That was a serious consular problem, and I ended up taking the strange lady to my house before we handled the problem, even though I was travelling that night. Incidentally, Ambassador Iroha knew Alhaji Bashir very well in Lagos but could not offer me any assistance with the problem at hand until we returned from Bujumbura. The lady found her way back to Lagos after spending two weeks with us. When she returned home to Port Harcourt, her family sent us a commendation gift of snails, which are the delicacy of that area of Nigeria, but we do not eat them.

Alhaji Mohammed Bashir continued to compromise highly-placed Nigerians, including Admiral Augustus Aikhomu, the Vice-President of Nigeria during the administration of General Ibrahim Babangida, claiming that he was defrauded of $500,000 in kickbacks on an oil deal with him. Security agencies arrested Bashir in 1989 without trial for false claims against the Vice-President, but he was later released under a secret deal. That was my second encounter with Nigerian men who were bent on tarnishing the name of Nigeria abroad and leaving problems for Nigerian diplomats to solve with their meagre personal resources. The first one was in Addis Ababa when Benibo issued an official letter stating that he had not married before in Nigeria and thus, he was qualified to marry an Ethiopian woman. He later ended up by carting away the household belongings of his host at the ECA; he sold them cheaply and escaped before his host returned from an official visit outside the country.

Incidents of this type carried out by unscrupulous Nigerians were rampant in most of Nigeria's embassies, and they would condemn the officers for refusing to render assistance to them. The officers are guided by headquarters rules and regulations to be tactful in handling the affairs of visitors, and their jobs are threatened by any act of infraction. The missions are not equipped with financial resources to cater for the demands of visitors, and in most cases the staff use their personal resources to render assistance to them, as happened to me in Brussels. The one in Addis Ababa almost implicated the administration attaché, since the officer violated extant directives from Headquarters not to render any assistance to him. These are some of the risks faced by Nigerian diplomats abroad, but the public continue to rain abuses on them without knowing their predicaments and limitations.

Record Keeping at Headquarters in Lagos

Due to the lack of adequate record keeping at headquarters, I was listed as one of those who had spent four years at post and was due to return to headquarters by September 1986. Mandatory posting at that time was four years at post and two years at Headquarters, but due to poor record keeping, it was recorded that I had served in three missions including Conakry, Guinea, although I was stopped from going at the airport. I did not want to be seen as a complainant, so I decided to disengage and leave the Mission along with those who had spent four years at post.

I handed over my schedules to an incoming officer, Korode Willoughby. During a phone call from Scott Omene, the Counsellor Staff, I mentioned to him that I still had one year at post to make it four years in conformity with the Foreign Service Regulations. After checking his records, he called and told me that they made a mistake and asked me to wait for further directives. But when the directive came I was given four months instead of a full year, because there were two senior officers of my rank already reported and keeping all of us would be unwieldy for the mission. These officers were Korode Willoughby and Joseph Keshi. The lack of adequate record keeping also affected me when I returned to headquarters, as I was listed as a lower grade level six officer instead of grade four. As such I lost the allocation of staff quarters, which was further compounded by the fact that I arrived in Lagos at a very odd time, in January 1987, when staff accommodation had all been allocated.

The MEA did not have any functional library, even at departmental level, so there was no proper record keeping of treaties, conventions, protocols and agreements signed between Nigeria and other countries. There had not been any proper archive for reference and research in the Ministry of Foreign Affairs before this book was written.

Besides the official work at the mission, I got involved in sporting activities at the American International School where my children were attending due to their transfer from the same kind of school in Addis Ababa. I was the only one from the Nigeria Embassy with children at that school. Each year there was keen competition among the children who showed interest in football, or soccer as the Americans call it, and in baseball. I was a coach in both the junior teams, since my children were in the junior classes. It was a period every parent and child looked up to because of the way it was organized in the form of tournaments with each team named after major European teams for soccer while the baseball teams were named after major US baseball teams. For the two years I was involved in coaching, my team won the trophies and I was presented with certificates and a trophy for my contributions to the Brussels Sports Association. Ambassador Iroha was so happy with my performance that he organized a reception in my honour and called on others to emulate my example in promoting

Nigeria's image through sporting activities. I tried, unsuccessfully, to promote baseball on return to Nigeria with my brother in-law, General Victor Lot, and his friend General Ishola Williams, but when they ventured into golfing, our aspirations could not be realized.

Nigerians in Belgium

One afternoon in 1986, the receptionist called to inform me that a Nigerian was in the Chancery to register his presence in Belgium as a football player and wished to see me briefly. He introduced himself as Stephen Keshi and said he was playing for a second division team, K S Lokeren in Belgium. I wondered if he was related to my colleague Joe Keshi, who one year later arrived to take over from me. Stephen Keshi was one of the first Nigerian footballers who ventured into Europe as an international football player, and he has since risen to stardom as both a player and coach/manager. Unlike many Nigerians, he visited the Chancery only to register his presence in the country rather than coming when there was a problem or to cause problems. That sense of duty and patriotism paid off handsomely for him until his death in 2016. He went to play for a French first division team, Strasbourg. He thus helped to build a good image of our country through football, and many others later followed him. It was unfortunate that he passed away, along with his wife, when Nigerian football was on a downward trend.

Brussels also offered me the opportunity to visit museums and monuments to learn more about the history of the country. The major battle was the Battle of Waterloo, which took place not far from the Ambassador's Residence at Waterloo. The 'Butte de Lion' or Hill of the Lion was built to commemorate the battle, which happened on 18 June 1815 when Wellington stopped Napoleon in his imperial ambition to conquer and rule the whole of Europe. The monument was erected by the King of the Netherlands on the spot believed to be where his son was wounded during the battle.

The other museum of great interest to me was the Royal Museum of Central Africa, which was built by King Leopold II at Tervuren. I had visited this museum before in 1977 when I was a student at the ISS, in The Hague. The museum depicted collections from the colonial Belgian Congo from 1897. As you enter, you feel an awareness of the kind of atrocities committed by the Belgians and their king, King Leopold II, who owned the Congo as his personal property from 1885 until it was transferred to the Belgian state in 1908. There are collections of artefacts, ethnology, minerals and ecology located on two floors of the museum. It is on record that over 30 million Congolese perished in the hands of King Leopold II through limb amputation and looting of villages which could not meet their demands for rubber, ivory and precious minerals for the enrichment of the king.

Leaving the Embassy late one evening, there was an unexpected visitor waiting for me at the Chancery gate. He stopped my car with the intention of smashing the windscreen and inflicting bodily harm on me. The security guards swooped on him to find out his problems. He told a long story about making frequent visits to the Chancery without his problem being solved, and since I was the "overall boss" he decided to settle his problem by attacking me, so that his case could be listened to or solved. I interrupted to correct him that I was not the "overall boss", because before me there was the Ambassador and the Deputy head of Mission. He retorted "but why are you called the head of Chancery if you are not the head?" He said he had bought a "Belgian car" at a garage in the town and paid for it in full but could not pick it up until he arranged shipment. When he returned to the garage they refused to give the car to him on the excuse that the previous company was in liquidation and the new owner could not honour previous commitments, even though the car was still parked on the same premises. He said he came to the Embassy several times for assistance but there was no one to help him, and wondered why Nigeria had established an embassy in Belgium when cases like his own could not be solved. Incidentally he had only been seeing the locally recruited staff, who in most cases took their own decisions since they had vested interests and in most cases created negative image problems for the Embassy and the Diplomatic Service.

After a lot of persuasion, I referred him to Chief Adegboyega Boyede, the scheduled officer, the following morning to deal with his case. Adegboyega (later Ambassador), the economic desk officer, handled the case skilfully. He visited the garage and pretended to be test-driving the car with a view to buying it from the new owner, but drove the car straight to the Chancery building, from which the negotiation was done in a position of strength in favour of the Nigerian.

That incident was not exceptional as such things were quite rampant in Brussels at that time, especially involving

Palestinians, Arabs and Congolese, who operated illegal garages and spare parts shops but kept on changing the names of the enterprises using the local laws of liquidation and acquisition. They did the same thing to Mr Etuk, the Administration Attaché in our Embassy in Athens Greece, who lost his own car to the rogues in the same manner. The Nigerian who attacked me at the Embassy in Brussels later met me at Lagos airport and came begging me for forgiveness for the embarrassment he had caused me in Brussels. But he questioned my function and designation as "Head of Chancery" and wondered if I was also the boss of the Ambassador and all the other more senior officers to me. I told him that I was only the administrative officer in the Mission and not the boss of them all. On this subject, I wish to quote from Sir Roger Carrick of the British Foreign Service, who was appointed Head of Chancery in Singapore in 1971. He said: "The Chancery is the political section in a diplomatic mission and the head of it is also a glorified office and personnel manager who is usually a middle level Foreign Service Officer." So 'Head of Chancery' is just diplomatic terminology (although not applicable or used by some countries) to refer to the head of administration and control of expenditure in a diplomatic mission. The position provides a separate function for checks and balances, but it has also created problems between the Ambassador and the holder of that desk in many missions. With the appointment now made from headquarters in the Nigerian Diplomatic Service, the Head of Chancery has a unnecessary sense of superiority over many other officers in the mission. I recall when I assigned Chiedu Osakwe as Head of Chancery in Geneva and he came to my office fuming in anger and asking me why I should assign such a degrading desk to him instead of an economic desk where he could learn and practise the art of negotiation. That situation has since changed with the enhanced position of controlling resources of the mission. Even senior officers jockey for it in recent times in Nigeria's Diplomatic Service and are appointed from headquarters based on the federal character principle. This principle is enshrined in the Nigerian constitution to ensure that appointments into the public service should reflect the geographical, religious and linguistic composition of the country.

My view of our sojourn in Brussels at that time was that we did not do much to improve or deepen Nigeria's bilateral relations with Belgium and Luxembourg. From my own desk, there were hardly any contacts with the Belgian Foreign office, NATO headquarters and the European Commission, apart from occasional visits by the Ambassador to the Development Cooperation Division (Division 8) at the European Commission. Even the promotion of visits by high officials of our two countries was not pursued. Maybe because Nigeria was not short of resources to execute its development agenda, as such technical assistance and advisory services were not of any significance to Nigeria at that time. That was why the EEC (now EU) often reminded the Embassy that Nigeria was not accessing the amount of technical assistance and aid earmarked for her development needs. Ambassador Iroha, who came from the business sector, organized several meetings with the private sector in Belgium to promote business opportunities available for them in Nigeria. But the military interventions by Muhammadu Buhari and

Ibrahim Babangida created instability that did not attract foreign direct investments into Nigeria.

On the multilateral diplomatic aspect of our assignment in Brussels, there was modest contribution by our delegation but the relevance of the Lomé Conventions, the third of which was under implementation during my service in Brussels, was being questioned. Was the ACP-EEC Agreement useful to our trade and developmental goals? I would say it was a novel innovation in its provisions of technical assistance and aid from the EEC to the ACP states. The Lomé Conventions incorporated preferential treatment and stabilization of export earnings from ACP countries. Lomé III provided mechanisms for the ACP states to determine their own development in accordance with their own priorities and diversities, in terms of culture, social values and natural resources. But it had drawbacks. The Convention required the purchase of ACP agricultural products such as food items at preferential prices, which endangered the development of ACP agriculture. The second drawback was the granting of preferential access to ACP agricultural products in the EEC for more favourable treatment, which tended to negatively affect the quality and competitiveness of ACP produce in world markets.

There has been significant transformation since I left Brussels in January 1987, as the ACP countries increased from 46 in 1975 to 68 in 1987 while the EEC transformed into the European Union in 1992 with an increase of membership from 16 to 25 members. Due to the doubts expressed as to whether the Lomé Conventions played any significant role in the development of the ACP states, attempts were made to improve on it by the Cotonou Accord.

This was because many of the ACP states depended on primary commodities and mineral products for their own development. It was also doubted if the technical assistance from the EU was significant. Most of the ACP countries, especially Nigeria, could not absorb the funds made available to them by the EEC. My experience in the few ACP countries I visited as well as during the Uruguay Round of multilateral trade negotiations tended to confirm the conclusions. It was also clear that the preferential treatment of ACP products sold into the EU did not materialise and even inhibited the development of ACP agriculture- a clear case of unintended consequences of the agreement in the development of the ACP group of countries, especially those in Africa. The main interest of the EU in the ACP as the main source of raw material for their industries also did not materialise due to competitive sources from the non-ACP countries in Asia.

With the recent withdrawal of the United Kingdom from the European Union (Brexit), the fortunes of many former British colonies, including Nigeria, in ACP-EU relations has been diminished or eroded. Their fortunes in the ACP-EU will be decided by the outcome of the negotiations between the UK and the EU. Many of them would likely rely on bilateral agreements with the individual countries for trade and investments, as was the case before the advent of the ACP-EU. Coincidentally the Cotonou Agreement, which was signed in 2000 to succeed the Lomé Conventions, was billed to end in 2020.

The inadequate bilateral contacts with Belgium could be attributed to the lack of emphasis and directives from headquarters until the appointment as Foreign Minister of

General Ike Nwachukwu, who made economic diplomacy a cardinal aspect of Nigeria's foreign policy. However, it was argued by some that that was not a new policy, but that he simply re-emphasized it because economic and commercial relations were already enshrined in our foreign policy objectives right from the time of Nigerian independence in 1960.

CHAPTER 4

PLANNING NIGERIAN FOREIGN POLICY

"Diplomacy is a disguised war in which states seek to gain by barter and intrigue, by cleverness of arts, the objectives which they would gain clumsily by means of war."

Randolph Bourne (1886-1918)

I returned to Nigeria in early January 1987 and found remarkable changes, both positive and negative. The most positive one, in my view, was the cleanliness of the whole country. The Marina, where MEA was located, was extremely clean compared to when I left in 1983 because of the "War against Indiscipline" pursued with vigour and zeal by General Muhammadu Buhari. The no-nonsense military regime also installed discipline among the people. Lateness to work was severely sanctioned; the same with shunting queues at public places. But there was grave violation of human rights and fundamental freedoms, where drug peddlers were executed without due process. Most members of the leadership of the ousted civilian administration of Shehu Shagari were detained without trial and a few of them died in custody. There was another new military regime, led by General Ibrahim Babangida (IBB), which adopted the structural adjustment programme (SAP) with untold hardship to the people. The Nigerian naira, which hitherto had been stronger than the US dollar ($) and at par with the British pound sterling, had been devalued to one US dollar, equal to three naira. That was the exchange rate used by the customs to compute the amount of duty for my car brought from Belgium as at January 1987. Corruption, which was fought by the Buhari administration, was on the increase and had been entrenched and appeared as if it was encouraged by the military leadership under IBB.

I was deployed to the East and Central African Affairs Division under the leadership of Samuel Ogundele and Ismael B. Muhammed, who were later appointed ambassadors but at different times. Suleiman Dahiru, my colleague and schoolmate at ABU Zaria, was in the same division and assisted me greatly to settle down. Most of the issues handled by the division were on apartheid South Africa, and there were many African National Congress (ANC) supporters taking refuge in Nigeria. Some of them were allocated staff quarters with us at the 1004 Federal Housing Authority at Victoria Island; notable among them was George Nene, who later became the first South African High Commissioner to Nigeria. I did not stay long in the Division as I proceeded on a one-month leave to enable me to clear my personal effects and settle my family, since I missed out on staff housing allocation due to the odd time I arrived and the fact that I was wrongly classified as a grade VI instead of grade IV officer due to improper keeping of records.

On return from vacation leave, I was deployed to Management Section in the Administration department. That was the first and last time I made a formal complaint against posting or deployment order for demoting me to a desk I regarded as inferior or degrading to me. I was the first university graduate with a master's degree to be sent to that Section. It was always manned by officers converted from the executive line of the Service, but to consider me for deployment to the Section was humiliating to me.

I went to Kevin Efretei in West African Affairs Division to assist me to reverse the deployment. Kevin took me to Mark Eze (later ambassador to The Gambia) to appeal on my behalf. Mark was the Deputy Director Administration and I was meeting him for the first time. He told us that he was sending me to that Section to sanitize the place and assured us that within six months I would be moved to an economic or political desk. He told us that another Foreign Service officer, Emmanuel Ademola Ogunnaike, was also deployed there to assist me. He said the Section was rotten with corruption and needed fresh blood. I wondered how he knew I would sanitise the place, as I had not known him nor worked with him before. I told Kevin that I was not convinced I was the most suitable person to work in that office.

As we left, Kevin told me a thrilling story about something that had happened in his division that morning. He said he had sent an urgent mail from one of the West African countries to a junior colleague to file, examine and submit to him for further action as demanded by the Foreign Minister. The officer could not finish the examination and took the work home with the confidential file, but armed robbers attacked him on his way and took everything including the file. The officer reported the incident to him but his director, Ambassador Gabriel Falase, took the officer directly to the Discipline Section and left him there! That story made my own complaint child's play and I grudgingly reported for duties at the Management section.

Unknown to me, many officers were lobbying to be deployed there, due to the contracts and monetary gains available, which I never knew existed. In fact, it was like a gold mine and was also an opportunity for me to get to know the officers in the Ministry. The section was part of the Administration directorate, headed by Ambassador Jibrin Chinade with Isaiah Udoyen as his deputy. Instead of staying there for six months, I spent two years there and it provided me with insight into the staff and management problems in the Ministry. It was a replica of Head of Chancery desk at post, as everyone, both senior and junior officers, was trooping in with endless requests for repairs and supplies at their offices or homes as well as general cleaning, lift maintenance, telephones, drinks etc. I was also appointed a member of the Junior Staff Committee which deals with recruitment, promotion and discipline of junior staff. It was man-management at the highest level and I made many friends, and some foes as well. At the end of my duties in that section I did not regret the deployment because I had learned a lot about the problems of the Ministry with all its intrigues and values.

The most intractable problem in the MEA, which

remains today, was power supply; we used generators, but it was impossible to keep them functioning for long hours. The other problems, linked to the same power supply, were the lifts and since all directors, the permanent secretary and ministers were on the top floors, I had a real battle on my hands, with endless complaints or requests from senior and junior staff.

After the lifts had not been functioning for almost a week through inadequate power supply Sefi Attah, the Permanent Secretary, could not bear it any longer as she had a bad leg and could not climb to the fifth floor. Ambassador Attah angrily shouted at me and directed that I should be deployed from that Section with immediate effect. Luckily for me Lawrence Agubuzu, the Deputy-Director Administration, who knew the problems with the lifts, posted me to a much better department, the Policy Planning Department.

What a relief. I found myself working with very experienced officers and I was supported by a cream of junior ones whom I believed were among the most intelligent Foreign Service Officers ever assembled together. My bosses were ambassadors Moshood Abiola as the Director-General, while Philip Binye Koroye and Emmanuel Otuokon were the directors. Dr. Philip Obioma Opara (just a step behind me in the Service rank) and some versatile junior officers added value to the work of the Directorate. Chief among them were Messrs Daniel Obasa, Olabode Adekeye, Sola Enikanolaiye and Audu Kadiri, among others. The work in the directorate followed the steps initiated by those before us, particularly by ambassadors Segun Apata and Olufemi George. Any issues referred to us were discussed by all officers round the table, with junior ones having more to say than the senior ones. By adopting this method, we achieved a lot on topical issues at the time, like the Bakassi peninsula problems between Nigeria and Cameroon, the Liberian crisis when it erupted at the end of 1989, the Gulf of Guinea Joint Commission and Southern Africa in transition and the dismantling of apartheid in South Africa.

I came into the Directorate soon after Major-General Ike Omar Nwachukwu was appointed Foreign Minister. He kept us very busy, and particularly my desk as the anchor person standing between the three senior officers and the junior ones dishing out policy papers on topical issues. Ike Nwachukwu created the Crisis Management Committee, in addition to the Policy Planning Committee, where we served as the secretariat. The Policy Planning Department was renamed Policy, Research and Statistics Directorate because of President Ibrahim Babangida's reform programme of 1988. The functions of the new Directorate were as follows:

a) Development Plans (Plans, Median and Perspective)

(b) Monitoring and Evaluation of Plan Implementation

(c) Secretariat of the Tenders Boards

(d) Research into the sectors over which the Ministry has jurisdiction

(e) Research into the internal organisation and operational modalities of the Ministry

(f) Sorting and Monitoring of Performance and Efficiency Targets of divisions and staff

(g) Constant collection and processing of data and statistics related to the Ministry

(h) Management of the Ministry's records and information resources such as Data Bank, Computer Services, Registry and the Library.

The Directorate was divided into two departments, namely Policy Planning and Research and Statistics, but we all worked as a team as if we were in one unit under the leadership of Ambassador Ola Moshood Abiola, supported by ambassadors Binye Koroye and Emmanuel Otuokon.

Ms Judith (later Ambassador) Sefi Attah, the Permanent Secretary, the one who was furious with me due to the lifts in the Management Section, found my work as the secretary of the Crisis Management Committee (CMC) to be invaluable and useful. I happened to have met Ambassador Attah in Brussels when she visited from Paris, where she was Permanent Delegate of Nigeria to UNESCO. Ambassador Attah later became my mentor and supported me when I was almost lynched by senior officers at headquarters for my continued stay at Geneva against their wishes on the directive of Ambassador Matthew T Mbu, the Foreign Secretary.

A question often asked by the public was who was responsible for the planning, articulation and implementation of Nigerian foreign policy. There is no doubt that the planning of foreign policy is the exclusive preserve of the President or the Head of State of any country, and Nigeria was not an exception. As the chief diplomat, the President was responsible for the planning, articulation and implementation of foreign policy. The Foreign Minister would assist him or her through the Ministry of Foreign Affairs. The direction a country takes concerning its foreign policy is the sole responsibility of the President of that country. It is a well-known fact that the foreign policy of a country is basically an extension of its domestic policy or is dictated by the socio-economic development of that country. Development at international level also influences a country's domestic policy through what is termed the "Boomerang Effect." An example of the boomerang effect in which developments at international level influenced domestic policy is the domestication of treaties, conventions and protocols which Nigeria had signed and ratified at the United Nations or bilaterally with other countries. These circumstances determine the type of work we were saddled with at the PRS under the close watch of President Ibrahim Babangida and Ike Nwachukwu, the Foreign Minister, who were the driving forces in Nigerian foreign policy architecture during our time. Of course, I cannot rule out the influence of external bodies like the Nigerian Institute of International Affairs (NIIA), the Nigerian Institute for Policy and Strategic Studies (NIPSS), the Armed Forces Ruling Council (AFRC) and the Defence headquarters, among others. But the main organ that had statutory responsibility for the planning, articulation and execution of Nigerian foreign policy was the MEA. However, our intervention in Liberia for example, to which Nigeria sent military equipment to assist President Samuel Doe to repel the invading rebellious forces of Charles Taylor, was not based on MEA recommendation. We learned of it through the media at the time we were meeting to proffer the best action to be taken by Nigeria.

Nigeria and the Liberian Crisis

The Liberian crisis had heated up by the end of December 1989 and I was invited to cover a meeting in the office of the Minister of State on a subject on which I had no idea; Liberia. Very senior ambassadors and directors were present. In my mind I felt this matter was purely within the schedule of the African Affairs Department as it was basically a political problem. But I was asked to deal with it from the policy planning perspective. It was a meeting akin to Crisis Management Committee (CMC) which fell under my schedule but since it was chaired by the Minister of State instead of the Permanent Secretary, it was something in between CMC and Policy Planning Committee (PPC). The Minister of State briefed the meeting that a member of the Armed Forces Ruling Council (AFRC) called and told him that the US Ambassador had visited him and discussed the situation unfolding in Liberia and wanted Nigeria to intervene and stop Charles Tailor's forces from entering Monrovia. From my recollection it appeared the US was favourably disposed to Prince Yormie Johnson instead of Charles Taylor, although both were in the same camp at that time. It was also reported that an American envoy (not the Ambassador) had earlier arrived at the MEA for an audience with the Foreign Minister and was directed to see Ambassador Ignatius Olisemeka, then Director-General (Regions), but he also turned away the American envoy because he was a political desk officer at the US Embassy and not the counterpart of the Director-General.

Ambassador Olisemeka wondered what the meeting was all about, as according to the newspapers of that day, the

Nigerian Government had already airlifted arms and ammunition to support President Samuel Doe. The meeting condemned the action of the US Embassy in sending a low-level officer to seek audience with the MEA officials, but its Ambassador went over and above the Ministry to the highest policy-making body of Nigeria. That action was contrary to diplomatic practice in the manner of channels of communications between the sending state and the receiving state, as enunciated in the Vienna Convention on Diplomatic Relations of 1961. That incident demonstrated the problems we often faced in MEA, renamed MFA in January 1992, when foreign envoys bypassed the well-known channels of communication and went direct to Ministries, Departments and Agencies (MDAs) or senior government officials. But we cannot blame them, because the MEA lacked basic working facilities to conform to the demands of an efficient Foreign Ministry.

The report emanating from Liberia was scanty, as our Embassy was ill-equipped to send detailed and relevant information. From other sources we gleaned that Prince Yormie Johnson and Charles Taylor were separately struggling to take over the Liberian capital from Samuel Doe, but the two forces later allied and formed the National Patriotic Front of Liberia (NPFL). It was also reported that Taylor's fighters had crossed into Liberia from a base in Cote d'Ivoire on 24 December 1989, while Johnson later broke away and formed the Independent National Patriotic Front of Liberia (INPFL). With so many conflicting reports it was not possible for the MEA to advise government unless the Embassy of Nigeria in Monrovia gave updated and factual situation on the ground.

Ambassador Olisemeka wondered what kind of advice the Ministry would give the Government, since the Federal Government had already taken a decision to send troops with arms and ammunition without any input from the Ministry. However, he agreed that more information was needed and called on the West African Affairs Division to monitor the situation and report back to the Ministry on a regular basis.

At the end of the meeting I did not render any reports because it was not part of my schedule, and I was not involved in the unfolding crisis again until I came face to face with the warring factions during a Peace Conference on Liberia in Geneva in 1993.

The Bakassi Peninsula Crisis between Nigeria and Cameroon

The Bakassi Peninsula had emerged as a major crisis when it was reported that Cameroonian gendarmes had attacked some villages in Nigeria for refusing to pay taxes. The gendarmes also chased away Nigerian fishermen in the area. The crisis was widely reported by the Nigerian media and Minister Nwachukwu wanted urgent action from the Directorate, from the policy perspective, even though African Affairs was deeply involved. Our usual approach involved working round the table with all officers participating and the younger ones having a field day. Luckily for us Ambassador Emmanuel Otuokon came from that area of Nigeria, and he was able to brief us effectively. The question then arose, where was the Bakassi Peninsula on the world map? We found that all the maps in our possession showed it deep inside Cameroon territory and not in Nigeria. All the geography books written by Nigerians, as well as the 1989 calendar hanging in our offices at that time, showed that the peninsula in question was not in Nigeria.

The Minister summoned a meeting of all Directors-General in the Ministry to discuss the problem. Beforehand we were tasked with the responsibility of preparing the background paper. My junior colleagues, namely Daniel Obasa, Sola Enikanolaiye and Philip Opara among others, swung into action and prepared an excellent draft. As we were discussing the draft before sending it up to our bosses my colleague from African Affairs, Charles Awani, entered my office and could not believe how the junior officers were so passionate in making their points and overriding my views even though I was their boss. I enjoyed such sessions very much, but my colleague phoned to sound a note of caution that such sessions might undermine my authority.

In one such session Sola Enikanolaiye, one of the most brilliant junior officers, proffered a novel idea to address the problems in the peninsula. He suggested that we should address the issue as an environmental problem because of the oil pollution in the area. He called for the establishment of a Joint Commission involving all the littoral countries of the Gulf of Guinea, namely Nigeria, Cameroon, Benin Republic, Sao Tome and Principe, Equatorial Guinea and Gabon. He said that if the Commission was created with the objective of addressing the environmental problems, it would invariably defuse the political crisis as well. In conclusion he recommended that the Commission should be called the Gulf of Guinea Joint Commission. As soon as we submitted our draft, ambassadors Binye Koroye, Otuokon and Moshood Abiola wasted no time in forwarding it to the Foreign Minister and the concept paid off in later years.

The Republic of Cameroon was said to have offered to host the first meeting as well as the Secretariat. Consequently, the Gulf of Guinea Joint Commission was established, but with Headquarters in Luanda, Angola, because of the work in the Policy Planning Department to which I had the privilege of contributing. That was one of the high points of achievement of the Ministry of External Affairs under my desk.

A lot had happened on the Bakassi peninsula, with the Greentree Agreement signed between Nigeria and Cameroon following the International Court of Justice (ICJ) judgment ceding the peninsula to Cameroon. The Greentree Agreement was signed at Greentree, near New York, on June 12, 2006 to peacefully implement the ICJ judgement on the Bakassi Peninsular crisis. The move to ease tensions between Nigeria and Cameroon by Presidents Olusegun Obasanjo and Paul Biya was further sealed through the establishment of the Cameroon-Nigeria Mixed Commission (CNMC), which has met the desired objectives of bringing the two countries to a negotiating table.

But during the greater part of 2012, there were many agitations for Nigeria to appeal against the judgment. Notable among such calls was one from Professor Bolaji Akinyemi, Nigeria's Foreign Affairs Minister, who left office just before the crisis between Nigeria and Cameroon erupted in 1989. In a speech entitled "Lead us not into temptation", he condemned Dr. Teslim O. Elias for saying that Bakassi was not in Nigeria but a Cameroonian territory. Professor Walter Ofonagoro, who was one time the Minister of Information, also claimed that there were new facts for government to use as evidence to support the grounds for appeal. But as I mentioned earlier, all the maps in Nigeria and the world showed that as of 1989 Bakassi was in Cameroon and not in Nigeria. Dr Nowa Omoigui, a medical doctor but also a respected historian on military matters, confirmed this. He wrote a detailed commentary entitled "The Story of Bakassi" in which he enclosed a copy of the letter written to the military Governor of Cross-Rivers state from Defence headquarters directing him only to assist the Nigerians living in that area without claiming sovereignty over the territory itself. It was therefore, a good decision that Nigeria did not appeal against the ICJ judgement and has left to rest the tensions created between the two countries.

Southern Africa in Transition

There were two events that happened in quick succession to each other in Southern Africa in which I was involved in my capacity as the secretary of the Crisis Management Committee. These were the rundown to the independence of Namibia in 1990 and the release of Nelson Mandela from prison on 2 February 1990.

The first issue was the conclusion of long and tortuous negotiations between Angola, Cuba and the Republic of South Africa on the withdrawal of Cuban and South African forces from Angola. It was triggered by the US calling upon Angola to withdraw the Cuban and Soviet forces from its territory, but Angola insisted that the South African forces must also withdraw from its territory and grant independence to Namibia in accordance with UN resolution 435 of September 29, 1978. The US agreed to act as the main mediator with the Soviet Union, which was acting behind the scenes in support of Angola. The negotiations ended with an agreement which was signed at Mount Edjo on 22 December 1988 by the three parties concerned.

As soon as we heard of this agreement, a CMC meeting was convened to deliberate on the way forward for Nigeria prior to the independence of Namibia. The meeting was very pro-active as it was decided that Nigeria should open an Observer Mission in Windhoek, the capital of the would-be independent Namibia. It was also decided that a retired career ambassador who had served in Southern Africa should head the mission, to be assisted by an officer in the MEA. Ambassador Rufus Omotoye, who had served as our high commissioner in Botswana, was appointed to head the Observer mission, with my colleague Joseph Keshi as assistant. These officers were to identify and purchase suitable buildings that would serve as Chancery, residence and staff quarters in that country. That was how Nigeria became one of the first countries to establish diplomatic relations with Namibia when it became independent on March 21, 1990. And to demonstrate the importance we attached to that relationship, President Ibrahim Babangida led the Nigerian delegation to commission our diplomatic mission in Windhoek on 22 March 1990, a day after the country gained independence.

The second issue in Southern Africa in which I played an active role was when President Frederik F.W. de Klerk repealed the ban on the African National Congress (ANC) and announced on February 2, 1990 that Nelson Mandela would be released from prison. The announcement took us by surprise and was big news all over the world. The Ministry's Crisis Management Committee, which I served as secretary, met immediately on the same day to deliberate on the way forward on Nigeria's policy with South Africa in view of the unfolding developments. The Ministry decided to organize a seminar titled "Southern Africa in Transition" in the Rotunda Hall at 23 Marina Street in Lagos. This was followed by another seminar two months later in London to reposition Nigeria in that country if South Africa became free from the apartheid regime and a democratic South Africa emerged.

I was on annual vacation in Jos when this seminar in London was arranged and Ambassador Ola Moshood Abiola, my boss, phoned me to tell me to return to Lagos and accompany Ambassador Olisemeka to London for the seminar. At the end of the seminar I missed my flight to Lagos and could not render the report of the meeting to Ambassador Olisemeka as I was directed, and that earned me the first and the last query made to me throughout my service years. In fact, it was my fault because my ticket read 18.00 hours but I misunderstood it as eight o'clock instead of six o'clock and thus missed the flight and had to fly the following day when I was due to give the report. By that query I learned a lesson from the Ambassador, who was one of the first generation of Nigerian diplomats, on the seriousness of non-rendition of reports of meetings in a timely manner, a lesson which I learned from for the rest of my Service career.

On the day of his release, Nelson Mandela stated that

he was committed to peace and reconciliation with the white minority population. He also made it clear that armed struggle was not yet over, since the factors that necessitated the establishment of the military wing of the ANC, the Umkhonto we Sizwe, still existed. He expressed the hope that a climate conducive to a negotiated settlement would be created after which there would be no need for the armed struggle. This was why the MEA took pro-active action to ensure that Nigeria was involved or carried along in the new changes in South Africa, although we still maintained the ban on travelling to South Africa or any trading links between our two countries.

Closure of Some Nigerian Missions Abroad

President Babangida took the Ministry of External Affairs (MEA) by surprise when he announced his intention to close some missions abroad during the end-of-year broadcast on 31 December 1988 without any input from MEA. In the first working day in the new year, which was January 2, 1989, Ambassador Attah convened a meeting of the CMC to deliberate on the matter and directed that I should work with my colleague, Scott Omene, the Minister/Counsellor (staff) in the Administration Directorate, to produce a draft document for further deliberations before we were caught up with closure of missions with strategic importance to Nigeria that could cause embarrassment to us.

We worked meticulously on this exercise dealing with the missions and their work schedules one by one. Our initial recommendation was the closure of 17 missions, but we had the novel idea of asking the Foreign Minister to discreetly find out from the President the list and the number of staff they intended to leave at each mission. To our greatest relief, the closure intended affected only 11 missions and the total number of officers appeared unlikely to exceed 498 Foreign Service personnel, including administrative and technical staff. This excluded locally-recruited staff and those from our home Ministries of Information, Commerce and the Department of Immigration, Customs and the NIA.

After the memo was presented President Babangida directed that all the Ministerial Departments and Agencies (MDAs) should close their outfits abroad and hand over their schedules to MEA officials but that NIA should be included in the ceiling of 498 staff. We argued against the frequent closure of missions abroad due to the wrongful claim that it would save costs. Some of these missions had immovable structures like chanceries and residences that would be wasted by such actions. Further, the closure often damaged bilateral relations with the host countries. The unilateral decision to close embassies as well as the Liberian saga without any input from MEA indicated that some Nigerian foreign policy matters were being formulated from sources outside the MEA.

The PRS Directorate was also confronted by another directive from President Babangida to move to Abuja within six months, without any input from the MEA. That was how the dilapidated office blocks meant for the Federal Ministry of Education at Maputo Road at Wuse Zone 3 Abuja were allocated to MEA as temporary office accommodation. The movement to Abuja was chaotic, just like the fire incident that destroyed the headquarters building on the Marina in

1981 and the movement to NEPA Building Awolowo Road Ikoyi and back to Marina. These movements resulted in the loss of important documents and archives which are still missing today. There was a small library when the MEA was in Lagos manned by the PRS, but I did not know what happened to it during the movement to Abuja as I was posted out to Geneva during the movement. At the time of writing these memoirs, the Ministry of Foreign Affairs has no functional library, even at departmental level, to use for research and documentation. The MFA also lost the plot of land earlier allocated to it at Garki with proximity to the Diplomatic enclave for its Headquarters building in Abuja until much later, when another one was made available in Central area.

The involvement of the Policy Planning Department in capital projects, in my view, seemed to have eroded or diminished its core functions in policy formulation and implementation, as attention was shifted from policy to projects or contracts instead of functioning as a real policy think tank as was the case prior to Decree 43 of 1988 on Civil Service Reforms.

By the beginning of 1990 there was speculation that I would be affected by the posting order of that year and that I was pencilled in to be the Consul-General in Jeddah. To confirm the rumour, I went to see Ambassador Jibrin Chinade, the Director-General of Administration and my former boss when I was working under him as the head of the Management section. Ambassador Chinade confirmed to me that it was his recommendation and that the Minister of Foreign Affairs had agreed to that proposal. I could not hide my feelings, as I was very excited by such good news.

It was good news because of the enormous responsibility attached to that post as well as the spiritual benefits it would offer me and my family. It would also enable me to widen and deepen the circle of friends I would make. That posting for me was even more important than an ambassadorial appointment.

I visited Makkah and Madinah in 1981 for the hajj when I was still in the services of Plateau State Government. During that year the number of Nigerian pilgrims was among the highest in the world, third only after Indonesia and Egypt. It was also the year President Sadat of Egypt was assassinated on Eid-el Mubarak day. When the BBC announced the news, I was one of the first people to hear it among the Nigerian pilgrims at Mina, because the only item I bought on arrival was a small radio to listen to world news. Since then I have loved and cherished going on pilgrimage to Makkah and Madinah, and for the MEA to post me there as Consul-General was the best news of my life.

Then the unexpected happened. Ike Nwachukwu was replaced by Dr. Rilwanu Lukman as Foreign Minister. Through intensive pressure from Rasaq Yunusa (later Ambassador), the Consul-General, to extend his tenure for another year, he claimed that he would soon retire from the Foreign Service and asked me if I could wait for another year. But that decision did not go down well with me and I requested a posting elsewhere, without naming any preference, because that was not the practice in the Service. I was then posted "to continue with multilateral diplomacy" as mentioned to me by Ambassador Chinade. I was happy nevertheless, since I would be involved in what I liked best, negotiations on issues instead of man-management with a myriad problem.

As some of us were preparing to move to Abuja or proceed to postings abroad, there was turmoil in the Middle East when President Saddam Hussein invaded Kuwait, making postings to the Middle East unattractive and dangerous. Many of my friends came to congratulate me for not going to Jeddah. Dr. Udo Moses Williams rushed into my office and gave me the spiritual aspects of the unfolding development in the Middle East. He said, "Man proposes, God disposes". I felt I should be grateful to God that I was not going to Jeddah after all.

CHAPTER 5

GENEVA: MULTILATERAL DIPLOMACY

"A diplomat who says 'yes' means 'maybe,' a diplomat who says 'maybe' means 'no,' and a diplomat who says 'no' is no diplomat."

Charles M. de Talleyrand, French statesman, 1754-1838

I was posted to the Permanent Mission of Nigeria in Geneva in late September 1990 and found the city much quieter than I expected and an environment very familiar to me in terms of the French language which I had picked up in Brussels. Our home was in Belleview in Versoix by Lac Léman (Lake Geneva) near the French border. Although the house was much smaller than at our residences in our previous posts at Addis Ababa and Brussels, it was in a splendid location which we enjoyed so much, particularly for weekend shopping at Ferney Voltaire in France, where we practise French conversation. Food items were much cheaper in France than in Switzerland due to the exchange rate between the Swiss franc and the French franc. Halima, my wife, picked up the French language much more easily as she enrolled in a formal French language school in the city. My children, Ibrahim, Ishaq and Yusuf, did well by brushing up the French they had learned in Brussels and were masters, often laughing and correcting us whenever we decided to speak or answer telephone calls in French.

Emeka Ayo Azikiwe, the son of Nigeria's first President, was our Permanent Representative to the UN offices in Geneva. There were also two senior colleagues at the level of Ministers in the mission, making three of us, which was regarded as top-heavy and difficult to manage with the resources available as well as the work schedules. My other two senior colleagues were Scott Omene and Okon Udoh (later High Commissioner to Kenya and DCM in Washington DC respectively). There was also Kabir Garba (later Ambassador), Olabode Adekeye, with whom I served in Addis Ababa and at PRS, Eric Bell-Gam, Chukudi Ihim (later a reverend), George Agim and Adullahi Kaoje Mohammed (Trade Attaché) among others, who were Administrative and Technical staff of the Foreign Service.

I was assigned the Economics desk dealing with the United Nations Conference on Trade and Development (UNCTAD). Scott and Okon were respectively in charge of the Conference on Disarmament and Uruguay Round of Multilateral Trade negotiations at the General Agreement on Tariffs and Trade (GATT), which is now the World Trade Organisation (WTO). Most of my duty schedules and meetings were at the Palais des Nations, which was established as the headquarters of the League of Nations and built between 1929-1938. It has served as the United Nations European office since 1946, even though Switzerland did not join the United Nations until 2002. Geneva still serves as the "Peace City" where most of the peace talks and arbitrations of conflicts in the world are held.

The Permanent Mission, which was located at Rue Richard Wagner, was small, and sandwiched within a block of flats; it was rented and quite unsuitable for the kind of work vested upon us. Geneva is the main UN centre for negotiations at technical level, while New York is where the political decisions are taken at the UNGA and the UN Security Council (UNSC). Ambassador Azikiwe devolved responsibility to the three of us to take decisions on matters under our schedules and to refer to him only those issues that require decisions at ambassadorial level. This was contrary to what I experienced under Ambassador Blankson in Addis Ababa, when I was directed never to make statements nor contribute to debates at the ECA without referring them to him. I was directed to listen, observe and report to him and never to speak without his prior knowledge, even at meetings of Counsellors. I wondered how I was expected to learn the art of multilateral diplomacy.

Although I had some experience in multilateral-cum-bilateral posts in Addis Ababa and Brussels, it was in Geneva that I would say I had the full experience of multilateral diplomacy. This was because we were neither accredited to the host country nor called an Embassy or High Commission but Permanent Mission to the United Nations. Multilateral diplomacy is also called conference diplomacy, since we were dealing with other delegates and not the host country. Our main functions were dealing with drafting resolutions and decisions based on national interests and in most cases based on group's positions, such as the African Group and the Group of 77. Since all statements, other than those made at informal consultations, are recorded they are carefully drafted and presented at plenary sessions and could be used for future reference. That was quite different from bilateral diplomacy, where most official duties are made with the host country and usually not recorded for future reference.

All the officers were highly intelligent, efficient and hardworking, especially my assistant, Chukudi Ihim, who briefed me on the issues under my schedule. He prepared all the briefs and talking points on all issues for my consideration and I wondered what time he had for himself and his family. At that time, the personal computer (PC) was not yet a major working tool available to officers, nor was it affordable, and none of us had one.

According to the organisation's information sheet, the United Nations Conference on Trade and Development (UNCTAD) was established by the UNGA in 1964 with the main objective of "maximizing trade, investment, development opportunities of developing countries and assisting them in their efforts to integrate into the world economy on an equitable basis. The primary objective of UNCTAD is to formulate policies related to all aspects of development including trade, aid, transport, finance and technology".

The UNCTAD Conferences met once in four years. The first Conference was held in Geneva in 1964, others were in

New Delhi, (1968) Santiago (1972), Nairobi (1976), Manila (1979), Belgrade (1983), Geneva (1987) and the one I participated actively in was in Cartagena des Indes in Colombia (1992). Apart from the Conferences, the other organs of UNCTAD are Trade and Development Board, UNCTAD Commissions and Working Groups and expert meetings on various issues, including transport, shipping, finance and investment. Negotiations and discussions on resolutions were always acrimonious with lengthy hours, which pitched the developing countries against developed member countries of the UN, none of which were implementable. With my economic background and services in Addis Ababa and Brussels it was not difficult for me to integrate easily and I was appointed the coordinator of the G77 on financial services for the UNCTAD VIII Conference. Chucks Ihim was posted to headquarters and I then worked with Abdullahi Kaoje Mohammed, the Trade Attaché, who assisted greatly in the preparatory process leading to the G77 Ministerial Conference in Tehran, Islamic Republic of Iran in December 1991 as well as the Conference itself in Cartagena, Colombia in February 1992.

Apart from UNCTAD, I was involved with Economic and Social Council (ECOSOC) matters and other UNGA Second Committee issues. I also took over the multilateral trade negotiations at the General Agreement on Tariffs and Trade (GATT) which was more taxing when Okon Udoh left for Headquarters. The ECOSOC was one of the main organs of the UN. Others are the UNSC, the UN General Assembly (UNGA), the Trusteeship Council (dealing with decolonization) and the Secretary-General, which are all based or meet in New York.

During one of the G77 meetings, the Chinese delegation came in to announce its decision to join the Group due to the onslaught China was subjected to by the Western European and Other Group (WEOG) on alleged violations of human rights in Tibet. Throughout my three and half years in Geneva there were WEOG sponsored draft resolutions against China on human rights violations, which were defeated with the support of the G77 member countries. Geneva also became the alternative venue for the annual sessions of the Economic and Social Council (ECOSOC) in 1992, as well as the preparatory committees for various UN conferences such as UN Conference on Environment and Development (UNCED) in Rio de Janeiro, UN Habitat, Istanbul as well as the UN Conference on Sustainable Development, Copenhagen, which kept us very busy.

The Ministerial Conference of the G77 in preparation for UNCTAD VIII was held in Tehran in November 1991. Abdullahi Kaoje Mohammed, the Trade Attaché, accompanied me to the conference. Fortunately for us our delegation was strengthened by the Permanent Secretaries of the Ministries of Commerce and Finance. I used this golden opportunity to raise the problems of inadequate funding for Nigeria's missions abroad. At that time, the Permanent Mission of Nigeria in Geneva owed officers more than six months in unpaid allowances, and months of areas in rents and local staff salaries. I was assured by Alhaji Ahmed Abubakar, the Permanent Secretary of the Federal Ministry of Finance, that priority would be given to my request on his return to Abuja, and it was. He informed me that as soon as he got to Abuja he took the MFA budget file to President Ibrahim Babangida and informed him that urgent action should be taken to fund Nigerian embassies abroad or else they would grind to a halt with negative influence on the image of his administration. Consequently, President Babangida directed the Ministry of Finance, in conjunction with MFA, to embark upon an exercise to verify the financial requirements of all missions abroad. At the end of the exercise, the Ministry of Finance was directed to fund missions directly through the Central Bank without recourse to the MFA. It was also decided that the Ministry's overseas budget should be designated in US dollars and funded directly by the Federal Ministry of Finance through the Central Bank, as there were indications that the funds for missions were diverted to other uses at Headquarters. With that decision, missions received adequate funding on a quarterly basis. Ambassador Femi George confirmed this in his memoirs, in which he wrote: "Between 1993 and the time I left Lisbon at the end of my tenure in August 1996, the mission did not have any financial problems. We paid all our bills when due..." That was the experience of all missions abroad during that period. There was no doubt that President Babangida enjoyed the confidence of the Minister of Foreign Affairs, General Ike Nwachukwu, and he attempted to fund the MFA very well. Unfortunately, that noble decision to fund missions directly, which I partly initiated, did not go down well with the senior officers at headquarters, who argued that the Federal Ministry of Finance was micromanaging MFA. It was truncated under Tom Ikimi and we returned to the status quo, and inadequate funding of missions abroad resurfaced again afterwards.

United Nations Conference on Trade and Development (UNCTAD VIII) in Colombia

The UNCTAD VIII Conference took place in Cartagena des Indias from 8-25 February 1992. The African Group of counsellors and first secretaries that were most active in UNCTAD were from Egypt, Algeria, Nigeria, Côte d'Ivoire, Morocco and Tunisia. Interestingly, all of them rose to the rank of ambassadors for their countries. Three of them were posted to Nigeria and the other to Vienna, where we met and recounted our time in Geneva, Tehran and Cartagena. That was one of the beauties of diplomacy in practice that favour career Foreign Service Officers over non-career appointees as principal envoys or ambassadors. In fact, one of them Ambassador Taos Farookhi of Algeria, was instrumental to my appointment as Chairperson of CTBTO Working Group 'A' for over four years even after I had left Vienna. She was also the person who was instrumental in my appointment as an expert member and consultant to review the Technical Secretariat of the CTBTO when she was the Chairperson of the G77. All these favours were done to me after I had left the mission and without my prior knowledge.

Cartagena des Indias is a beautiful Spanish colonial city and one of the most popular tourist destinations; it is preserved as a UNESCO heritage site. The Colombian Government pegged or jacked up the prices of hotels, reduced the exchange rate and charged for transportation, which they later relaxed after a formal complaint was lodged by the Conference. That action was a complete departure from our experience in Tehran, where most facilities, including transportation, were freely made available to the delegations. Due to the hot weather condition, almost all activities, including official dinners, were conducted in informal dress or "smart casual" dress". That was another piece of diplomatic protocol jargon to add to my vocabulary.

At a reception organized for heads of delegation plus one by the Colombian President, Cesar Gaviria, I was amazed to find many people of African descent entertaining guests. I found the same people at the coastal resorts selling mostly tropical agricultural products and artefacts. I wondered where they were from. I thought they came from Caribbean countries, but I was told that they were Colombians. I took a personal interest in finding out more about them during the weekend, when the Conference was not in session.

My informant and interpreter organized for me a visit to a resort about 50 kilometres north of Cartagena on a Sunday afternoon. The place was like Bar Beach in Lagos with people buying and selling farm produce such as papayas, tropical fruits, handmade crafts, artefacts, paintings, carvings etc. There were bars, discotheques and restaurants. All of them were black Colombians and looking more like the Yoruba ethnic group of Nigeria through their drumming and cultural artefacts. As none of them spoke English or French, only Spanish, communication was the main challenge for me as everyone was interested in getting closer to me to make friends. The word "amigo" (friend) was the first Spanish word I learned there. I was dragged into the discotheque and later to a restaurant, where food was organized for me freely. That was one of the friendliest receptions I ever had in a strange land where we hardly communicated together in a common language.

One man who spoke very little English came and beckoned to me to join him for a canoe ride in the small river estuary. I joined him and went far into the jungle, but I was becoming frightened because of the thick forest. He told me he was taking me to a village inhabited by people of African descent, but I was concerned about my safety and security because there was no mobile phone and I had not told anybody where I was, so we turned back and returned to Boca Grande, the part of the city where we lodged. It was a thrilling day for me, because I learned a lot about the country with its ethnic mix. It has a sizeable number of people of African descent, which is not well known to Nigerians as in Brazil, Cuba and other Latin American countries.

I later learned that Cartagena was one of the first sanctuaries of freed African slaves in the Americas. Before freedom came, this port city was used as a depot for the sale of slaves to neighbouring cities, and at one point there were accounts of the city being deserted and invaded by over 500 impoverished freed slaves. At a reception for heads of delegation, the Indian Ambassador to Colombia told me that Colombia was one of the most tolerant countries in Latin America in terms of the integration of ethnic nationalities. He told me that Colombians of African descent were numerous but concentrated in villages, where they did menial jobs and ran small-scale enterprises along the coastal towns, engaging in fishing and trading.

Due to the artificially exorbitant charges for hotels in Boca Grande and other surrounding areas, delegates had to keep changing hotels to find a good bargain, as the rates were arbitrary. A Zimbabwean colleague, Godfrey Chipare, thrilled us one evening and told us that he had been a "victim of a swindle by the Colombians" to the extent that he kept on moving in and out of hotels for a week until he settled into one which looked "reasonable". But getting services at a bargain price depended on negotiating skills, which he lacked due to the language problem. He said that the problem negatively affected his concentration at the Conference. My thought went back to Nigeria, where whenever we organized an international conference we offered everything gratis. I doubted if Nigeria ever broke even, let alone made a profit at the end of such conferences. These problems are one of the main reasons why many countries struggle to host international conferences.

The theme of the UNCTAD VIII Conference was "Partnership for Development", which was the outcome of the end to the Cold War, the changed international climate and growing globalization and interdependence. The Conference agreed that accelerated globalization had opened new opportunities, democratization, promotion and protection of human rights, rule of law, environment, and unequal access to markets, debts, and falling prices of raw materials. At the end of the two weeks of difficult negotiations, the Conference adopted the Cartagena Commitments, by which developed countries committed themselves to create a global economic environment favourable to accelerated and sustained development. The Conference laid the foundation of a new partnership for development based on sovereign equality of states and shared responsibilities. Both developed and developing countries committed themselves to tackling global problems such as migration and sustainable development. The

Conference concluded by calling for partnership for development from both developed and developing countries through growing interdependence and joint responsibilities.

UNCTAD VIII also agreed that henceforth all decisions and resolutions would be agreed by consensus, beginning with the Conference. But there was one issue which held the meeting for two days without agreement that was on reduction of military expenditures in developing countries to freeze resources for development and alleviating poverty. Although the novel proposal was acceptable to us in the G77, the discussions at the Conference on Disarmament and the NPT made us hold the Conference at a standstill. The delegation of Egypt and Nigeria, which I headed, insisted that developed countries should also reduce their military expenditure or even freeze it and release resources for technical assistance to developing countries for development. We insisted that developed countries should abide by their obligations under the NPT regime and reduce their weapons of mass destruction under general and complete disarmament and provide resources for peaceful uses of nuclear energy to developing countries. I never dreamed that I will deal with these matters twenty years later in Vienna as ambassador. That was an example of the beauty of the work of career diplomats, who continue to build on the experiences garnered elsewhere and by learning on the job from the bottom up which I admired so much in my career.

The Non-Nuclear Proliferation Treaty (NPT) entered into force in 1970. The treaty is well balanced as it provides for non-proliferation of nuclear weapons, disarmament and the right to peaceful uses of nuclear energy. The Review

Conference held in Geneva in 1990 was not conclusive, due to long-standing disagreement between the nuclear weapon states and the nuclear supply group. That conference informed our strong opposition to the call for only developing countries to reduce their expenditure on defence and security. The letter and the spirit behind the NPT agreement was that the non-nuclear weapon states agree to abandon nuclear technology for non-peaceful uses and the NPT nuclear-weapon states with nuclear technology agree to pursue nuclear disarmament aimed at total elimination of their nuclear weapons. At the 1990 NPT conference, many developing countries expressed their disappointment with the limited progress on nuclear disarmament, as the nuclear weapons states showed reluctance to disarm. It was due to these problems in nuclear disarmament that we held the Conference to a standstill until after two days of negotiations a compromise text was acceptable to us. Egypt and Nigeria were the two countries from the G77 that held the Conference to a standstill until compromise was reached and acceptable to us. It was at this conference that Japan announced to the delegates that she was instituting the Tokyo International Conference on African Development (TICAD) with the purpose of bringing Japan closer to Africa.

At the end of the UNCTAD VIII Conference, most delegates left through New York, Washington or to go directly to Europe, but I ventured to stop over in Miami, Florida to see the tip of the American south for two nights. My friends warned me that a Nigerian arriving from Colombia would attract attention in Miami, with negative consequences for me due to the narcotic drugs trade transiting Nigeria into Europe. I decided to try my luck because I really wanted to see Miami, as I might not have that opportunity again. To my great surprise, I have never been well received at any US airports throughout my numerous visits to New York and Washington. The immigration officer asked a few questions as to where I was coming from and what I intended to do in the city and then called one of his colleagues to help me out of the airport, recommending hotels near the beach as well as which complimentary bus to take. I observed that Spanish was widely spoken, and road signs were in both English and Spanish. That visit to Miami gave me some insight into the Cuban exiles as there were many in the city, owning hotels, shops and businesses. In general, they spoke against the Castro regime in Cuba and told me that Cuba was one of the best holiday destinations for US citizens, who travelled there secretly.

The treatment and the warm reception I received at Miami Airport in 1992 was just an exception and not the rule, and it was only by luck that VIP treatment was given to me. My subsequent stopover in New York JFK to Caracas to attend an OPEC Summit in Venezuela in September 2001 was a different story. I was literally detained for over thirty minutes and the return journey was even worse, despite my diplomatic passport and enhanced position as an ambassador. My luggage was ransacked and screened as if I was a criminal. I protested about name profiling or even racial profiling, but they would not listen to me. Later a senior immigration officer apologized and told me that the security agency recruited Mexicans who were not properly trained and that the 9/11 episode seemed to have put the diplomatic passport to test, as its value had been eroded by the war on terrorism. In fact, since then I have never used my diplomatic passport for routine journeys and have seen no difference between it and the ordinary passport, because it never added any value to entry and exit at most European and the US airports.

By October 1991 there were several changes in the Geneva mission as my two colleagues of the same rank, Scott Omene and Okon Udoh, returned to headquarters. Ten years later both were appointed ambassadors, Scott to Kenya and Okon as DCM in Washington. Ayo Azikiwe also left, at the beginning of 1992, after he successfully negotiated the Chemical Weapons Convention where he was the chairman.

Due to these changes the leadership of the Mission fell upon me as the Chargé affairs ad interim. I was not prepared for this and hoped that it would only be for a few months. I found myself handling many issues which hitherto had been handled by the senior and able officers who had just left, including Ambassador Azikiwe. For the first six months I focused my attention on the two highly-pressing negotiations at that time; namely the General Agreement on Tariff and Trade (GATT) multilateral trade negotiations and human rights issues, which surprisingly were becoming more important and needed our attention. Luckily for me, two highly intelligent and hardworking officers, Messrs Chiedu Osakwe and Cyril Uchenna Gwam, joined the mission to replace those who left.

General Agreement on Tariffs and Trade (GATT)

The GATT negotiations were very taxing, because we were

moving towards their conclusion and required full attention from all delegates. Most delegations, except those from Nigeria and a few developing countries, had reinforcements from their capitals. There were 16 negotiation groups, ranging from agriculture, trade related investment measures (TRIMS), trade related intellectual property rights (TRIPS), trade in services, commodities, trade dispute settlement, and many others. I assigned Chiedu Osakwe to join me in trade related matters and Uche to handle environment and human rights issues. Suffice it to say that Chiedu protested when I mentioned to him that he should take over the schedule of Head of Chancery and he wondered why I should reduce him to that desk, as he would learn nothing much in the field of negotiations and diplomatic practice. But in recent years the position of Head of Chancery is well sought after by many diplomats, due to the perceived monetary and political gains in the Chancery. The undue privileges assigned to that desk have reached a crescendo of envy and lobbying that made it necessary for Headquarters to take up the responsibility of assigning the schedules and posting of officers to that desk based on the Federal Character principle (explained in Chapter 3).

My encounter with the GATT negotiations showed a clear disparity in terms of quality and quantity of the negotiations for our delegation and developing countries in general. There were only two of us from our delegation, covering 16 negotiation groups which often met simultaneously. Abdullahi Mohammed from the Federal Ministry of Commerce was my assistant. Apart from India and Indonesia, which had Trade Representatives at the level of ambassadors, all other developing countries were covered by their UN Missions. Negotiations were not done by regional groupings like at the UN, such as G77, WEOG, Asian group, African group, and Latin America and Caribbean. To assist developing countries, UNCTAD established a technical unit to assist it. The African group also made unofficial arrangements to make joint statements calling for more concessions to developing countries, particularly in market access, agricultural products, financial services, TRIPS and TRIMS. The EU has a Trade Representative who also attempted to maintain the Generalized System of Trade Preferences (GSTP) given to its former colonial territories under the ACP-EU agreements under the Lomé Conventions. But developing countries were divided in the GATT, because many of them opposed the ACP-EU agreement, which was inimical to their trade into the EU market. The GSTP and non-exports discrimination principles of the GATT were not compatible with the ACP-EEC agreements to grant concessions to ACP countries in EU market. Therefore, there were several meetings at the EEC (later EU) Mission with ACP countries in order to blend the provisions of the Lomé Convention into the GATT. But some developing countries, non-members of the ACP-EEC like Egypt, India, Malaysia, Indonesia, Brazil, Pakistan, Morocco, Algeria and Argentina, were opposed to granting any concessions to the ACP countries.

The GATT multilateral trade negotiations needed inputs from various MDAs such as trade, finance, intellectual property, agriculture involving goods and services. Towards the end of the negotiations, the US, EU, Japan, Brazil, India, Argentina, and a host of others had their delegations headed by Ministers of Trade and

Commerce, and meetings were held on Saturdays and Sundays for considerable part of October and November 1993.

In addition to the presence of their Ministers, experts from their capitals were trooping in and out of Geneva for the trade negotiations. But for Nigeria, apart from the absence of an ambassador there were only two of us covering all the 16 negotiation groups as well as attended the Ministerial meetings. Abdullahi Mohammed, a highly efficient officer from the Federal Ministry of Commerce, and I were the only ones who negotiated Nigeria's position in the GATT (later WTO). The organisation was rule-based, and every country was expected to furnish its list of commitments on the level of tariffs on goods and services that could be imported into their territories. The tariffs could be one hundred per cent or more and all non-tariff measures were expected to be removed and put on tariffs, since there were no guidelines to us from Abuja.

Abdullahi initiated a list of commitments and levels of taxes on them and forwarded to Abuja but there was no amendment to it, so we presented it as Nigeria's contribution in the negotiations. The recall of Ambassador Azikiwe at such a crucial period without replacement for almost two years had negative consequences, as no matter how efficiently a lower officer handled an issue it was never given the same importance as if it was handled by an ambassador.

The Uruguay multilateral trade negotiations on every issue were tough, hard and tortuous and in minute detail, which ordinary diplomats like us found very difficult to deal with. Abdullahi did his very best to make valuable contributions, but on financial services and agriculture we needed inputs from relevant MDAs at headquarters. None was given to us, and yet we muddled through and got the best for Nigeria through the list of commitments we presented at the concluding negotiations in December 1993. But due to the lack of coordination between the various MDAs there were conflicting decisions that invariably violated the WTO provisions on non-tariff measures where imports of some agricultural produce were banned, like rice, as well as spare parts to protect our local industries. Nigeria was expected to impose maximum tariffs on those products instead of an outright ban. Nigeria was able to escape sanctions through the dispute settlement mechanism of the WTO because no contracting party protested the ban of the items. The US filed a case and won against the concession granted to the ACP countries by the EU for the importation of bananas and other agricultural produce under the ACP-EU Lomé Conventions. Nigeria was lucky to get away with many violations of the WTO rules, to the extent that some critics started questioning the benefits the country was deriving from the organisation when Nigeria signed the agreement at Marrakesh in 1994. I wondered if these critics knew that the Nigerian delegation that negotiated our commitments to the treaty was not properly composed or prepared, as headquarters abandoned their responsibility to low level representations at the concluding sessions of the negotiations in 1993. Worse still, the few months granted for me to conclude the negotiations did not go down well with some senior officers at MFA, who argued that I was not indispensable. The problem of selectivity and favour was the bane of the Nigerian Foreign Service; if one was not in the good books of the senior officials at headquarters or at post one, would suffer, to the detriment of the Service and Nigeria.

By the end of 1992, human rights questions were becoming important to Nigeria as we prepared for the World Conference on Human Rights in Vienna. There was also a searchlight upon Nigeria as we prepared for the 1993 general elections, with some NGOs advocating for free and fair elections. The Mission was also actively involved in the preparatory process for the UN Conference on Environment and Development in Rio de Janeiro, Brazil, in 1992. I was overwhelmed by these issues, in addition to my main desk at UNCTAD, which became less and less important in relative terms.

My experience of heading a mission longer than I expected in Addis Ababa had repeated itself in Geneva, as instead of a few months for an ambassador to be appointed to replace the one that had left, I found myself heading the Permanent Mission for two years.

Debates, decisions and resolutions at the human rights sessions were highly political, contentious, controversial and acrimonious and sometimes reports were beamed live by international news media. At this period, Nigeria was a member of the 53-member Commission on Human Rights and as such was expected to vote on decisions and resolutions of the Commission. The most contentious and highly political agenda item of the UN Commission on Human Rights was under Agenda item 12, later 10, titled: "country specific situations." Under this agenda item, resolutions were drafted, voted and passed against countries to name and shame them for their acute and systematic violations of the rights of their citizens. Luckily Headquarters was quite helpful by promptly guiding us on how to vote (for, against or abstain) on resolutions and decisions of the Commission.

But there was one draft resolution where we could not accept the decision of Headquarters to abstain. Apparently, due to the pressure by the US delegation through their embassies all over the world, Abuja directed us to abstain on the resolution against China in 1993. That draft resolution was the third in the series of resolutions by the Western Europe and other Group (WEOG) at the Human Rights Commission on the violation of human rights in China. Uche, the desk officer on human rights, informed me that he received a verbal message from Abuja that Nigeria should abstain on that resolution. But by our own analysis, if we abstained Nigeria would be isolated by developing countries, who had indicated that they would vote against the draft resolution on China. I dismissed the verbal advice he gave me to abstain because it was not addressed to me as the head of the Mission and not in writing. But the desk officer came back and insisted that it was a credible instruction addressed to us. I was unhappy because I was the officer in charge, but I wondered who the dark horse was who was dishing out instructions to my junior colleague without talking to me. I angrily decided not to check it with headquarters, as I sensed that someone wanted to undermine my position as head of Mission and to embarrass us.

Worried about what to do, and the fact that there was no written instruction for us to abstain, Uche and I then decided to contact Ambassador Attah, who was our

Permanent Secretary prior to her appointment as Ambassador to Italy. Ambassador Attah was very versatile on this subject matter and well respected in the Commission as an expert member of the Sub-Commission on Discrimination and Protection of Minorities. She had also served as Nigeria's Permanent Delegate to UNESCO in Paris, so we were in good hands if she agreed to come over to Geneva to bail us out of the dilemma by leading our delegation.

She willingly accepted and flew into Geneva in the morning and led our delegation during the votes on the resolution in the afternoon. When the vote on the violations of human rights in China was called for, the Chinese ambassador called for a "no action motion to be taken by a roll call of votes". Tactically, we directed the desk officer to cast the vote in favour of the no-action motion in support of the Chinese. Apart from that, Nigeria made a statement explaining why we had voted this way. Afterwards the leader of the Chinese delegation walked to our seats and thanked us for the valuable support we had given them and promised that they would reciprocate in the future, whether at the Commission or elsewhere. They also informed us that their capital had earlier intimated to them that our delegation would abstain and wondered why we had voted in favour of the "no action motion."

Replying, Ambassador Attah informed them that Headquarters advised the Nigerian delegation to abstain in the WEOG resolution against China but not on the "no action motion". She also told the Chinese that there was no directive from Abuja to vote against the interests of our Chinese friends. One of the US delegation from the capital,

Ms Susan Rice (later US PR in New York under President Barack Obama), accosted Uchenna Gwam after the votes and wondered why we had changed our position and voted in favour of China, because according to their information, Abuja had assured them that Nigeria was going to vote in support or abstain on the resolution.

When I returned to the office, Uchenna informed me that the director (International Organisation Department) had phoned from Abuja requesting the report of the afternoon session, particularly on how we had voted in the resolution against China. I was not bothered because there was no written directive to us on how to vote and even if there had been, a superior officer was leading the delegation, albeit unofficially. The decision to vote in favour of the "no action" motion by China was later reciprocated in many ways by China. Nigeria was subjected to severe condemnations by the international community, particularly the European Union, against human rights violations under the regime of General Sani Abacha. China did not only stand by Nigeria all through its period of international isolation (pariah position) during the regime of Sani Abacha but also gave technical assistance and advisory services to Nigeria in many fields.

That decision to disregard headquarters' unofficial directives was part of the policy by headquarters whenever they dished out instructions to our missions abroad by telling them to consider the elements of "local objection". The directive to abstain at the resolution against China met that criterion and we acted rightly, which reaped, and is still reaping, a lot of benefits from China. I was glad we took the right decision.

Worried by the continuous draft resolutions against China by the WEOG, the Chinese resolved to support the position of the G77, NAM and other developing countries at all UN fora. Ambassador Jamsheed Marker of Pakistan in his memoirs *Quiet Diplomacy* reported how he enlisted the Chinese to align with the G77 during the presidency of Pakistan of the G77 in 1992 and was called "G77 and China." At UNCTAD, the Chinese delegation repositioned itself effectively as a developing country more seriously than ever before. China also used the strengthened position to good effect at the Commission on Human Rights (CHR) to nail any future WEOG resolutions of human right violation against her. The last resolution against China at the CHR was in March 1994 and was massively defeated by the support of "G77 and China". The Nigerian delegation made a moving statement in support of China in the explanation of our vote. Ambassador Segun Apata, who read the statement, pointed out that China, with the biggest population, was feeding its population without external assistance, and we saw no reason to destabilise that country through politically motivated resolutions.

The World Conference on Human Rights, Vienna

The World Conference on Human Rights was convened in Vienna in June 1993. It was the second conference in twenty-five years. The first Conference was held in Tehran in 1968. In the preparatory processes for the conference, Nigeria and other African countries proposed many issues that would influence its outcome. We believed that there was the need to balance civil and political rights with economic, social and cultural rights. We also proposed the concept of inalienable right to development as an important component of human rights, which we pursued with vigour at the preparatory commission and at the conference itself. The Nigerian delegation succeeded in incorporating into the final document of the World Conference on Human Rights the concept of "toxic waste dumping as a violation of human rights". The issue of the transformation from Human Rights Centre to Human Rights High Commissioner was divisive, even within the African Group and the G77 and China. Nigeria was in support of the transformation from the Human Rights Centre (HRC) to the Office of the High Commissioner for Human Rights (OHCHR) like that of the UN High Commissioner for Refugees. Professor Ibrahima Fall (a Senegalese), the UN Under-Secretary-General in charge of the HRC, mounted a subtle campaign against the transformation from HCR to OHCHR through his Ambassador/Permanent Representative in Geneva, who had been there for over seventeen years. The Senegalese politicized the noble objective of raising human rights issues to higher level, to be manned by a High Commissioner for selfish reasons. Nigeria supported the change, but for fear of being isolated on the subject matter we subtly joined the consensus to oppose the move to transform the Centre, within the African Group and the G77 and China, until the Conference took the decision on it in Vienna.

Before June 12, Nigeria was not listed or mentioned anywhere in the Commission as a country violating human rights and fundamental freedoms. Nigeria had a very high profile in the Commission and continued to be elected into it due to the values its delegation brought to the work, both at the Commission and its Working Groups. Nigerian nationals were elected into various human rights treaty bodies' standing committees; the Sub-Commission on Discrimination and Protection of Minorities and the Committee on Elimination of Racial Discrimination (CERD). Nigeria was also a signatory to several human rights instruments and also domesticated the African Charter on Human and Peoples Rights as a demonstration of her commitment to the promotion and protection of human rights and fundamental freedoms.

The WEOG and particularly the US opposed the idea of an "inalienable" right to development and held the negotiations to a standstill by insisting that the Right to Development was no different from the overall human rights questions and should not be differentiated. There was also the issue of who was to enjoy the right, the state or the people? China, Cuba and many developing countries insisted on collective rights as against individual rights. These countries insisted that individual rights stem from the collective rights of states, meaning that rights are transferred to individuals from states. Cuba, in all human rights commissions and ECOSOC sessions, tables resolutions against the US economic blockade of Cuba as a violation of the collective rights of Cuba, which has impeded the country's right to development. The WEOG was behind the transformation of the Office of Human Rights to High Commissioner; as such we believed that a compromise would be reached at Vienna to balance the concerns of developed and developing countries, since we agreed that human rights was universal, indivisible and interrelated. Nigeria was the darling of many countries at the

Commission as many delegations were courting and enlisting our goodwill to support them for or against the resolutions at the Commission. But that goodwill changed overnight during the World Conference on Human Rights in Vienna in June 1993.

The Conference was well attended by Nigerian officials, NGOs and civil societies. Surprisingly I was not included in the delegation to Vienna, while over 18 officials came from the Ministry of Foreign Affairs (MFA) and Federal Ministry of Justice. I wondered why I was excluded from the list of the Nigerian delegation to the World Conference and wondered if it was because of the resolution against China three months earlier in which I had influenced our delegation to vote in favour of China against the decision of some powers at Headquarters. But it never bothered me, and I continued with my busy schedules in Geneva. Then a week into the Conference, Ambassador Attah arrived in Vienna from Rome for the Conference and went straight to the hotel suite of Chief Matthew T. Mbu, the Foreign Secretary, and complained that I had not been in Vienna for the Conference while those who had nothing to do with it were in Vienna idling about the place. That was how Uchenna Gwam called me late at night to come to Vienna for the World Conference. I had already lost ground on the negotiations on some of the key issues we were pursuing as I could not know what had transpired in some of them. Nevertheless, the most contentious issues were still on the table. These were the questions on the rights to development, toxic waste and human rights, the high commissioner for human rights and individual and collective rights. The reason these issues were on the table until my arrival was the general understanding at the drafting committee chaired by the Permanent Representative of Brazil that "nothing was agreed until all is agreed".

On arrival at the World Conference, I was directed by the Minister to join Marius Offor and Uchenna Gwam at the Drafting Committee of the World Conference. It was this Committee that negotiated and produced the Final Document and the Declaration of the Conference called "The Vienna Declaration and Programme of Action of the World Conference on Human Rights". Hence, this was the document most legal international human rights bodies refer to, in addition to the various conventions, protocols and treaties on human rights to the present day.

The Annulled Presidential Elections of June 12, 1993

The Nigerian delegation at Vienna was thrown off guard the day following my arrival when the BBC announced the annulment of the Presidential elections in Nigeria on June 12, 1993. It was one of the most difficult problems to deal with at the negotiations, because the conference rose in chorus to denounce the annulment and condemned in strong terms the violation of the right of Nigerian people to freely choose their leaders through elections. Luckily for Uche and me, the *creme de la creme* of the MFA were in Vienna for the Conference, so it was not a problem for the two of us alone to handle the hot potatoes.

As expected, ambassadors Olu Adeniji, the Permanent Secretary, Michael Ononaiye, Sefi Attah, Segun Apata and Marius Offor, Wale Sulaiman, Uche Gwam and I were present, and we had a formal meeting in the room of the Minister to proffer solution on how to respond to the barrage of criticisms from the delegations as well as the NGOs' forum, which suddenly shifted its searchlight to Nigeria. It was at that delegate meeting that Nigeria's instruments of ratification of the International Covenants on Civil and Political Rights, as well as the one on Economic, Social and Cultural Rights, were given to us by Ambassador Segun Apata for onward transmission to the UN Headquarters in New York. By the annulment, Nigeria had violated one of the most important articles of the conventions even before they were deposited in New York. Speculations were going around that Ibrahim Babangida deliberately signed the two instruments at the tail end of his reign to make it difficult for successive governments to govern the country. His choice of words, "annulment" and "stepping aside", dominated discussions for several months in many quarters on his real intentions.

As was always the case in the UN when delegations wanted more time to react to a decision they would announce that they were waiting for instructions from their capitals, even if their capitals had not been contacted. The Nigerian delegation decided to play down the matter and not to mention it in the general statement other than to say that Nigeria was committed to the promotion and protection of human rights and fundamental freedoms and that we were waiting for details from our capital. We were all hopeful that a new election would be held without delay. Apart from a few remarks in the corridor, the matter soon fizzled out, and we went on with the negotiations and decisions to conclude the Vienna Declaration and

Programme of Action of the Conference. Most of the concerns of our delegation were adopted, especially the inclusion of the rights to development, balancing economic, social and cultural rights to civil and political rights. The issue of Human Rights High Commissioner was also adopted, as well as the creation of independent national human rights institutions, which culminated in the establishment by the Abacha regime of our own National Human Rights Commission.

On return from Vienna after the World Conference on Human Rights, my schedule of duties changed dramatically as I was shuttling between the GATT and Human Rights Centre, which were in opposite directions. The latter was dominating our attention at the Permanent Mission, with debilitating effects on our image as a country violating human rights. The annual sessions of the Sub-Commission on the Prevention of Discrimination and Protection of Minorities (now known as the Sub-Commission on the Promotion and Protection of Human Rights) was held in August 1993, and we had an expert member, Ambassador Attah, and her Alternate, Ms Christy Mbonu (later Ambassador). During that session, it was no longer business as usual for the Nigerian delegation as NGOs and some delegations started making statements condemning the annulment of the Presidential election in Nigeria and the clampdown on protesters and their detentions incommunicado by the military regime.

Ken Saro-Wiwa and the Ogoni Bill of Rights

Ken Saro-Wiwa and some Ogoni people appeared at a

meeting of the UN Committee on Indigenous Peoples in September 1993. As I was busy at the GATT negotiations, Uchenna Gwam telephoned the reception (there was no mobile phone then) urging me to rush to the Palais des Nations, where the Committee was meeting Ken Saro-Wiwa and three Ogoni people who were addressing the Committee. They came under an NGO based in The Hague with consultative status with ECOSOC. But there was no way I could leave the GATT in a different location to meet up with what was happening at that end. Before I got there, Saro-Wiwa had left and all efforts to invite him to visit the Mission failed as he left Geneva soon after he made the statement and the launching of the Ogoni Bill of Rights, flag, constitution and other documents.

Uchenna later briefed me that Saro-Wiwa had made a statement claiming that the Ogoni people were an indigenous ethnic group in Nigeria under threat of extinction. He said that Ogoni oil was being extracted by the Nigerian authorities through Shell with devastating pollution and environmental degradation that had threatened their lives and properties. According to Uchenna, Saro-Wiwa declared that the people of Ogoniland people should be classified as "stateless people" to be protected under the UN Convention relating to Stateless Persons signed in New York on 28 September 1954. He also called for their rights to self-determination. To that extent he called on the UN to come to their aid, saying that otherwise within a few years the Ogoni would be totally wiped out from Nigeria. He also launched the Ogoni Bill of Rights, flag, constitution and national anthem. Copies were distributed freely at the UN and Uchenna picked some for me.

During the defence of our 10, 11, and 12 periodic reports on the Convention on Elimination of Racial Discrimination (CERD) on which we had Ambassador Hamzat Ahmadu as expert member, our delegation was overwhelmed by the attention the Ogoni matter had generated. Despite our plea that a strong delegation of experts from headquarters should come and present and defend the reports, none came to our assistance. So Uchenna and I agreed to present and defend the report. But before the session, Ambassador Ahmadu warned us that it was going to be difficult if a high-level delegation, well abreast with the matter, did not come from headquarters, because their briefs indicated that NGOs had filed petitions on violations of our commitments under the convention coupled with the statement made by Ken Saro-Wiwa. It was one of the most difficult issues we handled, as most of the Committee members were very hard on us on the treatment of minorities, particularly indigenous peoples like the Ogoni. We told them that all the 300 ethnic groups in Nigeria were indigenous, not only the Ogonis. We even recalled that oil was not only found in Ogoniland but in many locations and states of Nigeria. Oil was first struck and mined in 1957 at Oloibiri in Rivers State, and now nobody ever mentioned that location because the oil there had dried up. In defending some of the allegations, I mentioned to them that I belonged to one of the minority ethnic groups in Nigeria and we were also indigenous. I buttressed my response by mentioning the environmental degradation in my home state of Plateau, through tin mining, and said our people had not asked for self-determination. I concluded that if all the 300 ethnic groups in Nigeria sought self-determination there would be 300 new states created. I ended up by assuring the international community of the resolve of Nigeria to address the environmental concerns of the Ogoni people and all other oil-producing communities in Nigeria.

The Ogoni issue did not end with me in Geneva; it continued to haunt me even after I returned to Abuja in 1994. I will return to that issue later and the tragic deaths of Saro-Wiwa and nine others.

At the end of our presentation, the Movement for Survival of Ogoni People (MOSOP) sent negative reports to Nigerian media accusing Uchenna Gwam and me of defending the violations of human rights in their homeland by Shell.

The Liberian Ceasefire Agreement in Geneva

On 10 July 1993, Mr. B.D. Oladeji, one of my ablest officers, called my home and left a message that I should come to Gate 6 at the Palais des Nations, the old building which was the Headquarters of the League of Nations. Since there was no mobile phone I wondered what was so important to make the officer send such an urgent message, and also said I should be there as from 2000hrs (and this was also the weekend). I was curious because after the negotiations of the Chemical Weapons Convention (CWC), disarmament matter was not as important, especially after the end of the Cold War in 1991. This is where the Conference on Disarmament (CD) was located and when serious political or high-level crisis negotiations were held.

I arrived at gate 6 and found Oladeji already waiting for

me. He told me that according to intelligence reports, the Liberian factional groups were to hold a meeting in Geneva very late in the evening on Friday. The problem was how we could be smuggled into the meeting to monitor what the outcome would be. When we attempted to accredit ourselves to the meeting, we were turned down, since it was not an open meeting for all UN members. Luckily for us the ECOMOG Commander, General Olatunji Olurin, was there, and we told him of our intention to be accredited to brief Headquarters. General Ibrahim Babangida was the Chairman of ECOWAS, and the meeting was arranged preparatory to the ECOWAS Summit in Cotonou, Benin Republic. General Olurin accepted our request and directed the UN Secretariat to accredit both of us to the meeting.

Those present at the Geneva ceasefire meeting on Liberia were Alhaji G.V. Kromah, leader of the United Liberation Movement for Democracy in Liberia (ULIMO-k), and Charles Taylor, National Patriotic Front of Liberia (NPFL). These were men and women of Liberia who mostly resided abroad, as well as the ECOMOG Commander and UN officials. The meeting was aimed at a ceasefire before the peace agreement summit in Cotonou between all the warring factions, but the participants turned the meeting into jockeying to share political posts among themselves. The meeting was so secretive that even our capital was not aware of it, as they were preparing for the Cotonou Summit for the peace agreement.

The ceasefire meeting was the main subject matter. Then there was the issue of power sharing among the factional groups (of which there were many, but the dominant ones were ULIMO-k and NPFL) and the issue of the plight of the civilian population. Civil society members to be included in an inclusive government were discussed as part of the elements for inclusion in their agreement in Cotonou the following week. There was also the agreement for the inclusion of factional leaders in the transition government. The issue of the eligibility of factional leaders to participate in the future government of Liberia, through nominations and elections, was also agreed upon. It was also noted that apart from the representatives of those around the table there were several other factions that were not present, but they could be accommodated through inclusive interim government and quick election once the conditions permitted.

General Olurin, the ECOMOG commander, wielded enormous powers during the ceasefire agreement as he pressurized the factions, mainly ULIMO-k and NPFL leaders, to accept the terms of ceasefire agreement for the benefit of the masses of Liberia, instead of holding the meeting to ransom for personal gain. He urged them to end the fighting in the field and take the case to the peace meeting in Cotonou which was brokered by OAU and ECOWAS. He said that their concerns that they and their factional leaders should be included in the interim government of Liberia would be considered in the peace agreement. According to General Olurin, he told them that the first thing was the cessation of the hostilities in the war zones to facilitate the peace agreement.

It was with this pressure that the factional groups signed the ceasefire agreement on 25 July 1993. The agreement called for the establishment of the Liberian National Transitional Government (LNTG), which would include representatives of the signatory factions, ULIMO and NPFL. Soon after the meeting, which lasted for fifteen days and late into the nights and early mornings, I called Ambassador Daniel Hart, the Director West Africa, to brief him before we forwarded the report to Headquarters. The Ambassador was surprised that they were not aware of such a meeting at Headquarters. He said he was already proceeding to Cotonou for an ECOWAS meeting on Liberia and directed that our report should be sent to them through our Mission there.

The ECOWAS agreement in Cotonou included most of the elements the factional leaders generally agreed upon in Geneva. The agreement called for an ECOWAS monitored cease-fire and the disarmament, encampment and demobilization of combatants and granted amnesty to all combatants. The Cotonou agreement affirmed the ceasefire pact signed in Geneva and the establishment of the LNTG, which included the signatory factions (NPFL and ULIMO) as well as the Interim Government of National Unity (IGNOU). The executive power resided with a five-member Council of State, three of whom were to be appointed by each of the three signatory parties, while the additional two members were to be eminent Liberians nominated and selected by each of the signatory parties. The Cotonou agreement excluded the two rebel groups from holding office in the transitional government and was forced to seek power through the election to be held within seven months.

The year 1993 was eventful for the Nigeria Mission because of the developments at home. After the annulment of the June 12 presidential election, which triggered an immediate protest in Lagos and other parts of the country, coupled with the clampdown of protesters, NGOs had a field day accusing Nigeria of human rights violations, especially after the World Conference on Human Rights in Vienna. Coupled with the GATT negotiations, which were to be concluded that year, I had a real problem on my hands with the absence of an ambassador. In twelve months, Nigeria had three heads of state, Ibrahim Babangida, who "stepped aside" in August, then Ernest Shonekan as Head of the Interim National Government (ING), and Sani Abacha towards the end of the year, with Moshood Abiola declaring himself the elected president. It was a period of great confusion in the history of our country and no one took us seriously. Geneva being the seat of UNHRC as well as the Inter-Parliamentary Union (IPU), the Nigerian mission was facing a serious problem, especially the arrest and detention incommunicado of Chief Abiola, which was a grave violation of the International Covenant on Civil and Political Rights (ICCPR), which had been ratified by Ibrahim Babangida just before he had stepped aside.

The developments also affected the changes of Foreign Affairs Ministers, from Ike Nwachukwu to Matthew Mbu and Baba Gana Kingibe as well as Permanent Secretaries. These changes created all sorts of uncertainties and anxieties among Foreign Service Officers and friends of Nigeria.

The waiting game for the new Ambassador continued until the end of my tour of duties at the beginning of 1994. During that period, I heard that Ambassador Ejoh Abuah was being posted to Geneva and I recalled the Addis Ababa episode of 1984 being played in full again. For some reason I did not know, Ambassador Attah called from Rome advising me to leave Geneva as soon as practicable with the news of the incoming Ambassador, as if she knew about the unfolding problems that would bedevil the Permanent Mission in the months to come. As soon as I left the Mission, there were problems which threatened the recall of all the officers, and Ambassador Binfa Selchum directed me to solve the problems at headquarters, which I did after consultations with Uche Gwam and Chiedu Osakwe. But bigger and more intractable problems lingered on for years, and led to the recall of the Ambassador and his name being put on a stop list by the EU.

First meeting with the South African Delegation

Economic and social contacts between Nigeria and South Africa were still banned, despite the release of Nelson Mandela, because the sanctions against the apartheid regime were still in force. But South Africa was an active member of the GATT, and as such their delegation was keen to make contacts with the Nigerian delegation. The South African delegation to the GATT asked to pay a courtesy visit to me at the Mission. Since they were not members of the African Group and there was no official lifting of the ban on contacts with them, I decided to contact headquarters for guidance. There was an indication that the ANC would win the general elections in South Africa and Nelson Mandela would be President. As such the white-dominated South Africa embassies began the overtures to woo key African countries to do business with them. There were signs that some notable countries in Asian and Latin American embassies were in contact with South Africa. It took quite some time before I received the directive to meet with them at the UN, not inside our Mission because the Nigerian Government was awaiting the outcome of the election, and after all Nelson Mandela had stated that the armed struggle would not be over until after the election in 1994. The maxim that nothing was over until everything was over applied here perfectly.

We met with the South Africans at the GATT. Abdullahi Mohammed, the Trade Attaché, accompanied me to the meeting. The South Africans informed our delegation that Nigeria was one of the first countries in Africa south of the Sahara to have responded to their request for a meeting apart from those they were having contacts with even during the apartheid era. They called for early contacts with Nigeria for cooperation in commerce, social, cultural and tourism sectors. They informed us that their people were eager to visit Cairo, Nairobi and Lagos, which were banned for their tourists or businesses even though they were allowed a window of opportunity through sports. They told us that many of their tourists visited those cities to participate in a football tournament when the Confederation of African Football (CAF) accredited them. But their experience in Lagos was uncomfortable, as most of their people had lost their valuables in the hands of Nigerians and they went back disappointed. They asked our government to ease the sanctions and the ban on official contacts to enable our two countries to benefit from trade liberalization on the goods and services which were being discussed in the GATT. We assured them of the willingness of Nigeria to cooperate with them and our wish for successful, free and fair multiracial elections in South

Africa. From all indications, that meeting was the first official contact between Nigeria and South Africa in the process of the dismantling of apartheid prior to the establishment of diplomatic relations between our two countries.

The African Group in Geneva

The African Group was very active, as there was an OAU office with a Permanent Representative in Geneva who was coordinating and organizing the African Group meetings and African common positions at the UN except the GATT, which was negotiating based on national positions. This was because the North African countries were not members of the ACP, and as such the Lomé Convention's provisions were at odds with their national interest. Although the Moroccan delegation had pulled out of the OAU due to the Western Sahara, Morocco was very active in the African Group and was one of the first to pay its contributions in running the affairs of the Group. This was the same scenario in all the countries in my subsequent posts, and they often chaired the African Group. At one such meeting, Zaire came with two opposing sets of delegations, one representing Laurent Kabila and the other representing President Mobutu, and they wanted the African Group to support their accreditation at the UN Commission on Human Rights. As I had no instruction on what to do, I decided to call Abuja, and Ambassador Segun Apata, who had once served as Ambassador in Kinshasa, said we should advise the African Group to keep their hands off such matters and let them go to the conference secretariat for accreditation. He said at least they had their letters of accreditation signed by their Head of State or Foreign Minister and it was not the African Group that accredited delegates to conferences.

Armed with that directive, we advised them to go to the UN and settle their problems, and this was decided in favour of Mobutu's delegation; at least they were still in control of the capital. At a similar African Group meeting I came across Ambassador Tichaona Jokonya of Zimbabwe, whom I met in Addis Ababa, and he remarked humorously that I was always heading our Missions as chargé d`affairs and wondered why I was not being designated as Ambassador. I told him that I was still in the queue waiting for my turn, since we in Nigeria never jump the queue. Remarkably we met again in New York during the conference to facilitate the entry into force of the CTBTO in September 2001, when he was his country's Permanent Representative to the UN and I was the Ambassador in Vienna. We recounted our Geneva and Addis Ababa experiences and I told him that I had got to my turn in the long queue of those eligible for appointment, at which he laughed and offered me lunch to celebrate joining the club. I later met him again in Harare in 2005 as his country's Minister for Labour during our campaign for the UNSC permanent seat. Tragically, Jokonya died soon after from cardiac arrest by the end of 2005. I recount this to confirm my belief that career Foreign Service officers make better representation abroad than non-career officers in term of strengthening and deepening the bilateral relations between the sending and the receiving states. At least the devil you know is better than the one you do not know, and it is quite practical in diplomacy. We should, nevertheless, recognise the importance of non-career appointees in different fields who bringing expertise and experiences that add values to the work of diplomacy, but should be limited to specific posts and numbers.

The UN Committee on the Rights to Development

I was elected as an expert member of the Commission on the Human Rights Working Group on the Rights to Development. The Group comprised 15 experts appointed on their personal capacities. From Africa was Ambassador Mohamed Ennaceur (Tunisia), Ambassador Don Nanjira (Kenya) and I. The Working Group was funded by the UN Centre for Human Rights and most of the other members came from their capitals. The Working Group had two mandates:

a) To identify obstacles to the implementation and realization of the Declaration on the Rights to Development.
b) To recommend ways and means to the realization of the rights to development by all states.

The rights to development was first mentioned in the African Charter on Human and People's Rights, and was also reaffirmed in the Declaration and Programme of Action of the World Conference on Human Rights in Vienna on 23 June 1993. Our appointments were for a period of three years in the first instance. The first session was held in Geneva from 18-19 November 1993 and was chaired by Ambassador Ennaceur of Tunisia.

During the first session we took note of article 1 of the Declaration on the Rights to Development, which defines the right to development as "an inalienable human right by which every human person and all peoples are entitled to participate in, contribute to, and enjoy economic, social, cultural and political development in which all human rights and fundamental freedoms can be fully realized."

It was also agreed that the group should pay attention to the rights of minorities' indigenous peoples and women. The group identified the main factors in the enjoyment of human rights by all to be classified into three, namely national, international and regional levels. At the national level it was classified into states through popular participation; individual level and national institutions, NGOs and civil societies. It was also postulated that all human rights are universal, indivisible, interdependent and interrelated and linked in a non-hierarchical nature. It was also agreed that for the realization of rights to development, states needed political will as well as resources and capacities to implement the rights to development. At the first session, we agreed to list the obstacles to the realization of the rights to development as:

a) Failure to recognize the rights of people to self-determination. But this was contentious, because it encourages secessionist tendencies, as was the call by the MOSOP. When I mentioned to the Group that Nigeria has over 300 ethnic minorities apart from the three major ethnic groups, they burst out laughing and said they were promoting the birth of over 300 countries in Nigeria if each of them demanded their rights to self-determination. Since then one of them, the Ogonis, have done so through Ken

Saro-Wiwa.

b) Failure to recognize and prevent flagrant violations of human rights by states.
c) Failure to promote democracy and prevent capital flight, as well as disregard of human rights and fundamental freedoms by states through coercive measures.

The group concluded that there was a need for further comments from member countries, international organisations and civil societies on the obstacles and recommendations of ways and means towards the realization of the right to development. The Working Group decided on two meetings, in May and September each year. I did not know that this would be the end of my participation at the Working Group, although I had done much to contribute to its formation and at the first session.

Our appointment was on our personal capacities for a period of three years and funded by the UN Centre for Human Rights, if one was coming from the capitals, but when I left for headquarters in January 1994, some senior colleagues connived to cut short my further participation by claiming that I was unavailable to continue to serve in the Working Group. In fact, they even humiliated me by inviting me to prepare for and attend the meeting, but then called Chiedu Osakwe and castigated him for forwarding the invitation to me. They replaced me with Dr. Orobola Fasehun, who took over from me as the chargé d'affaires based in Geneva, thus forfeiting the financial benefits that would have been available to me and undoubtedly Nigeria through my participation from the capital. The decision was unreasonable, myopic and at variant to the usual practice in the Nigerian Foreign Service of encouraging officers to be appointed to UN posts on their personal capacities. It also showed lack of understanding on how I was appointed in the first instance. But that action did not dampen my spirit. Instead it energized me to do more to defend and promote Nigeria's interests in the years to come. That incident was the only sour taste I experienced during my thirty years plus in the Foreign Service, as the rest was carved in gold, so to say. And those senior colleagues behind that decision remain my best friends today, because I put everything behind me and carried on my work as best as I could. My reward was the three ambassadorial postings given to me at Lusaka, Vienna and Berlin, as well as the Consulate-General in Karachi, Pakistan which were rare in recent years.

I later understood from colleagues that the decision to stop me from attending the meeting of the Group of Experts was unconnected to the four months' extension granted to me by Chief Matthew Mbu, the Foreign Secretary to conclude the Uruguay Round of multilateral trade negotiations that culminated into the World Trade Organisation (WTO). But it was the prerogative of the Foreign Secretary to extend the posting of any Foreign Service officer as he/she wished, and mine was not an exception. I had already packed and shipped my personal effects before I received a call from Chike Anigbo, Special Assistant to the Foreign Secretary directing me to remain at post until further notice. The four months' extension created its own problems and uncertainty, as we had to buy new household utensils and bedding materials. We lived in limbo waiting for "further notice" which never came until the following year, when there was a change of the Foreign Secretary due to the military coup d'état of November 1993. It was then time for some senior colleagues to take their anger out on me for what they considered was an unwarranted extension granted to me by the Foreign Secretary, whom I never met. That was a clear case of the adage that "when two elephants fight, it is the grass that will suffer." I had even written a protest letter to the new Foreign Minister, Ambassador Baba Gana Kingibe, but I later withdrew it after Ambassador Attah advised me to do so. That turned out to be a wise decision, for which I reaped the benefits in later years in the Service by not being a complainer.

CHAPTER 6

DIPLOMACY BY A PARIAH STATE

*"I have discovered the art of deceiving diplomats.
I speak the truth and they never believe me."*

Di Cavour 1810-1861

*"Diplomacy is more than saying or doing the right
things at the right time, it is avoiding saying or doing the
wrong things at any time."*

Bo Bennett (Born 1933)

I returned to Abuja in January 1994 and was deployed to the American and Caribbean Affairs Department, but I wondered why I was deployed there, having just arrived from Europe and from a multilateral post. This was the same thing as happened to me when I returned from Brussels and was posted to East and Central African Affairs. Even if I was not posted to the multilateral desk, at least I would have been posted to the European Affairs

Department, since I had just arrived from that part of the world, to be debriefed before moving elsewhere. And due to lack of an office, I shared one allocated to another senior officer, Jonykul Onourah Obodozie (later Ambassador to DRC) and I proceeded on one month's leave to enable me to clear my personal effects and car. That was my last annual leave in the remaining 16 years in the Foreign Service, apart from the three months' recall for consultations from Zambia in 1999.

When I returned from the annual vacation, Onuorah Obodozie gave me a letter deploying me to the Second United Nations Division. He said the new Foreign Minister, Ambassador Kingibe, had even sent for me, but he was told that I was on vacation. I had never met the HMFA before and wondered who was behind this deployment, because it was a Division many officers lobby hard to move into. I later learned that it was Ambassador Kabir Ahmed, Director Administration who recommended me to the new Foreign Minister. I had never worked with this Ambassador before, but he had full confidence in me and was instrumental to my posting to Vienna as Ambassador many years later. Ambassador Ahmed later told me that it was through Ambassadors Moshood Abiola and Jibrin Chinade as well as his own observation of the manner I conducted myself to work generally. I imbibed the spirit of not lobbying for any posting or deployment to any Department throughout my years in the Service, and it paid me handsomely.

My former boss in Geneva, Ambassador Ayo Azikiwe, was the Director of the International Organisations Division (IOD) while Segun Apata was the Deputy Director in charge of the Second United Nations Division (SUND). Both officers were familiar with the issues at hand and very experienced with UN matters, particularly disarmament and human rights questions as well as the Commonwealth. Ambassador Azikiwe, before returning to headquarter in January 1992, had chaired the Conference on Disarmament that negotiated the Chemical Weapons Convention. I was assisted by many dedicated and intelligent officers. The most outstanding of them were Hakeem Olawale Sulaiman, Emmanuel Okpoju Egwa and Ramatu Ahmed. Ladan Sidi and Ngozi Ukaeje later joined my team and I found them invaluable.

I was assigned Third UNGA Committee desk, dealing with human rights questions and the humanitarian issues of the UN as well as the Commonwealth. I wondered why it was so as I thought I was most suited for Second Committee as an economic graduate to deal with ECOSOC matters, which I had been handling since I had joined the Service. Surprisingly human rights questions were among the most important and interesting subjects for the division, the MFA and the government due to the annulment of the June 12 presidential elections of 1993 and the consequent clampdown on pro-democracy groups which have murdered sleep to the military government. As soon as I settled down, Ayo Azikiwe was deployed to head the Consular and Legal Department and Segun Apata became the Director-General (IOD), with Dahiru M. Abubakar as the Deputy Director-General in charge of the SUND. The latter was later moved to head the Technical Aid Corps directorate and was succeeded by Nkem Wadibia-Anyanwu.

Because of the mounting pressure by national and international human rights groups such as National

Democratic Coalition (NADECO), Civil Liberties Organisation (CLO), Nigerian Bar Association and international NGOs such as Amnesty International, Human Rights Watch, as well as UN Commission on Human Rights, we were kept on our toes to respond to their allegations as well as official communications to the UN treaty bodies. This period coincided with the time Nigeria had just signed and ratified two international human right treaties without reservations. These were the International Covenant on Civil and Political Rights (ICCPR) and the International Covenant on Economic, Social and Cultural Rights (ICESCR), as any violations of their provisions would attract the wrath of the international community. It is strongly believed that the Abacha regime was not sufficiently aware of the implications of these Treaties. Was it a trap set up by his predecessor, Ibrahim Babangida, who signed the instruments of ratification a week before he annulled the June 12, 1993 presidential elections, and two months before he stepped aside, one may ask? But the mounting pressure against the military regime went on unabated and was even worsened by subsequent developments.

Attempted coup d'état against General Sani Abacha

The military regime announced on March 10, 1995 that there had been an attempted coup d'état to overthrow the government and that many military officers had been arrested and detained. Among these were General Oladipo Diya, the Chief of General Staff, Generals Shehu Musa Yar'Adua, Olusegun Obasanjo and several others. A Special

Military Tribunal (SMT) was set up to try them. It was chaired by a member of the Provisional Ruling Council (PRC) and all its members were military and police personnel. Some civilians and journalists were also arrested and detained; Ms. Christina Anyanwu (later Senator) was also implicated in the plot and tried by the SMT. Apart from this announcement, nothing was heard about their trial, which was conducted secretly, a violation of Article 14 of the ICCPR. Their detention incommunicado was also another violation of the ICCPR which attracted the wrath of the international human rights community. The list of those detained and facing trial was not known until after the trial, which announced that over forty persons had been convicted. Some of them received death sentences, others life imprisonment and the others long sentences of up to twenty-five years. My office was flooded by letters of appeal for clemency and condemnation as the trials fell short of the obligations Nigeria had freely signed and ratified two years earlier.

The sentences were later commuted to life imprisonment for those facing the death penalty and those with long sentences had them reduced. Unfortunately, General Shehu Musa Yar'Adua died in prison under mysterious circumstances. The condemnation of the process that led to their trials and convictions continued unabated as it was blamed on the secrecy of the trials and non-access to lawyers of their choice in accordance with the international legal obligations of Nigeria under the ICCPR. My desk in Block 'C' (often referred to as Siberia) was a beehive of foreign diplomatic personnel in Abuja, especially those from the EU and the US, whose ambassadors or high commissioners were still in Lagos with offices in Abuja. They used to organize lively evening events, to which I was always invited, during which they would try to gather information on human rights questions in our country. Baba Gana Kingibe was very active in such gatherings and was loved by many diplomats, but he did not last long as Foreign Minister because the military regime saw his diplomatic skills as against the combustive nature of the regime, and he was relieved of his position as minister.

The Military Tribunal law that tried and convicted General Olusegun Obasanjo and his former deputy Shehu Musa Yar'adua was signed by him to try the coup plotters, many of them my brothers in the Middle Belt who were executed in 1976. The same law was also used to try and execute subsequent coup plotters, notably Major-Gen Mamman Vatsa, Major Godwin Okar et al. Some critics commended General Sani Abacha for his magnanimity and the gesture of sparing the lives of those condemned to death, unlike his predecessors.

The execution of Ken Saro-Wiwa and eight others

Closely linked to the coup plotters was the case of the Movement for the Survival of Ogoni Peoples (MOSOP). The media reported one morning that four Ogoni elders had been murdered while attending a meeting on May 21, 1994. The elders were accused by the Ogoni youths of siding with the federal government and Shell Company. Shortly after the incident, Ken Saro-Wiwa and some members of MOSOP were arrested and tried by the Special Military Tribunal headed by Justice Ibrahim Auta, the Chief Judge of the

Federal High Court. There was also a claim of torture and intimidation by the Military Internal Security Task Force (MISTF) led by its commander Col. Okuntimo, who was also alleged to have received gratification from the Shell Company operating in the area. The UN Special Rapporteur against Torture and PEN sent urgent appeals calling for the release of Ken Saro-Wiwa and those detained and tried without due process in contravention of Nigeria's obligations to the international legal instruments. Chief Gani Fawehinmi, Olisa Agbakoba and Femi Falana, human right lawyers who indicated their intention to defend them, withdrew their representation in protest at the trial being conducted by the Special Military Tribunal instead of civil courts, as even the accused were held in military detention camps.

The tribunal delivered its verdict of death sentences for nine persons and discharged six others on 31 October 1995. As usual my desk was full of activity, as there were several protest messages from NGOs and international organisations condemning the verdict and calling for the discharge of the convicted persons because the trial had not followed due process. I was so overwhelmed by these requests that Ambassador Pius Ayewoh, my boss, asked me a funny question as to the meaning of "due process" which was occurring in virtually all the myriad of messages we received within such a short interval, when the PRC has not even ratified the verdict. The International Association to promote freedom to read and write (PEN), Greenpeace and several NGOs appealed for clemency. The MFA was in a major crisis as it tried to contend with the barrels of criticisms and condemnations of the trial. Unfortunately for me the Crisis Management Committee. which had been used to good effect during the time of Ike Nwachukwu, was moribund. There was no immediate action to contend with the impending crisis that would unfold as we all hoped that the Government would grant them amnesty as they had with the coup plotters. But we were wrong. Events unfolded rapidly and took us off-guard, so to say.

On November 8, 1995 Emmanuel Egwa, my junior colleague and assistant, walked into my office looking tense, sombre and worried. I sensed that there was something wrong with this versatile, resourceful and jovial officer, that he should look so sombre, an indication that my attention was needed urgently. I asked "Emma, what is wrong with you so early in the morning today?" He then told me that there was bad news with serious consequences for us in the Department and for Nigeria in general. According to him the PRC had decided to execute Ken Saro-Wiwa and eight others while six others had been acquitted, and the sentences would be carried out within the next few days. He told me that his sources of information were credible, and from the highest authority in the country.

I picked up copies of the ICCPR and the ICESCR and asked him to help me highlight boldly the relevant articles concerning the trials by special tribunals and the need for appeals in the case of death sentence, especially articles 4.6 (1), (2) and (3) of ICCPR which Nigeria ratified without reservations. The implications of hanging Ken Saro-Wiwa and eight others would be a gross violation of human rights as enunciated in these articles of the international instruments, which we had entered at our own volition.

I went to see Ambassador Timothy Mgbokwere, the

Permanent Secretary, and relayed to him the unfortunate development unfolding. I also drew his attention to the report of the Commonwealth Human Rights Initiative (CHRI), which had visited Nigeria a month earlier and written a damaging report on human rights violations in the country. That report would be presented to the CHOGM in Auckland, New Zealand, the following week. He directed me to give him a draft memo, as he would be receiving the HMFA at the airport to brief him. I was very hopeful that Chief Tom Ikimi, the versatile Foreign Minister, would prevail on General Abacha to either delay action by constituting a higher tribunal to act as an appellate body in conformity to the ICCPR or commute their sentences to life imprisonment.

I left the office armed with copies of the ICCPR and went to the house of one of the PRC members who was well connected to General Sani Abacha. I had never gone to his house in office clothing but informally, but on this occasion, I was well suited with documents in hand to catch his attention, as I knew how busy his house would be in the evenings. As soon as he saw me entered the well packed living room with many visitors he remarked, "where are you coming from with books clutched in your arms like Bassey Okon of the Village Headmaster? (*Village Headmaster* was a popular TV programme in Nigeria). I seized the opportunity to give reasons for my visit, which I told him was confidential and very urgent. He quickly moved to his dining table, ordered his cook to make food for me and sat down to listen to my problem.

I took with me two copies of the ICCPR clearly marking articles 46 (1). (2). (3) and drew his attention to what my junior colleague had told me about the Ogoni Nine trials, particularly Ken Saro-Wiwa, and the implications to Nigeria if the sentences were carried out without the right of appeal or due process. The words "due process" and "military tribunal" irked him, as I observed he was no longer interested in the subject matter and the attention he had given me dissipated. Nevertheless, he listened to my explanation that in any matter involving the death penalty, it should be subjected to appeal to a higher appellate body in the form of a higher tribunal to conform to our obligations under the ICCPR. He asked me who had signed and ratified the instruments by selling our sovereignty to an external body. I told him that it was the AFRC under Ibrahim Babangida in 1993, and some of the PRC were also members. After I had finished and handed over the two copies to him, he stood up and remarked angrily that I was lucky not to have been locked up, because it was a military affair and that if I had any problem I should refer them to my minister; after all I was not a member of the PRC. Ten minutes after that encounter, General Sani Abacha came in and they zoomed off, leaving me gulping my food at the table.

I travelled home to Jos the following day after checking with Tim Mgbokwere that the message had been delivered to Chief Tom Ikimi before he had left for the Commonwealth Heads of Government Meeting (CHOGM) in New Zealand. I love being in Jos in my small home located in a beautiful and quiet part of the city, and forgot the hot and turbulent affairs of Abuja and my desk. My mind went back to when Ken Saro-Wiwa had delivered the statement during the tenth session of the Working Group on Indigenous Peoples in Geneva in 1993 through The Hague-based Unrepresented

Nations and Peoples Organisation (UNPO). In that statement Saro-Wiwa had called for the self-determination of the Ogoni people under the guise that they were "indigenous people facing extinction in Nigeria."

I made it a practice not to listen to news nor read newspapers whenever I was in Jos with my family, so until I returned to Abuja I had no idea of what had happened on the 10 of November 1995 when Ken Saro-Wiwa and eight of his kinsmen were executed. I walked in a leisurely way into my office to find several messages from many sources requiring urgent action from me about the execution. There were messages from the Commonwealth Secretary General, the European Union Ambassador in Abuja, the Canadian High Commissioner, the UK Prime Minister, Amnesty International, Human Rights Watch and several NGOs condemning the execution. The Commonwealth Heads of Government (CHOGM) condemned the action and swiftly suspended Nigeria from the organisation for gross violations of human rights. The EU and other Western countries withdrew their ambassadors and High Commissioners from Nigeria to protest at the execution. Prime Minister John Major called it "judicial murder" and Nelson Mandela of South Africa spearheaded the suspension of Nigeria from the Commonwealth.

But instead of the Government making a holistic appraisal and properly articulating the implications in addressing the issue, it took a hard-line approach to the problems. The military regime retaliated by withdrawing our ambassadors from these countries. British Airways flights to Nigeria were banned, the EU and Canada recalled their ambassadors and high commissioners to Nigeria and diplomatic relations with Nigeria severed. There were also trade sanctions and travel restrictions imposed against some members of the military regime. But when the ambassadors from these countries returned to take up their seats in Lagos or Abuja, Nigeria refused to send her own back to their capitals in the belief that she was punishing them. All efforts by the MFA for the Government to appoint ambassadors or send those recalled for consultations fell on deaf ears. Some were even dubbed NADECO or saboteurs if they came from the south-west geopolitical region. Nigeria had fallen from grace to grass in the international human rights community, becoming a pariah and a failed state. One wondered how could Nigeria, which did not have any history of consistent patterns of violations of human rights, suddenly found herself during those countries well known for human rights violation, and even with UNCHR resolutions mandating special rapporteurs to visit Nigeria, monitor the violations and report to the Commission.

At the 51st session of the UNCHR in March 1995, Mr. Bacre Waly N'diaye, the Special Rapporteur on Extrajudicial Summary and Arbitrary Executions, reported on the grave violation of human rights in Nigeria following the annulment of the June 12 presidential elections and the detention of pro-democratic activists. Similarly, at the 52nd session of the UNCHR in 1996, the Commission condemned in strong terms the violations of the rights to life in the execution of Ken Saro-Wiwa and the eight other Ogoni leaders. It also mandated Param Cumaraswamy, the Special Rapporteur on the Independence of Judges and Lawyers, to report to the Commission about judges and lawyers in Nigeria. A similar mandate was also given to Soli

Jehangir, the Special Rapporteur, to report on all aspects of human rights situation in Nigeria.

My duties were to manage these streams of visitors and to engage them as much as possible to keep the damage to the barest minimum. The most important thing was to grant them access and co-operate with them, as refusal to do so would be more damaging to the image of the country. Auwalu Yadudu, the legal adviser to the head of state, set up an ad hoc committee on human rights which was chaired by Bukar Usman, the permanent secretary Special Services Office. Others were Sunday Ehindero, Assistant Commissioner of Police, who later became the Inspector General of Police, Jalal Al-Arabi, Office of the Secretary to the Government of the Federation (OSGF), Muhammed Tabi`u, the Executive Secretary of National Human Rights Commission, Buhari Bello (OSGF), Mustapha Musa Kida, National Intelligent Agency (NIA), Kabiru Muhammed, office of National Security Adviser and myself from MFA. The Committee worked tirelessly to ensure that Nigeria granted them access to all the non-military places they wanted to visit. I accompanied them to all the places, towns and cities they visited, particularly Rivers State, Lagos, Kano and Abuja. Some international NGOs such as Amnesty International and Human Rights Watch, the Commonwealth Human Rights Initiative and a host of others, trooped to Nigeria to report on the human rights situation. We were also expected to report periodically on our compliance with the international human rights instruments of which Nigeria was a state party. In 1996 I accompanied Auwalu Yadudu to present and defend

Nigeria's periodic reports on the ICCPR to the Human Rights Committee (HRC) in Geneva and New York. Uche Gwam and Sam Otuyelu (later ambassadors) joined the delegation in Geneva and New York respectively. The HRC condemned in strong terms the detention incommunicado and suppression of habeas corpus, which violated Article 9 of the ICCPR, and the establishment of the decrees without the rights of appeal, as it affected the rights to life (violation of Art 14.6 (1) and (2) of the ICCPR). The HRC called for urgent review of these laws to ensure that persons facing trial are guarantee a fair trial in accordance with Art 14 (1), (2) and (3) and those sentenced should have the right of appeal.

In response to these criticisms, Yadudu recommended a review of the laws of special tribunals to include the right to appeal to a higher tribunal, as it affected the death penalty. This was promptly approved and promulgated into law by the regime of General Abacha. That was a classic example of the "boomerang effect" in which international affairs influenced domestic policy in the practise of Nigerian policy.

During my reality checks for this memoir I stumbled on a document which confirmed my suspicion of the reasons for the action taken by the military regime to execute Ken Saro-Wiwa and the eight others, which was to avoid being a weak government, especially coming soon after the coup plotters were given lighter sentences. Those condemned to death in the coup had their convictions commuted to life imprisonment. Either of the two cases would have been met with drastic action to serve as a deterrent to others depending on which one came first.

According to Abacha's memo on the Ogoni trials to the

PRC dated Wednesday November 8, 1995, he cautioned that if members soft-pedalled, the administration would be regarded as weak. The memo also dismissed the call for the expunging of the death penalty from the nation's statute books and preferred military to civil tribunals. Amazingly, some PRC members suggested that the execution should be delayed until after the CHOGM meeting in Auckland, but that was rejected. Consequently, the Council condemned Ken Saro-Wiwa and eight others to death by hanging and acquitted six others, including Ledum Mitee, the Secretary-General of MOSOP.

There was a clear indication that the PRC exhibited ignorance to the international human rights instruments and the International Covenant on Civil and Political Rights (ICCPR), which Nigeria signed and ratified in June 1993 and deposited at the UN Headquarters in New York. Unknown to me, the day this memo was considered by the PRC was also the day I took the ICCPR instruments, belatedly, to one of the members of the Council, who sternly rebuked me for doing so. As indicated by Emmanuel Egwa, time ran out for any action MFA could do to avert the executions, which were hurriedly done without appeal. The fallout was devastating to Nigeria and the MFA was put in the firing line to defend the indefensible at the UN and international fora.

It was also amazing that Chief Michael Agbamuche (now deceased), the Attorney General and Minister of Justice, who was also present at the Council as a member, was unable to brief the PRC properly. Maybe he was the one who cautioned against the hasty execution as well as making the call for civilian trials rather than military tribunals. I would not know what role he played, because everything was done under strict secrecy. The same could be said of the chairman of the Special Military Tribunal and the other high court judges who tried and convicted those men and pronounced the death penalty without recourse to appeal. There was also an incomprehensible statement made by the Head of State that the coup plotters were pardoned because they had not carried out the plot. But Major-General Mamman Vatsa's coup plot was averted before they had carried out, yet they were summarily executed using the same law. That was a case of consistency of inconsistency in that statement. There were no international sanctions against Nigeria on the attempted coup by Mamman Vatsa, because Nigeria had not ratified the ICCPR and other human rights instruments that called for the right to appeal to a higher tribunal in matters involving the death penalty. After the ratification of ICCPR, it was no longer business as usual.

One of the concluding decisions of the Abacha memo was a directive to the AGF to consider the possibility of proscribing MOSOP and similar organisations in the country. Maybe it was in that regard that Bukar Usman, the Permanent Secretary (Special Services), established an ad hoc committee on human rights to compile all NGOs in the country with a view to re-registering them, as they were accused of receiving foreign funds to destabilize the country. But that exercise was dead before we started. At the first meeting MFA advised against the proposal and insisted that government should not indulge in the affairs of NGOs since the Corporate Affairs Commission (CAC) has the statutory mandate to register and sanction them, even though many are one-man organisations without formal registration. We argued that an attempt to restrict them from functioning would be counterproductive as it would amount to violations of their right to freedom of association. Auwalu Yadudu, the Legal Adviser to the Head of State, who understood the predicament the country was facing at various human rights fora, might have presented our advice succinctly to the Head of State and the subject matter was rested *sine die*.

Nigeria and Human Rights Questions

From 1995 until General Abacha died in 1998, human rights issues in Nigeria had reached a crescendo of criticism and condemnation by the international community. It had also eroded all the milestones Nigeria had recorded in this area as well as negatively affecting our diplomatic relations with many countries. Canada closed its High Commission in Nigeria. The street leading to the US Chancery in Lagos had its name changed from Eleke Crescent in Victoria Island to Louis Farrakhan Street in retaliation for "Kudirat Abiola Corner" on the street leading to Nigeria's Permanent Mission in New York. The Commonwealth Ministerial Action Group (CMAG) met several times to review the suspension of Nigeria and Pakistan, as the two-member countries violated their obligations to the Harare Declaration of 1991 on democracy and human rights.

The UN Commission on Human Rights (UNCHR) in Geneva and the UNGA in New York adopted resolutions condemning the violations of human rights and fundamental freedoms in Nigeria and mandated thematic Special Rapporteurs to visit the country. Several of them visited Nigeria and we did everything possible to cooperate with them according to UN requirements. Amnesty International also visited Nigeria and I accompanied them to Rivers State. The CMAG met in London from 10-11 July 1997 and expressed "strong concerns over the deteriorating situation in respect of human right and the rule of law in Nigeria". Equally strong concerns were raised about Nigeria's government transition programme which was perceived as being "without unfettered and free participation as well as its likely outcome." The report concluded by recommending to CHOGM that it should take more effective measures to "pressure Nigeria to live up to her obligations and commitments under the Harare Declaration of 1991." At the UNCHR and the African Commission on Human and People's Rights, there were several statements and resolutions condemning the human rights situation in Nigeria.

However, the military regime was ill-equipped or unwilling to respond adequately to these barrels of condemnations. Instead of listening to good advice and making changes, it put the blames on "detractors", the NGOs, and the National Democratic Coalition (NADECO), whose members were in exile abroad and mounting pressure at international fora, particularly the UN in New York and in Geneva. The MFA took hard and combative measures to respond to these criticisms by defending the action of the military regime.

Auwalu Hamisu Yadudu, the Legal Adviser to the Head of State, understood our predicaments during several meetings we attended together. One was in New York to present Nigeria's periodic reports to the Human Rights

Committee, where one of the members had known him at Colombian University Law School and raised some embarrassing questions concerning the rights to life, military tribunals trying civilians without the rights to appeal as was the case with Ken Saro-Wiwa. At the end of the meeting Auwalu, Sam Otuyelu and I discussed the steps that must be taken urgently on our return to Abuja. Yadudu initiated the move to establish the independent National Human Rights Commission which was one of the recommendations of the Vienna Declaration and Programme of Action of the World Conference on Human Rights in June 1993. The other action taken by Yadudu was the amendment to the military tribunal trial of civilians involving death penalty, which included the right to appeal. These measures were applauded, albeit temporarily.

One morning I decided to pay a courtesy call on Ambassador T. Daniel Hart, director in the Office of the Minister, and he told me that Ambassador Wadibia-Anyanwu, my boss, and I should get ready to accompany the Minister to Geneva that afternoon. The purpose of the journey was a UNHRC meeting, but I wondered why we had not been informed that the Minister was attending and would deliver a speech. I was surprised because that was my schedule and I would have drafted the speech for the Minister, but I was side-lined, for reasons best known to them. I wondered why, and it left me wondering if my previous drafts were not good enough or too mild and less combative and against the spirit of the regime.

I rushed back to inform my boss and she screamed that she was not ready to travel that afternoon. We did not even know for how many days we would stay abroad and there was nobody willing to tell us. She directed me to find out from the Director of Finance and Accounts (DFA), Mr. Sangodele, but he declined to tell me how long we would be staying and the allowances that would be given to us. I however, persuaded my boss to get ready to leave for the airport to wait for the Minister.

Ambassador Wadibia-Anyanwu, Martin Uhomoibhi and I were in the entourage of the Minister to be given visas on arrival at the Geneva airport. Martin (who prepared the statement instead of me) then decided to give us the ministerial statement that was scheduled to be delivered on the morning of our arrival. The statement had already been approved by the Minister, who was also with us in the Presidential plane, and we decided to work on it inside the plane to make last-minute changes to errors of substance, after which Martin rushed to get it re-typed at the Permanent Mission. Even though the substance was intact the combative language, words and phrases were substantially amended. Chief Tom Ikimi, the Foreign Minister delivered it with excellent oratory and was received with loud applause. I was not sure if the applause was for its contents or the delivery. As a result, the changes we made were not noticed and it helped in diffusing the wave of criticisms at the Commission.

Fourth World Conference on Women: Beijing, China

Women's issues were also becoming important and my assistant on this subject was Ramatu Ahmed, who was very resourceful and had good contacts within the Presidency and National Commission for Women as well as the

National Council for Women's Societies. The former metamorphosed into the Ministry of Women's Affairs at the federal and state level while the latter was a quasi-governmental NGO. A preparatory meeting of African Ministers of Women for the World Conference in Beijing was held in Dakar, Senegal from 21-23 November 1994. It was the Fifth African Ministerial Conference on Women, held preparatory to the Fourth World Conference on Women in Beijing in 1995. It was organized jointly by the Government of Senegal and UNECA as a follow up to the UNGA resolution of 1992. The major objectives of the Conference were to review the progress made since the Nairobi Conference in 1985 to identify obstacles to women's development. It was also to prepare a concrete Action Plan which would accelerate the advancement of women in Africa. The Conference prepared country reports of sub-regional and regional workshops. The NGO forum preceded the Conference from 13-15 November 1994. There were workshops and seminars on critical areas of concern such as peace, violence against women, health, family planning, the environment, women in business and in the media etc. About 1,000 women all over Africa took part in both the NGO forum and the Ministerial meeting.

The Conference adopted an African Platform for Action with eleven critical areas of concern to accelerate the advancement of women. They included the following:

a) Women's poverty, security and lack of economic empowerment;

b) Inadequate access to education, training science/technology;

c) Women's role in culture; family

d) Women's health, family planning/population and environment/natural resources management;
e) Women and the peace process;
f) Women's political empowerment;
g) Legal and human rights;
h) Mainstreaming gender data;
i) Communication information and arts and the girl child;

The strategy for implementation was also outlined involving governments, NGOs, civil society, the OAU, ECA, UN and the World Bank.

The experience of connectivity and communication within Africa manifested with me on our way from Lagos to Dakar. We boarded an Air Afrique plane for Dakar to Abidjan, Cote d'Ivoire, with my luggage checked directly to Dakar. We changed the aircraft in Abidjan but when we arrived at Dakar my luggage did not arrive. I had on me only the shirt I had worn for the journey. It took the airline five days before my luggage was traced and brought back to me; I was told it had been sent to Paris via Abidjan.

There was a similar experience with the Chief Justice of Nigeria, Justice Mohammed Uwais, who transited at Karachi on his way to Mumbai but his luggage from Lagos did not arrive. He went ahead, and his luggage arrived after he had concluded the meeting and gone back to Nigeria. We had to arrange to send back the luggage to him. With this experience, I resolved never to travel without some extra clothes in my carry-on luggage, no matter how short the journey was, particularly in countries where there was nowhere to buy new clothes.

I took time off at the weekend and visited The House of

Slaves (Maison des Esclaves) on Gore`e Island, about three kilometres from Dakar. Like Badagry in Lagos, there was the 'door of no return'; any slave who passed through it did not return to African soil again but was shipped to the Americas. The House of Slaves was built by the Dutch in 1776 and was used to ship over 20 million slaves across the Atlantic Ocean. Most of the inhabitants of the island were former slaves who were to be shipped across, and they were saved when the French abolished the slave trade in 1848. The relics of the slave trade remain in their original form, such as the slave house with its cells and shackles, which is now a Museum. UNESCO has designated it as a World Historical Site.

The Fourth World Conference on Women was held in Beijing, China from 4-15 September 1995. After the Dakar meeting the government established the Federal Minister of Women Affairs and appointed Judith Sefi Attah, who was our Ambassador in Rome, as its first minister. She took over the new Ministry at a crucial time when the preparatory process for the Conference had been concluded. But it was no problem for her to settle down as she was familiar with most of the major issues as an expert member of the UN Sub-Commission on Discrimination and Protection of Minorities.

For reasons not known to me, there was a hasty deployment for Ambassador Segun Apata, my director, at the high point of the preparatory process for the conference. He was posted out of the IOD as director and another versatile director, Ambassador Remi Esan, was posted from African Affairs to replace him. I was shocked by such movements because Segun Apata had put all the effort in to ensure the success of the Woman's Conference. Another hasty decision was to replace the President of the National Council for Women Societies (NCWS), Laila Dogonyaro, with Zainab Maina, who later became Minister of Women's Affairs. In addition to these changes, all NGOs earlier registered for the NGO forum were cancelled and new names were submitted. But the dateline given by China for the registration of NGOs had passed, so these changes created many problems for us in the department. The major problem was having to send a list of NGOs for accreditation in Beijing in June when the NGO list had already been closed by the Chinese as far back as March. All efforts to replace the names of NGOs accredited for the Conference were rejected by China. That informed the decision to register all Nigerian NGOs and civil societies as part of the official delegation. Because of this problem we registered well over 1,000 delegates to the Beijing Conference, the highest among UN members and embarrassing to Nigeria as we were seeking technical assistance from the international community.

Chief Tom Ikimi, the Minister, approved the participation of only two officers from the Ministry of Foreign Affairs, namely, Ramatu Ahmed and me, and the UNDP sponsored two junior officers, Ladan Sidi and Ngozi Ukaeje. It was only with great difficulty that Sam Otuyelu and Adenike Ukonga, from our Permanent Mission in New York and Embassy in Addis Ababa respectively, got approval to attend the Conference. Since there was no Ambassador in Beijing, Ambassador Olugbenga Ashiru in Pongyang (later Foreign Minister and now passed away) was charged with the responsibility of coordinating the participation of Nigeria at the Conference. We also enlisted the previous two retired Nigerian ambassadors to China, Emmanuel Oba and Ade-Adekuoye, to join the Nigerian delegation, which we found very useful throughout the two-weeks period.

With such a large delegation, one would expect effective participation at the various negotiations of the Plan of Action and in the Declaration. But there were very few women who were conversant with the issues. That was partly due to the fact that a new Ministry of Women's Affairs, headed by Ambassador Attah, was hastily established less than six months before the Conference and most of the Directors, apart from the Minister, were transferred from state services with very little experience of international relations and negotiations. I had the goodwill of the women who relied upon the few of us from MFA for guidance and we were treated very well, including welfare. Apparently, all the women departed the Conference without the final documents and they returned to Nigeria only to turn our office into a "mecca" of some sort, looking for copies of the Beijing Declaration and Programme of Action. At the Conference I was expected to brief Maryam Abacha, the leader of the delegation, daily, but it was not possible because the meetings went on late into the night and at times ended in the early morning. I ended up briefing Ambassador Attah, whom I accompanied to several ministerial meetings of the Conference.

At the end of the Conference, I took time to visit tourist sites in Beijing. The most attractive one to visitors to China was the Great Wall at Badaling, about 80km from Beijing. It was said to have been built in 1504 during the Ming

Dynasty. It is about 7.6 kilometres long and 1,015 metres (3,330ft) above sea level to protect the city of Beijing, but it was the route taken by the Mongols who overran Beijing and established the Yuan Dynasty from 1368-1644. As with all visitors who were able to successfully climb the Wall, I was presented with a magnificent and colourful certificate on my downward trip as a mark of victory. It is also said in China that "He who Has Never Been to the Great Wall is Not a True Man", an inscription engraved on a stone statute which was also written on the certificate presented to me at a small fee.

After the African Women Ministers' Conference in Dakar in 1994, Maryam Abacha mentioned the idea of an African First Ladies Peace Mission to address the issue of women in conflict, which was an important article in the Programme of Action of the Beijing Conference. She was concerned about the plight of women and children in the war-torn countries of Liberia and Sierra Leone. Maryam Abacha launched a programme of relief material which was supported by many state governments and stakeholders in the humanitarian fields and massive relief material was airlifted to Liberia and later Sierra Leone. She started it as an ECOWAS First Ladies' initiative and later expanded to interested African First Ladies. It was an ad hoc and not an institutionalized programme.

Women's Summit in Amman, Jordan

One Sunday morning of June 1996, I received a call from the office of the First Lady directing me to be at the Presidential wing of the Nnamdi Azikiwe International

Airport Abuja by 14 hours with my passport, as I was to accompany Mrs Abacha to Jordan. That message was at variance to the laid-down Civil Service rules and regulations. The channel of communication was for the directive to have come to me through my bosses and not directly to me. I had no option but to comply with it, so I went to brief my director, Ambassador Remi Esan, at home, but he had been in the office since morning. He was there with Segun Apata and Audu Kadiri working on a document entitled "Way forward to ease sanctions against Nigeria." It was in preparation for a meeting of the Commonwealth Ministerial Action Group (CHOGM) scheduled for London that would review the sanctions against Nigeria. The three officers were among the most intelligent, resourceful, committed and hard-working in the MFA. Unknown to them, that exercise on Sunday was what led to their exit from the MFA, except for Audu Kadiri, who was a junior officer. I understand that in one of their recommendations they called for the release of political detainees, but the military government took exception to that phrase. The military establishment refused to agree with them that there were political detainees in Nigeria. The government concluded that since the two senior officers came from an ethnic group, they were sympathetic to Moshood Abiola and belonged to the National Democratic Coalition (NADECO) and a security risk to the military administration.

I got permission from my director and rushed to meet up with the First Lady and her entourage at the airport, then left for Amman. The Summit of First Ladies was under the patronage of King Baudouin 1 Foundation, the King of the Belgians. Queen Fabiola, the widow of the king, coordinated the summits with the co-operation of Queen Noor of Jordan. We got to Amman, obtained our visas at the airport and were received by our Embassy in Baghdad, which had concurrent accreditation to Jordan. Amman is a pleasant place and since the meeting was hosted by Queen Noor, we received royalty throughout the visit. The meeting was on the roles of women in rural development and we were taken on a tour of the projects of Queen Noor, Jordan's First Lady. King Hussein declared the Conference open and Queen Noor chaired it.

The two-day conference was followed by a tour of the tourist sites in Jordan, most importantly the Dead Sea on the river Jordan and Petra, one of the Seven Wonders of the World. The Dead Sea borders Jordan, Israel and Palestine, and we floated on it due to the hypersaline water. We took many jerry cans of holy water from the river Jordan on our return flight back to Nigeria, as we were told that it has healing power and can be used for therapeutic beauty and cosmetic treatments. We also visited Jordan's most important Christian Baptism site, mentioned in the Holy Bible as "Rabbi, that man who was with you on the other side of the Jordan, who is now baptizing, and everyone is going to Him" (John 3:26). We were told that the Hashemite Kingdom of Jordan had preserved the site in its natural state since the time of Jesus Christ. The site was also mentioned as the "Bethany beyond the Jordan where John was baptizing" (John 1:28) and is one of the most important Christian sites in the world, together with the Church of the Nativity in Bethlehem and the Church of the Holy Sepulchre in Jerusalem. Both Pope John Paul II and Pope Benedict VI visited this site in 2000 and 2009 respectively and addressed Christian pilgrims.

The visit to Petra was also informative. It is described as the "rose red city, half as old as time." It is also called by travel magazines the "Ancient Nabatanean city in the South of Jordan". Petra was a prehistoric city, is half-built and half-carved into the rock and was an important caravan centre for incense of Arabia, Egypt, the silks of China and spices of India. The Tomb of Aaron, the brother of Moses in the Bible, who was a Jewish High Priest, was said to have been buried on Mount Hor adjacent to the city of Petra. It is an attractive site for Jewish tourists that visit Jordan and Petra. The ancient Nabatanean city of Petra is a fascinating archaeological site of architecture, and some of it is being replicated even today in many cities in Europe, US as well as in Nigeria.

On the Thursday I woke to the good news that Maryam Abacha had indicated interest in visiting Jerusalem and praying at the Al-Aqsa Mosque (Dome of the Rock) during Friday prayers. This is Islam's third holiest site after Makkah and Madinah, and we were all excited. But there were logistical problems on how to cross the Israeli checkpoints to and from Jerusalem. We did not have Israeli visas and it was not possible to arrange them within such a short time; we were told it would take at least five working days. Moreover, Fridays and Saturdays are holidays in both Jordan and Israel and the first working day was Sunday. Ambassador Ignatius Olisemeka, one of the icons of the Foreign Service, was the Nigerian Ambassador in Israel and I think he advised against the visit due to security concerns.

My mind went back to the assassination of King Abdullah bin Al-Hussein I of Jordan at the mosque on 20 July 1951, when he went there to perform Friday prayers.

He was assassinated by a Palestinian because of a rumour that he was negotiating a separate peace with Israel in company of his grandson, who later became the King of Jordan. My quest to visit Al-Aqsa mosque was fulfilled ten years later during an official visit to Israel at the invitation of the Israeli Foreign Ministry, which offered me the opportunity to see more closely the intricate problems between Israel and its neighbours.

We returned to our beautiful city of Abuja, but our entourage started to criticize the city in comparison to what they had seen in Amman, particularly the painting of houses. In Amman, everywhere was painted in sparkling white or bright colours. Abuja was not, yet it was beautiful and safe in comparison to other cities in Nigeria.

Human Rights Questions at the UN

One of the most difficult moments for us during one of the sessions of the UNHRC came after we had worked very hard to stop a resolution against Nigeria being adopted, with assurances from many developing countries that they would vote against the resolution or abstain. We even agreed with the WEOG that instead of condemnation, the resolution should encourage the military regime to conduct free, fair and credible elections. But on the day the resolution was tabled for action it was announced that the five political parties had adopted Sani Abacha as their Presidential candidate, thus transmuting from military head of state to civilian President. Casting doubt on the intention of the military to hand over the government to civil rule, Chief Bola Ige, one of Nigeria's foremost politicians, referred to the five political parties as "five fingers of a leprous hand". The writing on the wall was clear.

That announcement came as the greatest disappointment for the Nigerian delegation and the Commission adopted a resolution condemning human rights violations in Nigeria and mandated thematic Rapporteurs to visit the country and report to the Commission within one year. China and Cuba voted against the resolution, while most African members of the Commission abstained. Zambia voted in favour, which irked Nigeria, leading to the withdrawal of the 25 Technical Aid Corps (TAC) volunteers sent to Zambia in protest. The action by the five political parties and the broadcast that followed it was a repeat of the incident during the World Conference on Human Rights in Vienna when the Presidential election of 12 June 1993 was annulled. Although I was not at the CHOGM in Auckland, New Zealand, in 1995, the same kind of humiliation and frustration was experienced by the Nigerian officials. I wondered why such damaging decisions were taken to coincide with major international gatherings with maximum damage to our Foreign Policy. Those of us at the MFA were much more concerned and directly affected by the negative publicity against our country. All efforts to advise government properly was rebuffed and even sanctioned, as was the case with my two former bosses who were summarily retired from the Service without due process for advising that political detainees should be released to ease the pressure and avoid the sanctions against our country. The summary retirement of these two senior officers sent shivers to the already intimidated staff of the MFA which might have led to the death of many of them.

On return from Jordan to my busy schedules at the SUND, I was also engaged with several activities for Maryam Abacha, such as delivery of relief materials to war-torn Liberia, Sierra Leone and DRC under the African First Ladies Peace Mission. I attended the preparatory committee (Prepcom) of the Summit of First Ladies in Kuala Lumpur in 1998. Even though Maryam Abacha did not attend, due to the demise of her husband, Justice Fati Abubakar attended the Summit and I accompanied her with my boss, Ambassador Wadibia-Anyanwu and Christy Mbonu. The Summit was the same as the one held in Amman, Jordan under the patronage of King Baudouin 1 Foundation of Belgium. What struck me most in Malaysia was how that country revered the palm tree as a symbol and an engine of their development. Everywhere we went, both in the city and the rural areas, there were symbols depicting palm trees adorning hotels, restaurants, street lights and shops. The majestic hotel called the Hotel of Golden Roses, where we lodged, provided comfort above any of the best hotels in Nigeria and at a price three times less, and was built on a tin mining site. It is on record that in her development efforts Malaysia imported palm tree seedlings from Nigeria and turned it into a huge success and a national symbol. There are also many attractive resorts and ponds all over the city of Kuala Lumpur, some of which were also built on former tin mines. But in my own home state of Plateau, these sites are an eyesore. Our land had been degraded and rendered useless for agriculture and human habitation. Before the discovery of oil, tin and columbite were among the major sources of Nigeria's exports earnings. Both

Death of General Sani Abacha

Nigeria and Malaysia were members of the International Tin Council.

On Friday 5 June 1998, I took permission from my boss's ambassadors Wadibia-Anyanwu and Pius Ayewoh to travel home for the weekend. It was the practice in the Foreign Service that all senior officers must take permission from their immediate bosses before they travelled out of their stations, even at weekends or public holidays, and leave their telephone contact details in case of emergencies. I loved visiting my home in Jos because of the beautiful weather, as well as the location of my modest home during many highly-placed Nigerians and Europeans who owned homes there. It is in a crime-free and the most peaceful part of the city due to the presence of the Nigerian Air Force, like the Defence Housing Authority in Karachi in Pakistan, which was my next posting. It is called Gold and Base, which was the name of the company owned by expatriates engaged in tin mining during colonial time on the Plateau, and some of the colonial-style housing still exists there today.

Before I left Abuja, I stopped at the National Masjid for Jumma prayers which normally ended by 14:30 hours, leaving time for me to get to Jos before dawn. But on that day the prayers did not end as expected and I was wondering what was happening, so I asked someone sitting next to me and he said it was a national week of prayers for the country. Some Christians were assembled at the National Women's Development Centre, since the National

Christian Centre was still under construction, while the Muslims were in the National Mosque. The Muslims were expected to recite the Holy Qur'an a hundred times before the prayers would start. When the recitation ended the Imam started the sermon and called on Allah to "remove the obstacles to peace and development in our country". He emphasized that even if it was the government or anyone responsible for the lack of peace in the country that Allah should guide them right and bring changes for the benefit of the Nigerian people. He was emphatic in his sermon, as if he foresaw the unfolding development in the country.

The national prayers followed a week where two million people had marched at the Eagle Square parade ground, not far from the masjid and the uncompleted Christian Centre, calling for General Sani Abacha to contest the Presidential election. There was also a spectacular animation display by North Korea, portraying the virtues of the military regime of General Abacha and that of the First Lady. The North Koreans were pleased with the $6 million cash donation given to them by Nigeria when they were struck by flood disaster. In addition to these, there was the Kanu-led 'Youth Earnestly Asked for Abacha' (YEAA) to continue as Nigeria's civilian president. Several mushroom organisations sprang up all over the country cashing in on the confusion by enriching themselves. But General Abacha did not make any statements on these issues and there was no indication that he was behind any of these moves, which to me were part of their right to freedom of expression and peaceful assembly, a fundamental human right as enshrined in the Universal Declaration of Human Rights of 1948.

The events of that weekend unfolded dramatically and rapidly. I arrived in Jos quite late and Halima was already worried and informed me that there was a phone call for me from Pius Ayewoh to return to Abuja without delay. She said that on Monday 8 June 1998, Maryam Abacha was holding a workshop with the Commissioners of Women's Affairs all over the federation as well as the wives of Military Administrators. She said that Mrs Abacha had asked me to attend and deliver a paper on the implementation of the Beijing Declaration and Plan of Action.

My journey back to Abuja was on Sunday June 7 rather than the usual Monday morning. My car broke down on the way and I managed it to the National Women's Development Centre (formerly Maryam Babangida Women's Centre), where the workshop was to be held, and took a taxi home. When I got home I found thieves had burgled my home and carted away most of my valuables by entering through the roof. The following day was raining, so going to the venue of the workshop without a car was a big challenge to me, and I was ill-prepared to deliver any paper. Nevertheless, I managed to reach the venue, but I was late and all invited guests were already seated and waiting for the First Lady to come and open the workshop. There was an empty chair for me at the high table, but protocol did not allow me to walk in late when Ministers and high delegation were already seated. An hour beyond the opening time was too much, as Maryam Abacha was known to be punctual at events, unlike most Nigerian officials. She even spoke openly against the "African time syndrome."

Suddenly Dr. Hajo Sani, the Minister for Women's

Affairs and Social Development, walked briskly past me without responding to my greetings. That allowed me the opportunity to move to the high table. Dr (Mrs) Safia Muhammed, one of the icons of the Ministry of Women's Affairs, and pioneer director when the new Ministry was established, whispered to me that there was a problem in the land. She said General Sani Abacha was in a coma or even dead and since there had been no formal statement to that effect she did not know how to make the announcement to the participants who had been assembled from all the 36 states of Nigeria.

I advised her to announce the postponement of the workshop till the following day to allow the First Lady to come and declare it open. My reasoning was that since Gen Abacha was a Muslim, there was no way his death and burial would not be announced immediately according to Islamic injunctions. But I was not surprised by his sudden death, because I knew he was ill. There were many occasions when he had not received the credentials of ambassadors accredited to Nigeria, even after elaborate preparation by the Protocol Department. The Protocol Department and the State Chief of Protocol (SCOP) had difficult tasks in handling these issues at the Presidential villa. Due to the sanctions and partly due to his ill health, Abacha rarely travelled out of the country, even to the UNGA in New York. He had even expected to travel to Burkina Faso that day for an OAU Summit where the MFA and the advanced team had already gone.

As we dispersed, some jubilant youths were thanking God for answering their prayers for the death of Abacha, whom they claimed had been the main obstacle to peace and tranquillity in the country. My mind went back to the sermon at the Friday prayers three days previously. There were all sorts of rumours as to the cause of death, but the most authentic sources pointed to natural causes. Whatever the cause, we believe that Allah gives life and takes life as at when He deems it fit. As Muslims, we thanked Allah for his life on earth and the role he played in the development of our country despite the misgivings by his foes.

The new Head of State was General Abdulsalami Abubakar, the then Chief of General Staff, while the Chief of Naval Staff, Admiral Mike Akhigbe, became the Vice-President. I knew the latter well due to his constant visits to the MFA, both official and personal, to meet his classmate Habeeb Elabor, a good colleague of mine in the PRS. General Abubakar seemed to have a good grip of the main problems of Nigeria at that time as he took important steps to solve them. He released all political detainees and made moves toward releasing Moshood Abiola, who tragically died in detention. All those who fled the country, including the NADECO members, were encouraged to return without conditions. He constituted a Constitutional Conference to review the 1979 constitution, and what pleased everyone was the announcement that the election should be conducted, and power handed over on May 29, 1999. Nigeria was transformed overnight from an international pariah state to an international poster boy.

Like a pack of cards, Nigeria returned to her enviable position as an important player in international affairs. The EU lifted sanctions and membership of the Commonwealth was restored. All actions on UN resolutions against Nigeria were discontinued. Those countries that had closed their embassies, like Canada, reopened them hurriedly. My desk, which was a hotbed of criticism on human rights abuses in the country, was changed overnight and turned into a place other country were courting for support on their resolutions against other countries or in defence of their own. The MFA, which was effectively in a coma in the community of nations, came to life as the era of despair due to non-posting of staff and ambassadors abroad ended abruptly. Ambassador Ignatius Olisemeka, one of the most senior career Foreign Service officers, was appointed Foreign Minister. He brought life to the MFA and put Nigerian diplomacy along a path of progress and respectability.

It was in this climate that I was posted to open a Consulate-General in Karachi, Pakistan. I had no briefing on what was expected of me in my new assignment other than what I had read in the Vienna Convention on Consular Relations of 1963. This is a different agreement from the Vienna Convention on Diplomatic Relations of 1961. Severance of the latter does not imply severance of the former, even though in most cases the functions of the former are included in the latter in most missions abroad. I left hurriedly without any formal briefing and without any condition of service attached to the post, nor the Station Charter, which should have specified my main duties and expectations in the new mission, as well as the Consular Districts we were to cover in Pakistan's six Provinces. The posting was a great relief for me as my desk on human rights was very difficult and tortuous for us and the conduct of diplomacy was by no means easy during the pariah period. My boss Ambassador Wadibia-Anyanwu wondered why I had been posted to Pakistan as well as Tijjani Otepola and Chief Boyede, who were the responsible officers for the posting briefs and had themselves been posted to Islamabad and New Delhi respectively instead of influencing our postings to other more amenable and lucrative posts. I told her that I had never influenced postings as a matter of policy and I had no idea who had made the proposal.

In any case I went to Pakistan and found it one of the best missions I had ever served. I regretted being moved from there to Lusaka after barely one year, even though I had higher status as High Commissioner.

I had a good impression of working closely with Maryam Abacha, a mother of all, intelligent and hardworking, who handled her duties with zeal and determination, which resulted in three most viable projects that stand out above all others, even today. These projects are the Women and Children's Hospital (renamed National Hospital), the First Ladies' Peace Mission, which I was closely involved in after the Beijing Conference on Women in 1995, and the establishment of the Federal Ministry of Women's Affairs. She influenced the establishment of the latter after the Dakar Conference of African Women in preparation for the Beijing Conference. It was formerly called the "National Commission for Women" before it was upgraded to a fully-fledged Ministry. Most of the staff were her confidants and associates from the states civil services or universities.

Working with Nigerian women during and after the Beijing Women Conference of 1995 endeared them greatly to me. It made me appreciate the need to empower women through affirmative action in the form of education, credit facilities for businesses, health and political appointments for sustainable development in our country. I would have wished to see some of our parks, streets, centres, plazas and public buildings named after prominent women who were behind their establishment, like the National Woman Development Centre (formerly Maryam Babangida Women's Centre), National Hospital and the Ministry of Women's Affairs. This recognition would encourage women to put in their best efforts in the MDAs they were appointed into. There seemed to be only two streets named after women in Abuja, Okonjo-Iweala Street and Margaret Ekpo Street, and although they had been named after women who had initiated their establishment they were later renamed without good reason. These were political and moral decisions which were beyond my power as a career diplomat with limited influence. After all I had more serious work to do in my next assignment in Karachi.

At the GATT negotiations in Cairo, 1992

At the GATT negotiations on trade in services in Cairo 1992

At G77 Conference on UNCTAD with Alhaji Abubakar
and Roddy Nwokeabia in Teheran in 1991

Presentation of Credentials to President Chiluba of Zambia 1999

Laying a Wreath at the Freedom Square in Lusaka Zambia 1999

At UNCTAD VIII Ministerial Conference in Teheran with AK Muhammed, 1991

The Great Wall at Mutianyu

With a German Counsellor at negotiations on disarmament and release of resources for development at UNCTAD VIII, Colombia, in 1992

Inspecting the guard of honour at the Hofburgh Palace in Vienna in 2000

Presentation of Credentials to President Thomas Klestil
at Hofburg Palace May 3, 2000

With President Thomas Klestil at Hofburg Palace, 2000

At an OPEC Ministerial Conference in Vienna with
Dr. Rilwanu Lukman and Mohammed Barkindo

With General Abdulsalami Abubakar and Dr. Lukman
at OPEC Secretariat, Vienna

General Abubakar with Dr. Lukman and Sayid Abdulai
DG OPEC Fund at the Residence in Vienna

With Alhaji Sule Lamido and Halima at the Residence in Vienna in 2003

General Abubakar visits Mauthausen Concentration Camp in Linz, Upper Austria

The gateway to the Torture Chamber at Mauthausen in Upper Austria

With Benita Ferrero-Waldner, Austrian Foreign Minister, and Alhaji Sule Lamido at the historic Hall of the Vienna Congress of 1814-1815

Presentation of Credentials to Carlos Margarinos, UNIDO Director General, 2000

Presentation of Credentials to Antonio Maria Costa,
Director General (UN Office) in Vienna, 2000

Presentation of credentials to Mohammed El Baradei
Director General IAEA, in Vienna, 2000

Visit to Salzburg in Austria with Jane Odeka and Halima in 2003

With my staff Bukun Onemola and Dahiru Adamu after the presentation of credentials to the IAEA Director General

Presentation of credentials to Wolfgang Hoffmann,
Director-General, CTBTO, in Vienna in 2007

At the UNIDO Conference in Vienna, 2001

Co-Chair with Ambassador Starr of Australia to review the organisational structure of CTBTO in Vienna in 2004-5

Ambassadors should collaborate closely with nationals of the sending state in the receiving state

Inspecting the guard of honour at Schloß Bellevue in Berlin before presentation of credentials to the German President on June 4 2007

Presentation of credentials to Horst Kohler, the German President, on 4 June 2007

At the G-8 Summit in Germany June 2007

With Horst Kohler, the German President, at Schloß Bellevue

With Angela Merkel, the German Chancellor, at her residence in Berlin, 2010

President Musa Yar`Adua at the Residence in Berlin in 2007

Halima and Eva Köhler at Schloß Bellevue, Berlin,
for New Year reception 2008

Ambassadors' visit to Bayern Munich in Germany 2008

Receiving a medal from the German President, with the President of Togo looking on, after a football match with the German Foreign Ministry

Ambassadors visit to Hannover in Niedersachsen Germany

Halima and Eva Kohler at New Year's reception for
Ambassadors' spouses at a New Year reception in Berlin, 2009

With Horst Kohler, the German President, during a
New Year party in Berlin

At the US July 4 reception in Berlin. From right to left Ambassador of Ethiopia, the author, Ambassador of Niger and Dem Pauline Tallen, Deputy Governor of Plateau State

My farewell to the German President, Christoph Wulf, at Schloß Bellevue on July 7, 2010 and my exit from the Foreign Service

CHAPTER 7

KARACHI: CONSULAR DIPLOMACY

"A real diplomat is one who can cut his neighbour's throat without having his neighbour notice it."

Otto Von Bismarck (1815-1898)

"Diplomats are just as essential to starting a war as soldiers are to finish it. You take diplomacy out of war and the thing would fall flat in a week."

William Rogers (1879-1935)

I did not really know what persuaded headquarters to post me to open this mission, which was recommended many years ago by Ambassador Baba Gana Kingibe, during his services as Nigerian High Commissioner to Pakistan. I had no inkling of what was going on at the Posting Committee, even though my two directors were members. None of them could tell me. Not that I was bothered about where I would be posted as it was not in my character to delve into the affairs of other departments, even if it affected me. The only time I knew that a posting exercise was going on was when one of my junior female officers approached me to assist in influencing her posting from Trinidad and Tobago to a place in Africa. I took up the matter with my director by arguing that as a married officer, the lady would wish to be close to her husband in Nigeria, and he agreed with me; she was posted to Tunisia.

I had a stopover in Islamabad from Kuala Lumpur, Malaysia where I accompanied Justice Fati Abubakar, the then first Lady of Nigeria, for a Summit of First Ladies. I was just stopping over to have a feel and glimpse of the assignment from purely diplomatic to consular diplomacy, which was quite new and strange to me, but since the city I was to operate from was more than one hour away from our mission in Islamabad, there was not much to do. The High Commissioner Razaq Yunusa, who incidentally was the officer who had blocked my posting to Jeddah by asking for an extension in 1990, received me warmly and even accommodated me at the residence. We arranged that pending the actual opening of the Consulate-General in Karachi, all our financial needs would be borne by the High Commission until our funds were received. I returned to Abuja and completed the preparation for UNGA in New York and left for Islamabad, taking with me two of the five officers I was to work with. These were Messrs Thomas Aguiyi Ironsi and Onyemaechi, the Finance Attaché.

We travelled to Karachi in search of office accommodation and staff quarters. Karachi was the capital of Pakistan before it was moved to Rawalpindi and then to Islamabad in 1963. There was a large concentration of consulates in the city of over 18 million people. As the commercial capital of Pakistan with many industries, it was highly polluted, and crime was high. We found suitable accommodation with the Defence Housing Authority, all in the Defence 5 District, the safest part of the city. Crime in this area was near zero, with heavy security patrols. The area is called Defence Quarters because the land was allocated to the Pakistani military, but they sold it to wealthy Pakistanis, the politicians, businessmen, diplomats, and most of these people live overseas. The Bhutto family home was a stone's throw away from our residence. Buildings in this Defence Quarter were of the highest quality. It is a city within a city, as the other parts where most of the people live are of poor quality. The streets and utilities, like water and electricity, were in good supply.

Duties of a Consular Post

I did not have any Station Charter for my duties in Karachi and they were cut out for me by resorting to what was spelled out in the Vienna Convention on Consular relations of 1963. These are:

a) Protection of the interests of the sending state and its nationals in the receiving state;

b) Enhancing trade relations between the sending state and the receiving state.

Nigeria was the only African country with a Consulate-General in the city. It did not take us more than three months before we discovered why the Consulate-General had been opened. There were many commercial opportunities for Nigerian businessmen and women in the area, most of them small to medium-sized enterprises. Clothing, textiles, solid minerals, armament, guns and ammunition, a seaport, and therefore commercial diplomacy was the essence at this post.

The Pakistan Defence Officers' Housing Authority, as the name implies, primarily came into being for the welfare of the serving and retired officers of the Armed Forces of Pakistan. It is the largest and most prestigious residential estate scheme, while others are located in other provinces of the country. The scheme provides the best educational, recreational, cultural and civil facilities. Defence Five, where we resided, was the most prestigious of all the Districts 1-6 when we arrived the city in 1998.

I presented my Letters of Commission at the Pakistani Foreign Ministry in Islamabad within two weeks of arrival, devoid of any formal ceremony. Without this ceremony of presentation of the Letter of Commission and receiving an exequatur from the host Foreign Minister, I could not function as the head of the Consulate-General in Karachi. As the only African country with a Consulate-General in the city, the Chancery became a "mecca" for seeking assistance from all African countries from Egypt, Tunisia, Algeria, South Africa, Kenya and many West African nationals were trooping to the Chancery with complaints of harassment from the Pakistani police. There were cases of illicit Nigerian drug peddlers using the city as stepping stone to reach Afghanistan, and a few were detained in Karachi prisons. There were many consular cases in the neighbouring Provinces such as Punjab and Balochistan, but since there were no clear-cut Consular Districts assigned to us to cover we could not pay consular visits to them unless our High Commission in Islamabad directed us to do so. We confined our tasks to the Sindh Province alone. The name of Sindh was derived from the Indus River that separates it with Baluchistan and the Iranian Plateau. There was a provincial office of the Federal Ministry of Foreign Affairs in Karachi, which was responsible for the day-to-day contacts with the large number of diplomatic Consulates in Karachi, numbering over 50.

Since Karachi is the commercial and financial capital of Pakistan, we made commercial and trade-related issues the most important duties of the Consulate-General, followed by consular, cultural and social issues. Due to the large number of Pakistanis that had worked in Nigeria during our oil boom period who had taken residence in this bubbling city it was easy for us to operate, because there were well-established commercial contacts with some Nigerian States' Chambers of Commerce. They had some contacts with the Kaduna and Kano states' Chambers of Commerce and Industries. Our main task was to link them with the NACCIMA and MAN at the Federal level. There was also the Islamic Chamber of Commerce and Industries (ICCI) with its headquarters in Karachi.

We became very active in the work of the ICCI, which was established in Istanbul, Turkey in 1978, with the aim of strengthening closer collaboration in the fields of trade, commerce, information technology, insurance and reinsurance, shipping, banking, promotion of investment opportunities, and joint ventures in the members' countries, including those with smaller Muslim populations like

Uganda, Rwanda, Burundi, Zaire, Zambia, Cameroon, Benin and Togo. The Secretary-General and the Deputy Secretary-General were from Oman and Cameroon respectively.

The controversy over whether Nigeria was a fully-fledged member of the OIC or an observer necessitated discussion with my colleagues at the Consulate-General. As far as MFA was concerned, Nigeria had not withdrawn from the OIC. It was only a decision following the outcry by some section of Nigerians that it was decided to lower our active participation. High level participation at its Conferences and Summits were attended by traditional rulers and Muslim organisations in Nigeria and at the level of directors at the MFA, which had changed during the Yar'Adua and Goodluck Jonathan's administrations when meetings were attended at high levels. But as far as we were concerned, the Consulate-General was established to promote and facilitate commerce and industrial activities between Nigeria and Pakistan, so the work of the ICCI was very important to us and as such we participated actively in its activities that were relevant to our duties.

The other important pre-occupation of the Consulate-General was consular assistance to Nigerians, and invariably to Africans. Because of this involvement of the mission all crimes committed by African peoples were reported to be by Nigerians. One such incident was the arrest and detention of 12 Kenyans and Tanzanians for various offences; they were reported in the media to be all Nigerians. When we visited them, and discovered that they were not Nigerians, we protested to the DAWN newspaper and urged them to publish a rejoinder to correct the misinformation, but they refused because all black peoples from Africa were deemed to be Nigerians. They said that their people did not know about the other African countries, and Nigeria was the only country they knew. However, the Republic of Cameroon was known for football. They also thought that Ghana and Kenya were provinces of Nigeria, like their own Sindh Province, so they could not rescind their publication. What surprised us most was that Algerians and Egyptians were also calling upon our Consulate-General for consular assistant, because their embassies were in Islamabad.

Dubai in the United Arab Emirates was just emerging as a centre for commerce, and we visited to equip and furnish our residence and Chancery. To our surprise we found that most of the items of clothing and textiles sold in Dubai were products made from Karachi and Mumbai.

Trade Fair for Military Armaments in Karachi

A Naval Defence Exhibition (NAVDEX) which attracted many participants from all over the world including the Command and Staff College, Quetta, National Defence, Rawalpindi was held in Karachi. The Nigeria delegation included the Chief of Naval Staff and many naval officers who were Military Administrators and the top brass of the Nigerian Navy. We were amazed to see the kinds of products that were made in Pakistan in the field of armaments on display, including armoured personnel carriers (APCs) and submarines, with collaboration with the French armament industries. Highly advanced and sophisticated armament products manufactured in Pakistan were exhibited. Our delegation lamented our own efforts in these areas. The naval officers from Nigeria told us the sorry state of the Kaduna Defence Industries Corporation, which was now manufacturing furniture instead of armaments. They blamed Nigeria's lack of success in this area to corruption and mismanagement. I informed them that Nigeria was second only to Pakistan in the corruption perception index of Transparency International (TI) at that time, yet Pakistan was still better than Nigeria. The main difference between our two countries was the fact that most of the armament industry in Pakistan was controlled by retired military officers with assistance from the government of Pakistan. But in the Nigerian situation, her retired generals and military personnel go into all sorts of business unrelated to armament industries, such as politicking, contracting, commerce and farming. The Nigerian government was not even encouraging and assisting retired military officers to go into military industry like in Pakistan, as depicted at the Naval Expo.

There was an Air Commodore Ate from the Nigerian Air Force attending a course at the Pakistan Air Force College in Karachi during our time there. This prestigious college was founded in 1958 as a Staff College and later upgraded to Air War College and it attracts Air Force officers from Nigeria through the bilateral agreement between our two countries. I understand that the curriculum of the College was as high as Sandhurst in the UK and in India, where our officers were also trained. The Nigerian War College (now National Defence College) was established in early 1990 based on a curriculum like these and of high standard as well, and is also open to a few military personnel in other countries. There is a need for the Government to encourage and support our retired government personnel to manufacture needed military equipment in the country instead of depending on imports from abroad. Why should Nigeria depend upon the supply of military equipment from abroad to fight insurgents and terrorism within her shores? At least we should look inwards by making our own defence capability functional and import only complementary items that could not be produced locally.

My wife Halima, who is a linguist and has a penchant for languages, picked up the Urdu language very quickly in the bazaars and at receptions and our contacts, with the many friends we made. The ease with which we made friends in Karachi in such a short period amazed me. There was no day of the week when there wasn't a reception to which we were invited. Apart from the large diplomatic receptions, wealthy locals were competing with one another in organizing receptions and parties. They were also very active in organizing events about the countries they represented. Many such requests for Honorary Consuls for Nigeria were made but, for reasons not known to us, Nigeria did not encourage the practice. I do not see anything wrong with Honorary Consuls because they provide certain services that are useful to the countries they represent, at no extra cost. The only thing they do is to fly the country's flag and represent your country at events and receptions and provide business and cultural information to the public in areas your country could not reach diplomatically.

There were cases of Nigerian scams. The '419' scams (named after the relevant Nigerian criminal code) were rampant and they were cashing in on gullible Pakistanis who wanted to reap where they had not sown. One such case came to my attention at the Chancery. An Honorary Consul of Barbados came into the Chancery to report a case to me involving about $300,000 in a business deal with a Nigerian. According to the deal he was expected to wire the sum to an account in Barbados as an investment, and within 3 months it would yield $900,000 and his share of the deal would be $750,000. As he was narrating to me how the money would be made and the kind of business, I asked him if he had sent any money yet. He was a bit nervous as I asked my question. When I repeated the question to confirm if he had sent any money before we got into detail of finding if it was genuine business or not, the man jumped out of my office and rushed out of the Chancery. He returned to thank me for saving his $300,000, which he had authorized his bank to wire to the business. Any time we met at reception he would mention how I saved him from committing suicide. Several other such cases were reported to us involving nebulous businesses formed with a view to making quick money. We then made it a duty to put up notices at the Chancery and the Chamber of Commerce to warn people about such scams to make quick money, saying that if it was too good to be true they should contact the Consulate-General for advice. There were also very many businesses that were without problems. However, businesses in sugar, cement, salt, textiles and finished products were discouraged due to the Dangote monopoly.

The main reception we organized was the democracy day on 29th May, 1999. It attracted many diplomats; businessmen and many old friends of Nigeria who had worked in our country during the oil boom of the 1970s and early 1980s. As the reception ended Aguiyi Ironsi (later Ambassador) came up to me and told me that there was a problem. He said that there were four top members of the Pakistan Muslim League, one of the formidable parties challenging the Pakistan Peoples' Party (PPP), who were stuck in his office and could not walk out due to the amount of alcohol they had taken. He said they had found sanctuary in his office and had had an overdose. Halima shouted *"subhan Allah!"* and wondered why they call themselves "Muslim League". They were the leaders of the ruling party of Prime Minister Nawaz Sharif in Sindh Province. With a lot of persuasion, we managed to get them home.

Whenever I visited Islamabad I stayed at a hotel where most of the workers were from Afghanistan and they used to tell me news about the Taliban to the extent that I bought several books about the Taliban, not knowing that they would soon dominate the world of terrorism and politics. The most attractive places to visit in Pakistan are the King Faisal Mosque in Islamabad, the Khyber Pass in the North-West Frontier Province and the historical city of Lahore. I managed to visit only the first one as I was appointed High Commissioner to Zambia after less than ten months in Karachi. I received the appointment as High Commissioner to Zambia with mixed feelings, as I had started to enjoy our stay in Karachi and made a lot of friends during the short stay. Although I was appointed to a higher position I was not very excited, particularly as it was in a country with fewer basic facilities and less glamour than Pakistan.

Before I left Karachi, there were a few incidents of terrorist attacks in the city, but none in the Defence Housing Authority where we were located. The most devastating act of terrorism was at the US Consulate-General, where part of the building was destroyed, fortunately with no loss of life. The other attack was at the office of the Chief Minister of Sindh Province to coincide with the visit of Prime Minister Nawaz Sharif to the city. But despite the increasing security concerns, nevertheless Karachi was a very lively city and we loved it very much. The Diplomatic community was also very large as most countries retained their Consulates in the old capital when the capital was moved to Rawalpindi in 1960 and later to Islamabad in 1963.

Aga Khan University Teaching Hospitals

I had cause to visit a doctor named Dr. Mohammed Amin Kharadi, who organized surgery on me at the Aga Khan University Teaching Hospital, Karachi. The hospital is a sprawling and splendid place and one of the largest hospitals I have ever seen. The surgery was done, and I was highly impressed with the efficiency of the workers, although the cost was very minimal. I saw many nurses from Kenya who told me that they were under scholarship from the Aga Khan Foundation. They also informed me that the Foundation had a college in Nairobi as well as a clinic for heart and cancer treatment, which was later upgraded into a fully-fledged University named after the Aga Khan. To them, the Aga Khan "was a very good Asian" who had touched the lives of many people in East Africa, particularly in Kenya and Tanzania. The Aga Khan University Teaching Hospital in Karachi was opened in 1985 with 500 beds. The one in Nairobi had 250 beds and the nurses I met in Karachi were being trained for it. That was a practical example of South-South cooperation among developing countries, which I admired and cherished so much. I later learned that the first Aga Khan hospital with 96 beds had been opened in Mombasa in 1944. Others with 80 beds and 61 beds were opened in Dar es Salaam and Kisumu in 1964 and 1952 respectively.

I left the hospital full of envy and wished that the Aga Khans could have visited us in Nigeria with similar gestures in the educational and social fields due to the quality of services rendered so efficiently and cheaply. I regretted not having a meeting with the Foundation to drive my urge to invite them to visit Nigeria or arrange cooperating meetings with Nigerian doctors, because then I departed to Lusaka to take up my post as high Commissioner, albeit briefly.

CHAPTER 8

ZAMBIA SHALL BE FREE

"All the monies in this world are either red or blue. I do not have my own green money, so where can I get it from? I am not taking a cold war position. All I want is money to build the Tanzam Railways."

Julius Nyerere (1922-1999)

"Diplomacy is a continuation of war by other means."

Chou Enlai (1898-1976)

The modern history of Zambia could be traced to the visit of the missionary expedition of David Livingstone, who arrived on the Zambezi River in 1851. David Livingstone named the river after Queen Victoria (later Victoria Falls), the reigning Queen of England at that time, while the town was named after him. Livingstone town later became the capital of Northern Rhodesia until it was moved to the central town of Lusaka in 1935. Before independence in 1964, the country was in a joint federation with Southern Rhodesia (Zimbabwe) and Nyasaland (Malawi) and was called the Central African Federation of Rhodesia and Nyasaland with power dominated or resided with the white population based in Southern Rhodesia. The Federation, which was established in 1953, came to an end on 31 December 1963 and led to the independence of Malawi (July 6, 1964) and Zambia (October 24, 1964), while the minority white population in Southern Rhodesia unilaterally declared independence (UDI) from Britain in 1965.

I received my credentials from General Abdulsalami Abubakar at a ceremony at the Aso Rock Presidential Villa along with many of my colleagues, and was directed to proceed to post immediately before the change of leadership on May 29, 1999. That was the date scheduled by the military to hand over power to the elected government of Chief Olusegun Obasanjo. Before I got to Lusaka, the Acting High Commissioner, Emmanuel Ademola Ogunnaike, and the Head of Chancery, Ahmed Daura Gafai, had already decided for me to present my credentials, which were done within two weeks of arrival.

My greatest shock on arrival was the lack of resources to run the mission. Due to the shortage of hard currency in the country, the mission's account was opened in London but there was nothing in it. I presented my credentials to President Frederick Jacob Titus Chiluba, after which I rushed back to Karachi to wind up and bid farewell to the numerous friends there.

The Democracy day of May 29 was observed as an official public holiday and marked by parties in all our missions abroad. President Obasanjo announced the recall of all ambassadors who had been appointed by Gen Abdulsalami Abubakar and we were given 30 days to return to headquarters for "consultations." I was then faced with the problem of where to ship my personal effects. Would I send them to Lusaka or to Abuja? There was also the problem of pulling out my children from schools in Karachi in the middle of the term. The challenges were so enormous that I decided to leave my personal effects in a warehouse in Karachi at extra cost to the shipping agent, while I pulled my children out of school back to Nigeria. The senior ones were admitted to the University of Luton, UK, as the move to send them to Canada was not successful due to visa refusal. I was surprised that the Canadian High Commission could deny my children visas despite adequate financial support and excellent results from them while giving visas to children of my junior staff with less financial standing. Even after settling down in their universities in the UK and the US, an attempt by them to visit their friends in Canada was refused due to the refusal in Islamabad. I could not understand the Canadian visa regime throughout my diplomatic career, both in Abuja and other missions I served as ambassador.

I informed my host country, Zambia, that I was being recalled to headquarters for consultations. Keli Walibuta, the Foreign Minister, was a pleasant and intelligent personality whom I met several times within a short time, because I participated at several meetings hosted by Zambia to broker peace in the DRC.

As part of the inauguration of the Obasanjo administration on 29 May 1999, many Heads of State and Government were invited, some of whom were close neighbours to Zambia. It surprised my host that the Zambian President Chiluba was not invited, despite the known track records of Nigeria and Zambia during the apartheid period when Zambia was the venue of the Front-Line States, of which Nigeria was a member despite its location in West Africa. Even after the liberation of Southern Africa from apartheid, Chief Obasanjo was a member of the Commonwealth Eminent Persons Group with Zambian President Kaunda. That bond of friendship was expected to manifest in long-lasting relations between the two countries and President Obasanjo was highly respected in Zambia, but that was not the case with his inauguration of May 29, 1999 as Nigeria's president. The Zambians took exception to this omission or commission and they quickly attributed it to Nigeria supporting former President Kenneth Kaunda to recapture the presidency from Chiluba.

To stop the former President Kaunda from contesting the election, Chiluba instituted an amendment to the Zambian Constitution stopping anyone whose parents were born outside Zambia. Kaunda was traced to Malawian parenthood, and as such he was ineligible to contest the Zambian presidency. The Ndola High Court declared Kaunda stateless and Chiluba attempted to deport him, but the Supreme Court restored his Zambian citizenship. His son, Wezi Kaunda, was killed on November 5, 1999 and most embassies and High Commissions paid condolence visits to Kaunda, including me. The Zambian authorities under Chiluba were very unhappy about not being invited to the Obasanjo inauguration and we informed headquarters accordingly. But the former President Kaunda was knocking at the door of our Mission to visit Nigeria and congratulate his friend, Chief Obasanjo. We also advised against making the visit public as it would harm relations between our two countries, but Ambassador Dele Cole, the Special Adviser on Foreign Affairs, facilitated the visit of Kaunda to Nigeria without input from MFA and against our advice.

As I was recalled to headquarters, I watched the television coverage of President Kaunda's reception by Chief Obasanjo at the State House. I knew that if I returned to Lusaka I would have a difficult task to explain to our host the circumstances of the visit. That visit was reported widely in the Zambian news media with comments that President Kaunda was promised large sums of money for presidential campaigns by Nigeria. The incident put a sour taste in our relations with Zambia, albeit temporarily.

After three months in Abuja I was nominated ambassador by the Obasanjo Government and posted to Vienna, Austria. I returned to Lusaka for three months to wait for my agremént and to wind down for the new posting, which would involve both multilateral and bilateral diplomacy in Austria.

During the courtesy calls I made to my colleagues in Lusaka, I also bade farewell to them at the same time and most of them were surprised that an ambassador should decide to leave his post within such a short period. My visit to the doyen of ambassadors, John Kangai of Zimbabwe, was informative. Basking in the euphoria of having just been allocated a large farm confiscated from white farmers by President Mugabe, he told me how happy he was to own such a large farm. I asked him what was he going to plant or cultivate there and how he was going to manage it while serving abroad. He was incoherent in his response. He said that all ministers, politicians and ambassadors were allocated farms and he planned to continue to cultivate what was being grown by the white farmers. He told me that maize and tobacco would be good on his farm, but the problem would be machinery and management. John later met me in Vienna as the Zimbabwean ambassador to Austria and permanent representative to UN offices in Vienna and we continued our good friendship. Unfortunately, he died towards the end of my tenure of duties in Vienna and I believe he never put his farm to good use, as he never went back home for many years, having moved from country to country as an ambassador.

Visiting Economic and Tourist Sites in Zambia

I made it a duty to visit some important places and people in all the countries I was posted to, and Zambia was no exception. I visited Michael Sata, leader of the Patriotic Front Party, and Rupiah Banda, and I was eager to meet or see the graves of prominent Zambians like Harry Nkumbula. During the apartheid period we read President Kaunda's book "Zambia Shall Be Free", which was a must-read for us in Nigerian colleges and universities. Most of the people I visited decried the new laws haunting their country, the so-called "bad laws" made by President Chiluba to stop people whose parents were not Zambians. They recalled that before independence, Zambia was part of the three nations Federation of Rhodesia and Nyasaland. Zambia was Northern Rhodesia, Zimbabwe was Southern

Rhodesia and Malawi was Nyasaland, and people moved freely and intermarried easily within the Federation. Zambia bordered eight countries with fluid boundaries, namely Malawi, Angola, the Democratic Republic of Congo (DRC), Tanzania, Zimbabwe, Mozambique, Namibia and Botswana, and it was difficult to find a person whose parents were both Zambians by birth or descent, and had lived in the country consecutively for twenty years to contest for the country's presidency. Although this "bad law" was made to stop ex-President Kaunda, Chiluba himself was traced to have come from DRC and was born in that country's Kisangani hospital.

I visited the Copper Belt at Ndola, Kitwe and Chingola. Copper was the backbone of the Northern Rhodesian economy during colonial rule as well as the main economy of post-independence Zambia. But its economic importance was severely damaged by a crash in the global copper prices in 1973 and was worsened by the nationalization of the copper mines by the Government of Kenneth Kaunda. Copper mining also extended to Lubumbashi in the DRC. We visited three large copper mining conglomerates, namely Mopani Copper Mines plc. Kitwe, the Xstrata at Kansanshi and the Zambia Consolidated Copper Mines Ltd (ZCC M). There were signs of decay and under-capacity production at all the mines we visited due to the fall in the prices of copper and cobalt on the international market. I was informed that most of the investors were Canadians, British, Australians and Chinese. Exports were by rail and road haulage to South Africa, Tanzania, Mozambique and Angola.

I recalled reading about the history of the Tanzam Railway, which was built by the Chinese to haul copper from

Zambia to Tanzania for export abroad. It is also called Tazara or Uhuru Railways and was built by China from the Tanzanian port of Dar es Salaam to Kapiri, Mposhi in the Copper Belt from 1970-1975 at a cost of over $500million. It was the largest foreign aid project by China at that time, intended to ease the dependence of Zambia on Rhodesia and South Africa for the export of copper to the world market. It was about 1,800 miles long. I indicated an interest in taking a ride on this train, but I was advised that it had deteriorated badly due to inadequate maintenance and financial difficulties.

I also visited the town of Livingstone and the tourist resort of Victoria Falls. Established in 1905, the town was named after the British missionary explorer David Livingstone and was the capital of Northern Rhodesia until 1911. It still featured colonial buildings, as seen in the main road. I was down with a severe fever, so I went to see an Asian doctor and it gave me the chance see the inside of one of the buildings with fireplaces and decoration like those of the old buildings in Edwardian or Victorian England. I was not fortunate enough to visit the famous Livingstone Museum due to my ill health, so I reduced it to a safari tour and the Victoria Falls. The town of Victoria Falls in Zimbabwe lies across the Zambezi River and is separated by a bridge which we used to cross over into Zimbabwe just to feel the differences between the two countries. I changed a few US dollars to buy a souvenir from the Zimbabwean town of Victoria Falls and the exchange rate compared more favourable to that of the Zambian kwacha. But when I returned to Zimbabwe in 2005, I almost collapsed at the Harare Hilton hotel when I gave dinner for three and the bill presented to me was over 1,300,000 Zimbabwean dollars! I was forced to call my colleague, Ambassador Tony Osula, to come to my assistance as there was no way I could pay such a huge bill. He just laughed and told me that it was only worth about $80 US or less!

We drove to see the memorial of David Livingstone just by the Victoria Falls and saw monuments and names of people who lost their lives during WWI and WWII, but curiously there was no name that appeared African. I asked our tour guide and he laughed over it and said that since he had been doing that job for over ten years, no one had ever asked him that question except me, because most of the tourists that visited were Europeans and South African whites, Asians (Chinese and Japanese), so it was not an issue of interest to them. He told me that Livingstone town had a white and black settlement and that we were in the white settlement as such there was no way an African killed in combat during those wars would be recognized as important enough to warrant being mentioned.

We went on safari to observe and photograph animals and wildlife and ended up with the canoe ride into the Victoria Falls where one side is Zimbabwe and the other is Zambia, all in the same river, and the Falls itself. The most fascinating and tallest part of the Falls gorge, called locally Mosi-oa-Tunya ('the smoke that thunders'), is in Zambia, while the longest part is in Zimbabwe. The peninsula cliffs of the Falls are in Zambia, while the outer cliffs are in Zimbabwe. Our visit coincided with the period of the bird flu epidemics ravaging Europe and other countries worldwide, so there were devices put in place for us to wet our feet and the tyres of our car on the main highways between Lusaka and the places we visited outside the state capital. I wondered if Nigeria had any similar devices in place, but there was none when I returned home.

On my return to Lusaka, I called on the Secretary-General of the Common Market for Eastern and Southern Africa (COMESA) located at Ben Bella Road, Lusaka. The organisation is aimed at promoting regional cooperation in trade and investment. It was established in 1994 by Southern African Development Cooperation (SADC) countries, but curiously members included Sudan, Egypt, Libya, Djibouti, Eritrea and Ethiopia. I wondered why Nigeria could not be a member in view of the large volume of informal trade between Nigeria and Zambia, as I found a sizeable number of Nigerian motor component dealers in the country, whereas countries as far away as Libya and Egypt were members. After all Nigeria contributed immensely to the liberation of Southern Africa as a Frontline State, so any economic benefits through this organisation would be useful to our businessmen and women. I recommended our membership in this organisation to headquarters, but did not get a favourable response until I left the Mission for Vienna.

Diplomatic Problems with my Departure from Zambia

My agremént as Ambassador to Austria was delayed since the Austrian ambassador agreement, which was requested from Nigeria before mine, was also delayed by Nigeria. That was an example of pure reciprocity in diplomatic practice. Dr Christopher Parasini, who later became controversial with the Nigerian authority, had his agremént delayed as mine was delayed by Austria. But my successor in Lusaka, Ronke Adefowope, a political appointee, was eager to take her post in Zambia, so I decided to leave for Nigeria and waited for my own agrément. According to diplomatic practice, it is unusual to have two ambassadors from the sending state in the capital of the receiving state at the same time. The former must leave before the arrival of the new one to be accorded full protocol and diplomatic protection by the receiving state. It is also unusual for the departing envoy to depart the mission without taking leave of the host president, or whosoever the credentials were presented to on arrival, to enable him or her know that the former ambassador has departed and a new one has arrived and is ready to be received. That explains why the credentials include the recall of the previous ambassador and they are presented together at the presentation ceremony.

I made the request to bid farewell to my host, President Frederick Chiluba, through the usual diplomatic channels, as well as saying farewell to the relevant directors of the Zambian Foreign Ministry. Surprisingly there was no response and no arrangement for me to see and bid farewell to the President, despite two or three reminders. I conferred with my deputy, Emmanuel Ogunnaike, and we decided that I should depart the High Commission and send the usual *note verbale* to the Ministry of Foreign Affairs and all heads of mission accredited to the country without any protocol officer seeing me off at the airport. That was unusual.

At the VIP lounge of the airport I met the foreign minister, Keli Walubita, who was arriving from South

Africa, and I informed him that I was leaving Zambia on transfer to Austria. He regretted my short stay in the country and wished me well in my new endeavour. I later learned that a small political and diplomatic storm was brewing following the well-publicised visit of Kenneth Kaunda to Abuja with the claim that I followed him as he canvassed for resources from President Obasanjo to campaign for the next election. I was very surprised with that insinuation. We had advised against the visit, since the host president was not invited for the inauguration.

The private visit to Nigeria by Kaunda soon after the inauguration of President Obasanjo and the way and manner he was received, and his visit was reported by the media in Nigeria and Zambia created a temporary irritant in our relations. It was aggravated by the fact that I was also in Abuja on recall or "consultation". The Zambian authorities were also angry at the way Nigeria, under Abacha, withdrew the 25 TAC volunteers posted in Zambia in retaliation for their vote in favour of a resolution against Nigeria at the UNCHR in Geneva in March 1998. They saw it as a humiliation for what they called the "peanuts" assistance given by Nigeria, but due to the long-standing excellent relations between our countries, these irritants were nipped in the bud and the TAC volunteers resumed work in Zambia after I left the country. I was glad that I left when I did, as it was becoming more difficult for me to function, through no fault of mine or that of the MFA, but purely because of the over-zealous Special Advisor to the President, who facilitated Kaunda's visit to Nigeria without considering our advice against it.

The Nigerian High Commissioner to Zambia was also

accredited to Malawi, but because I had no accreditation to present to President Muluzi of Malawi, I left the affairs of Malawi to my deputy, Emmanuel Ogunnaike. Malawi was preparing for a presidential election, so Emmanuel was very busy with monitoring and reporting the events there.

The Austrians granted my agremént after their own request was granted, more than six months from the time they made the request. This was always the case with Nigeria; delaying such requests but often knocking on the doors of foreign missions in Abuja to hurry up their own. But here the Nigerian authorities were right in delaying the request, because the Austrian Ambassador became controversial and almost created a problem for me. Their own appointee was a Member of Parliament and from a controversial party which was in coalition. Because of this our apparatus responsible for scrutinizing the credentials of ambassadors rightly delayed the request, but because my own request was pending in Vienna we had to grant their request, which later became a problem for our two countries. I will return to that in the next chapter.

CHAPTER 9

VIENNA: SOUNDS OF MUSIC

"All wars represent a failure of diplomacy."
Tony Benn (1925-2014)

The modern history of Austria could be said to start from the Austro-Hungarian Empire, which was ruled by Emperor Franz Josef (1830-1916) as the Emperor of Austria and King of Hungary. Archduke Franz Ferdinand and his wife were assassinated at Sarajevo in June 1914 by a Serbian nationalist who triggered World War I (1914-1918). After the Napoleonic wars, the Congress of Vienna was convened and chaired by the Austrian Prince Klemens Wenzel von Metternich from 1814-1815. The Allied Forces that defeated Napoleon were Austria, Prussia (Germany), Russia and Great Britain. WWI led to the end of the Habsburg Empire in 1919 and Austria became a Republic. WWII, led by Austrian-born Adolf Hitler, led to the death and persecution of many socialists, Jews and intellectuals. In 1955, Austria declared its neutrality during the Cold War between the East and the West. The capital city, Vienna, housed the second European offices of the United Nations Organisation as well as the International Atomic Energy Agency. Thus, the posting of Nigerian diplomats to Vienna involves both bilateral and multilateral functions. Most of the developed Western countries have two or three ambassadors in Vienna for bilateral relations with Austria, and for UN Offices and the Organisation for Security and Cooperation in Europe (OSCE). Some countries, like the State of Israel and the Islamic Republic of Iran, had separate Representatives to the International Atomic Energy Agency (IAEA) other than the United Nations Offices at ambassadorial level.

I arrived to assume duties in Vienna in the cold winter of 2000 and was received by the Embassy staff, led by Dahiru Adamu (now late). The ambassador's residence was in one of the most prestigious parts of Vienna, 19 District, surrounded by vineyards overlooking the Kalenburg Hills. I was once a guest of Ambassador Jonathan Kabo Umar in this house in 1983 during a meeting on OPEC investment promotion conference. I presented credentials to President Thomas Klistel four months later, on May 3, 2000. The presentation of credentials, according to Austrian protocol, was for a group of six ambassadors. An impressive ceremony at the Presidential Palace was followed by a short exchange of pleasantries devoid of any substantial discussion. The President's speech was tailor-made, very short and seemed standardised for all ambassadors accredited to the Federal Republic of Austria.

Austria is a federation of states, like Nigeria, with nine provinces including Vienna. The most frequently visited by

Nigerian businessmen and women was Lustenau in Vorarlberg, with a common border with Switzerland and Germany and a booming trade in lace which expands to the other neighbouring countries of Switzerland and Germany. Lace businesses are small scale and family-owned. President Obasanjo banned the importation of the product to encourage and promote Nigerian-made material through investment rather than trading. Despite the ban, the trade continued unabated through smuggling, which created the problem of enforcement. One of my first business missions was to visit this area, which is a stone's throw across the border cities of St. Gallen and St. Margarethen in Switzerland, which we used to visit for the same material when I was serving in Geneva.

I came across some Nigerian women making large orders and I inquired how they could ship the item despite the ban into Nigeria. They just burst out laughing and said that until Stella Obasanjo started wearing apparel made in Nigeria they could be stopped from importing the items to Nigeria "through their own means". They even showed me an item called "Atiku" which was named after the Vice-President of Nigeria under Obasanjo, and told me the ban was a joke.

The Chancery building was one of Austria's historical monuments, bought at the same time as the residence in 1982. It is in the neighbourhood of the embassies of Germany, Italy, Iran, the UK, the Russian Federation and the Netherlands, but was in severe disrepair. It was located on a street named after Klemens Wenzel von Metternich, the Austrian statesman and Foreign Minister who chaired the Congress of Vienna of 1814-1815. To redeem our image regarding the poor state of the Chancery and paucity of funds, we decided to trick all those entering the building for any services, be it for visas, commerce or courtesy calls on me, by transforming the entrance into my office, the visa section and all public areas with the best facelift ever, using marble. The trick worked, as all those who visited gasped at the beauty of the Chancery, including the Japanese and US multilateral ambassadors who visited me. The same commendation was made by Chief Bola Ige less than one month before his assassination, and he repeated the same when he spoke to me in fluent Hausa and made remarkable comments to me about the Embassy, even though the rest of the building was collapsing. I told him it was my "419 scam" on the public and visitors to the Embassy and he said "*kada ka damu da kanka, wurin yana da kyau da sha'awa dayawa*" (Don't worry yourself, the place is good and beautiful). My main point here is that our embassies have always had the problem of lack of funds, so we cannot fold our hands without taking initiatives to improve on our working conditions with the little available to us.

The goal of attracting foreign direct investment rather than trade was high on my agenda, in accordance with headquarters directives. After a round of courtesy calls to my colleagues I got down to this matter with vigour. I was fortunate to have very capable, intelligent and committed officers at my disposal, whom I deployed in the field, including at the United Nations Offices and the OPEC. Dahiru Adamu was the economic desk officer in addition to other assignments bordering on security. Sani L. Mohammed, Rauf Bukun Onemola and Abel A. Ayoko were assigned to the UN offices, while Okey Emuchay was the political desk officer and Lawal Gana oversaw administration as Head of Chancery. That collection of officers was a wonderful asset to my work and apart from Dahiru Adamu, who passed away after his posting, all others rose to high positions as ambassadors in their career, which makes me proud.

We started our investment drive by visiting the Austrian Federal Economic Chamber, which manages the Austrian External Trade missions and delegations in many parts of the world, quite distinct from their embassies, including Lagos. This is like our NACCIMA and MAN, and we proposed an MOU between the two chambers in the form of the Austrian-Nigerian Chamber of Commerce and Industries as a platform for the exchange of information, including trade fairs in each other's capitals. They informed us that these kinds of agreements did not translate into increased commerce or trade between our two countries. Even trade delegations were not successful. In development assistance, Austria development cooperation provides helps directly to tertiary institutions and projects focusing on the poorest developing countries and disadvantaged regions. Nigeria was not classified under this category. Austrian development cooperation is classified into two categories, namely cooperative countries and partner countries. Nigeria is one of the focus-countries of the Austrian foreign policy concept, "Africa 2000", and is also one of Austria's most important trading partners in Africa. The criteria for technical assistance included respect for human rights, promotion of democratic institutions and good governance, gender equality, and environmental protection. Education attracts special attention, and this was where special assistance was given to some universities in northern Nigeria, particularly the University of Maiduguri, as well as an exchange of students to learn the Fulfulde and Hausa languages.

The Federal Economic Chamber also own Austrian Trade, which is the official foreign trade promotion organisation with over sixty trade commissions in about 70 countries. Austrian Trade coordinates and represents the interest of Austrian businesses within and outside the country. Our modus operandi then was to identify and visit the most important Austrian companies that had links with Nigeria. There was a long list of companies in this area, especially during the boom days of Nigeria, including steel, motor manufacturing, hospital equipment and road construction.

Voest-Alpine Stahl AG, located in Linz, the capital of Upper Austria, was one of the largest steel companies in the world in terms of volume of products and turnover. This company had built the Aladja steel company near Warri in Delta State, but the Nigerian company went under due to mismanagement and corruption. The company was to supply products to the rolling mills at Jos and Katsina, which have also gone under and have been abandoned as Aladja must be revamped and reactivated before Jos and Katsina can operate. The good news was that prior to our visit they had already contacted the relevant ministry in Nigeria and contracts would be signed to reactivate the abandoned project in Warri. The company also told us that the "Nigerian factor" concerning the electricity and power generation did not allow them direct supply of products at cheaper rates. They informed us that the company bid for the supply of transformers, which they manufacture in their factory, but the contract was awarded to a supplier who did not produce such items and they had to approach them to produce the items at more than twice their prices. Worse still the supplier wanted used items or fabricated ones, but they refused because they would violate their trade ethical rules of doing businesses with clients abroad.

The other company of interest to us was a motor manufacturing and assembling plant which built a factory in Bauchi in the early 1970s. The Obasanjo administration appointed a board to govern this company in Nigeria, but the parent company had diversified into different products other than truck manufacturing.

The truck manufacturing company was located at Steyr, a town with the same name in Upper Austria. On the day of our visit the street leading to the company complex was dotted with Nigerian, Austrian and company flags. Protocol was excellent, and they were welcoming. They told us that the truck division of the company had ceased to exist and had been sold to the German company MAN, and that the only vehicles they made were armoured personnel carriers (APCs) as well as military equipment. However, due to the large number of trucks still in operation in many countries including Nigeria, their spare parts manufacturing unit was still operational. They told us that they would not return to Bauchi to revamp the company in truck assembling, even though the Obasanjo administration had appointed a Board of Governors for it without contacting them.

Professor A B C Nwosu, Minister of Health, arrived in Vienna and informed me that he was to sign a management agreement with VAMED, an Austrian company, to equip and manage eight university teaching hospitals located in the six geopolitical zones of Nigeria. These were university teaching hospitals located at Zaria, Ilorin, Ibadan, Lagos, Port Harcourt, Maiduguri, Enugu and Jos. We had no idea about VAMED, but after reality checks and checks on the viability of the company with its trade records for equipping and maintaining hospitals, the minister returned to sign the contract to maintain the eight hospitals in phases. Strangely enough, after I left Vienna there were incidents of alleged shady deals by the Nigerian Senate Committee on health, the Minister of Health and the chairperson of the House of Representative Committee on health about the project.

Austria is a beautiful country, with clean air, good roads and good rail and airport links. I preferred travelling by road to enjoy the good air and appreciate the landscapes and the castles that dotted the country. Apart from my own visits there was the official organized annual skiing competition by the Austrian foreign minister, Benito Ferrero-Waldner. In addition to the official tours, there was an NGO that ferried diplomats every quarter to some interesting tourist sites around Vienna. The annual January receptions by the Austrian president for the bilateral ambassadors was very interesting and gave us the opportunity to interact closely among ourselves, since most of us from the developing countries could not afford the luxury of three ambassadors in Vienna.

Before my arrival in Vienna there was a celebrated case of a Nigerian, Marcus Omofuma, who died in the hands of Austrian police while on deportation on May 1, 1999. The incident sparked demonstrations by Nigerians and Africans in Vienna. The Austrian authorities set up an investigative panel and concluded that the Nigerian used violence and attacked the police, and that was why he was gagged and chained, leading to his death inside the plane with a stopover in Romania. They offered to pay some compensation on the burial expenses and a small amount of money to the victim's family, which turned out to be his German girlfriend and a child she had had by him. Some one-man NGOs sprang up here and there making claims to represent Marcus Omofuma and continued to defend and even facilitate the illegal trafficking in human beings into Austria and some European countries.

It was such a group of NGOs that stumbled into a diplomatic dispatch by my counterpart, Ambassador Christophe Parasini, in which it was claimed that he blamed Nigerians for falsification of documents which, according to him, were all fake. He went on to mention unpalatable things about the Nigerian government, rampant corruption, rigging of elections and concluded that all documents used by Nigerians and their officials are fake. A copy of the diplomatic dispatch, which was supposed to be confidential, was leaked to the Asylum Court by NGOs and copies were circulated widely in the media. That led to a series of actions that threatened our bilateral relations, as well as my continued stay in Vienna as Nigeria's Ambassador.

Without serious deliberation on the consequences to our bilateral relations, Ambassador Dele Cole, the Special Adviser to President Obasanjo, visited Vienna during my absence and learned about the incident. He was furious and recommended the recall of the Austrian Ambassador in Abuja, who was to be declared *persona non-grata*, and this was granted without recourse to the MFA. I received a directive to convey the message to the Austrian Foreign Ministry to recall their Ambassador in Nigeria. Fully aware of the consequences to me and to our future bilateral relations, which would obviously be reciprocal, I decided to inform Alhaji Sule Lamido, the Foreign Minister, and I was invited to Abuja for consultations. Since it was a decision by the President without any input from MFA, it was difficult to refer the matter back to him for reconsideration. But I saw nothing wrong in doing so. Consequently, the Ministry sent one of its best officers, Ambassador Godfrey Bayour Preware, the Permanent Secretary, to visit Vienna and confer with the Austrian Foreign Ministry. The way Ambassador Preware handled the matter showed him at his best, and he was able to convey the message in such a way that it would not harm relations between our two countries. There was no dateline given to them to withdraw their Ambassador. However, it was pointed out that their Ambassador might not be able to function effectively, which would harm Austrian interests in Nigeria. But Ambassador Parasini was a member of Parliament (MP) from the neo-Nazi Freedom Party, which was in coalition with the Socialist Democratic Party to form the Government, so it was difficult for action to be taken without affecting their political arrangement or my continued stay in Vienna as Nigeria's Ambassador. Ambassador Parasini was blamed for careless handling of the diplomatic dispatch, which was supposed to be confidential or top secret and was leaked to NGOs and the media. But he was not recalled, since no dateline was given. This could have resulted in my own recall as well. Incidentally Dele Cole, who made the recommendation without input from MFA, was soon relieved of his post and sleeping dogs could lie until both of us concluded our tours of duty.

I arrived in Vienna at the time Austria was under sanctions from its European partners after the Freedom Party joined the Socialist Party as coalition partners in government. This followed the 1999 general elections in which the pro-Nazi far-right Freedom Party led by Jorg Haider won over 27 percent of the votes in the general election. The Freedom Party is nationalistic, anti-immigration and anti-Europe. Haider also supported President Saddam Hussein in the run-up to the Gulf War. This development led to outcry from within the country and internationally. Jewish organisations around the world condemned the coalition government which culminated in the state of Israel recalling its ambassador from Vienna. To stop the international condemnation of Austria, Jorg Haider resigned the leadership of the Freedom Party but retained his post as Governor of Carinthia. Benita Ferrero-Waldner, the Austrian Foreign Minister, was very active in her campaign within the EU-partners to get the sanctions lifted to restore the image of Austria in the community of nations without delay.

As far back as 1979, I developed a love for the Vienna Philharmonic Concert held on January 1 every year and I made sure to watch the live television broadcast as well as ordering the cassettes and DVDs as my main musical entertainment. While in Vienna, I was home to this event and enjoyed it so much as well as the evening concerts at the Concert Haus which was an enjoyable pastime.

The Austrian Parliament has an annual programme of commemorating the liberation of prisoners of World War II at Mauthausen on 16 May 1945, to which heads of mission accredited to Austria are invited. After the ceremony at the Parliament I decided to visit the concentration camp complex, located near Linz, the capital of Upper Austria. Lalou Blast Suarez Savantes, my driver, warned me to be strong-minded before visiting the place because of the atrocities committed there during World War II. He said that even 60 years after the feeling of the atrocities and the guilt associated with them are beyond human imagination, as ordinary Austrians never wanted to be associated with it, nor ever visited the place.

As we approached the complex, we saw monuments built by many countries whose nationals had lost their lives in the concentration camp: Russians, Poles, Israelis, Italians, Spaniards and many others had erected monuments and fresh flowers dotted the area, left by tourists visiting the place. Inside the complex was a horrible sight. The camp was constructed in 1940 by slave labour on the banks of the River Danube to produce granite quarry for the Nazi economy. It was the largest such camp and used mostly for the extermination of dissidents, intelligentsia and people of higher social class. Most of those who died were Soviet and Polish officers. It was estimated that over 300,000 people died at the Mauthausen camp by use of lethal injection, mobile gas chambers, or carrying granite blocks up 186 steps to the top of the quarry on the "stairs of death" (still visible). There were also icy showers to kill prisoners by taking cold baths at temperatures below freezing. The tour ended with a film show and I ended up shedding tears, as if it was still happening.

On different occasions I took two prominent Nigerians

on a visit to Vienna to the camp, General Abdulsalami Abubakar and Alhaji Abubakar Rimi. At the end of the tour, General Abubakar remarked that he had never seen nor witnessed that kind of "man's inhumanity to man" before.

The only high-level official visit to Vienna was by the Foreign Minister, Alhaji Sule Lamido, who held meetings with the amiable Austrian Foreign Minister, Mrs. Ferrero-Waldner, on a wide number of issues ranging from democracy, rule of law and protection of human rights to development cooperation in Nigeria and Africa in general. Austria commended Nigeria for her role in Africa, particularly in the ECOWAS sub-region.

At the end of the bilateral talks and as the two ministers were leaving the room, Alhaji Lamido, who was a keen lover of paintings, stopped to look at a large painting in the room and the Austrian Foreign Minister informed him that the Congress of Vienna had also been held in that same room in 1814-1815. She pointed to the painting of the Foreign Ministers of the principal negotiators: Austria, Prussia, Russia, Great Britain and France. Incidentally our Chancery building is in a street named after an Austrian Foreign Minister, Klemens Wenzel von Metternich, who was among the principal negotiators and chairman of the Congress. It should be recalled that the Congress of Vienna was the first such international conference to forge a peaceful balance of power in Europe at the end of the Napoleonic Wars and the dissolution of the Holy Roman Empire. The Congress served as a model for the League of Nations and the United Nations.

At a luncheon we organized for Sule Lamido and all multilateral ambassadors at the Vienna International

Centre restaurant, an incident happened concerning the seating arrangements. Jane Asu-Odeka a versatile, hardworking and efficient officer on protocol in the MFA, oversaw the arrangement, and she was constantly in contact with me on phone about this matter. I had wanted all the ambassadors of major countries in Africa and the P-5 countries to sit on the same table or close by the Minister, which was done, to the extent that my own seat was behind the minister to give room for the doyen of African ambassadors (Angola) who had clocked twenty years in Vienna. As soon as we got in, Alhaji Sule Lamido rightly shifted one of them and replaced it with mine, and that was the British Permanent Representative who enabled me sit with the Minister.

That incident irked Ambassador Peter Jenkins (Britain). Towards the end of the luncheon he left the room in protest and the Minister directed me to consider the problem after the luncheon, which I did. I sent a formal letter of apology with the assurance that Nigeria had excellent relations with the United Kingdom. That incident showed how improper seating arrangements could spark protest at diplomatic receptions.

Organisation of Petroleum Exporting Countries

The Nigerian ambassador to Austria was also accredited to the United Nations Offices in Vienna (UNOV). These are the International Atomic Energy Agency (IAEA), the United Nations Industrial Development Organisations (UNIDO) UN office of Drugs and Crime (UNODC), Comprehensive Nuclear Test Ban Treaty Organisation (CTBTO), United

Nations Commission on International Trade Law (UNCITRAL), UN Office for Outer Space Affairs (UNOOSA), UN Committee on Peaceful Uses of Outer Space (COPUOS). In addition to these UN bodies, the Organisation of Petroleum Exporting Countries (OPEC) and the OPEC Fund are covered by the embassy. Since there was no accreditation to the OPEC and OPEC Fund whenever they met in the country we attended their meetings and reported to MFA accordingly. However, at the time I arrived in January 2000, President Olusegun Obasanjo was the Minister for Petroleum Resources and he could not attend the regular sessions of the OPEC ministerial meetings. Rilwanu Lukman, the Special Adviser on Petroleum Resources was appointed the Secretary-General of the Organisation, so the responsibility fell upon me to attend the ministerial meetings. The appointment of the OPEC Secretary-General to replace Rilwanu Lukman was inconclusive for two consecutive meetings because the Iranian and Saudi Arabian delegations were opposed to the candidates. Each of them presented candidates but there was no consensus, and Lukman continued in an acting capacity in addition to his position of special adviser. The most important issues facing the organisation at that time were the reviews of quota allocations, the price of petroleum and the admission of members and observers like Russia, Mexico, Angola, Egypt and Ecuador. Ecuador was a member but was leaving and returning to the OPEC fold depending on their domestic politics.

Saudi Arabia was the most conservative regarding any major changes that would affect the future of oil prices and output. In one of their meetings and after intensive discussions, the ministers agreed to peg the oil prices at a range of $25-28 dollar per barrel instead of a fixed price. According to this formula, when prices fell below the range, they would reduce production to shore up prices and when prices rose above the ceiling, they would increase production to bring down the prices. The other contentious issue was the quota allocation, as Iraq at that time was not producing to capacity and not exporting due to sanctions. There was also the knotty issue of environmental protection, as OPEC countries were under pressure to cut down or reduce dependence on oil to protect the environment. Mohammed Barkin-do was very active in this issue within the UN Framework Convention on Climate Change (UNFCCC).

As for the appointment of a Secretary-General, there were several consultations by the ministers. Since Rilwanu Lukman was the Acting Secretary-General for almost a year he wanted to be confirmed, but there seemed to be a problem with his position as special adviser to President Obasanjo. My briefing was to play safe so that the status quo could remain as Acting Secretary-General until the next meeting in late 2000. But at a breakfast meeting to take the decision after the Iranian minister insisted that their nominee would not stand down for the Saudi candidate, it was clear that a stalemate would occur at the June session which would favour Nigerian Rilwanu Lukman continuing as Acting Secretary-General. Since I had a hidden agenda and was hoping for a stalemate, I did not press for any decision at the session. But the Saudi minister, Ali Na'im, approached the Venezuelan Minister, who was the President of the OPEC, to ask if he could accept the post and the latter nodded in agreement. Within few minutes the deal was struck. It took us all by surprise how such a simple whisper could seal the decision. When the roll call was to be made I requested for a short break for consultation with my delegation, but it was too late as the Indonesian minister (later President of his country), who was sitting next to me, whispered that it was the best solution for all of us to support the Venezuelan minister. I ended up conferring with Lukman in the Hausa language, and he agreed that we should join the consensus. As a result, Rodriguez Ali Araque of Venezuela was elected by consensus as the Secretary-General of the OPEC.

Soon after this decision a summit of OPEC heads of state was held in Caracas, Venezuela, from 23-28 September 2000. It was the second summit of Heads of State of OPEC member countries after 25 years and all of them attended the Summit except for Saudi Arabia, which sent the Foreign Minister. President Obasanjo was at the summit and that was the first time I came very close to him. I enjoyed the morning breakfasts with him, during which he would attend to many issues of State. He is an intelligent and wise man, but somehow, I never liked him after reading his first book "My Command" when I was still an undergraduate. I was also unhappy when I got the hint that he was contesting for UNSG when I was in Geneva in 1991. But in Caracas he impressed me when I listened to him at breakfast on the vision of Nigeria, and his problems with Vice-President Abubakar Atiku, which were just brewing.

I woke up to joyous applause in the hotel lobby in Caracas on 24 September. There were cookies and flowers and a shout of "happy birthday!" I was surprised by that gesture and wondered how they knew about my birthday, until I realised that I had filled in a form and left my passport with them on arrival. I wondered if such a gesture had ever been made for hotel guests in my own country! That was tourism at its best, I thought.

During the Summit I was seated next to the Indonesian delegation and I noticed that their President was making statements extempore without reading anything. I later discovered that President Abdurrahman Wahid was vision impaired and was being dragged up and down by his daughter. I could not imagine how tolerant the people of Indonesia were to have elected a blind man as their president. Despite his handicap, he was active and made meaningful contributions. Incidentally, his oil minister, Susilo Bambang Yudhoyono, later became President of Indonesia and moved the country to greater heights despite the tsunami disaster the following year. The Indonesian policy of "Confidence Diplomacy" influenced the title of my memoirs, with slight modification. It was those policies that I admired, policies which have moved that country to greatness despite their running out of petroleum resources and withdrawal from the group of oil exporting countries (OPEC).

President Hugo Chavez made a long and powerful statement at the opening of the summit, and despite its length it was a masterpiece. Delegates were thrilled by the oratory and the forceful delivery of a long and enjoyable speech in which he dismissed the accusation that oil prices were too high. He compared the price of oil per barrel to that of water, Coca Cola and gin and tonic and stated that the prices of these items were far higher than the price of oil, which hovered between 22-28 US dollars per barrel at that time. But soon after the summit, it shot up to between 80-100 US dollars, which was blamed on the instability in the world political situation, coupled with the war in Iraq two years later.

Nigeria and the International Atomic Energy Agency

Rauf Bukun-Onemola, my highly resourceful officer on the IAEA desk, had planned that Nigeria should vie for the Chairmanship of the Board of Governors from 2000-2002. He sensed that the Algerian Ambassador, Mukhtar, was canvassing for this position when Brazil's term expired in September and it rotated to Africa. To be the Chairman of the Board, the country must be a member of the Board of Governors. As such Nigeria did not want to be a member until the chairmanship rotated to Africa. That was a clever decision by the desk officer and he briefed me before I presented my credentials to Mohamed Elbaradei, the IAEA Director-General. During the presentation of my credentials, the Director-General briefed me on the activities of the Agency, especially those of great importance to Africa in general, and urged Nigeria to sign the Additional Protocol of the IAEA Safeguard Mechanism to fully benefit from the IAEA activities. He also mentioned the need for Nigeria to set up a regulatory authority for the peaceful use of atomic energy. Technical assistance and advisory services were also top on the agenda of IAEA activities to developing countries especially in manpower development, radioactive material and cancer screening, among others.

After our election to the Board we indicated our interest

in the Chairmanship of the Board of Governors at the meetings of the African group and the G77, but Ambassador Mukhtar of Algeria reacted furiously because he had obtained the endorsement of the OAU Candidature Committee in Addis Ababa as the African candidate. But we insisted that Algeria had occupied the Chairmanship before when it was the turn of Africa. We argued that that information was not known to the OAU Candidature Committee, so we had our capital endorsing our candidacy. For more than two months of arguing we refused to back down to their pressure, since we had our Headquarters standing firm behind us. More so, Algeria was the last Chairman when the seat was Africa's turn. This argument swayed many delegates towards us and at the end of one of the Board meetings, Mohamed Elbaradei told me that we should not step down for Algeria because they had occupied the seat before and most delegations were sympathetic to Nigeria and would support our candidacy if the matter was decided by voting. He then told me that he would use his good offices to ask the Algerian Ambassador to step down for us, which he did. A few days after, the Algerian Ambassador phoned to tell me that he would stand down for Nigeria in view of the excellent relations between our two countries as well as our personal relations.

That's how we were elected Chairman of the Board of Governors of the IAEA for the first time in the history of the Agency since Nigeria joined the organisation in 1961. Professor Ibrahim Umar, the Director-General of the Energy Commission of Nigeria did an excellent job as the Chairman and I assisted him as the alternate for the period 2000-2002. Rauf Bukun Onemola was the desk officer on this subject matter and discharged his responsibility credibly.

One of the most important outcomes of our Chairmanship was the establishment of the Nigerian Nuclear Regulatory Authority (NNRA) headed by Professor Shamsideen Elegba as its pioneer Director-General. The NNRA works with the IAEA to promote safety to secure peaceful nuclear technologies. Within one year of my arrival, Nigeria signed and ratified both the Comprehensive Safeguard Agreement and the Additional Protocols. That action led Nigeria to establish the Nigerian Nuclear Regulatory Authority (NNRA) with advisory services and technical assistance from the IAEA

We were also fortunate to have at headquarters two highly efficient and hard-working colleagues familiar with the issue of disarmament and non-proliferation who were the Directors of International Organisations (IOD) and First United Nations Division (FUND) in the persons of ambassadors Simeon Adekanye and Enny Onobu respectively, who helped us pursue the issues we handled in Vienna. The signing of the IAEA Safeguard Mechanism and Additional Protocol were pending for action which we got prompt approval to accede to them without much delay. Even though Nigeria has no nuclear programme but as a state party to the Non-Nuclear Proliferation Treaty (NPT), she was expected to sign and ratify the Comprehensive Safeguards Agreement and Additional Protocol. This would give the IAEA authority to verify that Nigeria does not use its nuclear programme for non-peaceful purposes. According to the NPT regime, the nuclear weapons states were expected to commit themselves to nuclear disarmament and non-proliferation of nuclear weapons, while non-nuclear weapons states were expected to receive technical assistance and advisory services to develop nuclear power for peaceful uses such as electricity generation, scientific purposes etc. But the nuclear weapons states have reneged in their obligations to full and complete disarmament as well as the provision of adequate technical assistance and advisory services to non-nuclear weapons states.

Iran's Nuclear Enrichment Programme

During our chairmanship of the IAEA Board of Governors, the issue of preventing the Islamic Republic of Iran from developing nuclear weapons was overshadowed by the war in Iraq, and the issue of the Iranian development of nuclear technology for non-peaceful uses was not taken seriously, as Iran insisted that it was for peaceful uses in the generation of electricity. Iran, which had three ambassadors in Vienna with one specifically designated only to the IAEA, continued to develop and enrich uranium for non-peaceful uses in contravention of her commitments to the NPT regime. During the 2000 NPT Review Conference in New York, Iran defended herself credibly and seemed to have won the acceptance of most developing member countries, including our own, that she did not violate her obligations under the Treaty as her nuclear programme was for peaceful uses.

How was Iran able to do this despite cases of proven "non-compliance"? It was pointed out that the same facilities needed to generate electricity from nuclear fission could also be used for nuclear weapons programme. For reasons of solidarity, the G77 was sympathetic to the Iranian course since the nuclear weapon states (NWS) had reneged in their obligations to the NPT regime in nuclear disarmament as well as inadequate technical assistance and advisory services under the IAEA for the non-nuclear weapon states (NNWS) to develop their nuclear energy for peaceful uses. The only unanswered issue was that Iran was not fully cooperating with the IAEA. Similarly, their claim of developing nuclear fuel for peaceful nuclear energy as well as the enrichment of uranium materials was not convincing. The nuclear fuel was what delayed the development of Nigeria's nuclear energy programme until she signed and ratified the Additional Protocol before the Nigerian Nuclear Regulatory Authority could import the fuel from China.

The EU3 (France, Germany and UK) started bilateral negotiations with Iran in Brussels and compelled Iran to sign the Additional Protocol to the IAEA Safeguard Mechanism, which was regarded as a milestone towards curbing the Iranian nuclear programme, but Iran did not ratify nor abide by it. The US Permanent Representative, Kenneth Brill, was not convinced by the steps taken by the EU3 and kept on pressurising the Board of Governors to refer the matter to the UNSC, which was resisted mostly by developing member countries. The argument was that Vienna can handle the matter within its responsibility, since it did not constitute any threat to international peace and security. The so-called "Vienna spirit" in which resolutions and decisions were adopted by consensus through the Chairman's Summary, did not allow the resolutions to be adopted by votes. The Iranians continued to play a cat and mouse game with the EU3 on the terms and definitions of their agreement as to whether they were expected to "suspend uranium-enrichment activities" or to their "cessation". According to the Iranians, they were expected to do the former as against the latter, which the EU3 demanded. The Russians and the Chinese were playing passive roles on the Iranian issues and stood strongly behind the "Vienna spirit" along with most developing member countries.

At times even, small wording details on the resolution against Iran or the Chairman's summary tended to delay action, as was the case one morning when a small amendment to delete the word "definitive" from the US draft which used the phrase "definitive conclusion" held up the meeting for almost two days! These types of delaying tactics by delegations were very common, just to buy time on issues they were not comfortable with. With these intractable arguments, the Iranians held up the issue of referral of the resolutions to the UNSC until much later by buying time in their favour until after I had left Vienna.

United Nations Industrial Development Organisation

The United Nations Industrial Organisation (UNIDO) was established by the UN on November 7, 1966. The main functions of the Organisation were to promote and accelerate the industrialisation of developing countries, with three main themes as follows: poverty reduction through productive activities; capacity building in trade related matters; energy and environmental activities.

I was not very actively involved in this organisation, partly because it did not have any contentious issues under debate and because I had an efficient and hardworking officer, Sani Muhammed (who later became Ambassador to Egypt) as the desk officer. According to UNIDO fact sheets, the organisation aims to "promote and accelerate sustainable industrial development in developing countries and economies in transition". The organisation was actively involved in Nigeria with a Residence Representative. Its core functions are research and dissemination of industrial-related information, and as a technical cooperation agency. But the organisation was facing financial problems, as the US was not actively involved. So, the capacity to render assistance and support to enterprises was heavily impaired. However, there were frequent visitors from Nigeria to the headquarters of the organisation, notably Ministers of Commerce and Industries and senior government officials.

One of our most important involvements, however, was the election of Kandeh Yumkela as the Director-General of the organisation. Kandeh, a Sierra Leonean, was the UNIDO Resident Representative in Nigeria and we rallied many countries to support his candidacy, which he won in 2005 after I had left Vienna. He succeeded Carlos Magarinos, to whom I presented the letters of my appointment as the permanent delegation of Nigeria to UNIDO.

Comprehensive Nuclear Test Ban Treaty Organisation (CTBTO)

The Executive Secretary of the CTBTO Provisional Technical Secretariat (PTS), Wolfgang Hoffmann, invited me for lunch within one month of my arrival in Vienna, and discussed the need for Nigeria to sign and ratify the Treaty.

He recalled Nigeria's well-known commitment to disarmament and non-proliferation of nuclear weapons. He reiterated the role of the Nigerian delegation during the negotiations of the Treaty at the Conference on Disarmament (CD) in Geneva as well as our commitments to the NPT and Africa Nuclear Free Zone Treaty (the Pelindaba Treaty). I recalled what had transpired between me and my former boss, Remi Esan, when he sent a memo for the signing of the Treaty in 1996 but it was rejected with some questionable comments about what would Nigeria gain from the Organisation. Since the Treaty bans any testing, even scientific testing for peaceful research in laboratories, it was felt that it was not in our interests to sign it. Other remarks were about why Nigeria should belong to an organisation that prevents scientific progress through experiments for peaceful uses. But due to Nigeria's commitments on nuclear disarmament and abhorrence to nuclear testing in the Sahara by the French in the early 1960s, as well as the role we played in the negotiations, it was strongly recommended that Nigeria should join the bandwagon to sign and ratify the Treaty.

By the end of 2000, Nigeria had signed and ratified the CTBT, which endeared us high in the organisation. Inalegwu Victor Ogah (later Ambassador) was my desk officer on this organisation and did very well to register Nigeria's position in it. He was also elected to serve on many of its bodies, including the Committee on Budget and Coordination. I was also elected the Chairperson of the Preparatory Commission (the highest decision-making organ of the organisation) from January-June 2002. We also played an active role at the Ministerial Conferences promoting the entry into force (EIF) of the Treaty.

After I left Vienna I received a phone call from Maria Laose, (later Ambassador) informing me that the African Group and the G77 and China had recommended my name for appointment as an expert member to review the organisational structure of the Provisional Technical Secretarial (PTS) of the CTBTO. There were other experts from Australia, Canada, France, the Russian Federation, Malaysia, Mexico, South Africa and Germany. I was to co-chair with Richard Starr, a retired Australian ambassador. Our appointment was on our personal capacities and funded by the organisation. We worked on the review exercise for one year and produced an excellent report which was applauded by member countries as the blueprint for the future functioning of the organisation. Our major recommendation was for the PTS to work along functional lines. We recommended that the International Data Centre division should be responsible for all operational functions while the International Monitoring System Division would handle all supporting functions of the PTS. At the end of the review exercise there were some major changes in the personnel of the PTS, mostly affected by the seven-year service limitation as the organisation was already over seven years old by 2006.

The seven-year service rule was strictly enforced and supported by our review exercise. To this end most of the Divisional Directors retired, as well as the Executive Secretary, the Chairperson of Working Groups A and B in the persons of Ambassador Tibor Thot of Hungary and Dr. Ola Dalman of Sweden, who had served in that capacity since 1996. I was then elected the Chairperson of Working

Group A, which deals with the administrative and financial matters of the Organisation. Mr. Hein Haak from the Netherlands replaced Ola as the Chairperson of Working Group B, which deals with the technical and scientific issues. I served in that capacity for five years, until I retired from the Service in 2010. The MFA, in fact, approved my continuation even after retirement, but the approval never got to me as it was erroneously sent to our Mission in New York instead of Vienna or Berlin where I was serving. That was why Nigeria lost the position to Brazil.

The entry into force (EIF) of the Treaty was a matter of great concern to member states categorized into Annexes I and II. Nigeria belongs to Annexe I states which have no nuclear arsenals, but the Annex II states were those classified as nuclear weapons states, or had substantive nuclear arsenals at the time of the negotiations of the Treaty. According to the provisions of the Treaty, unless all these Annex II states have signed and ratified the Treaty it would not enter into force. A few of those states are yet to ratify the treaty, namely India, Pakistan, North Korea, USA, Israel, China, Egypt, and the Islamic Republic of Iran. But only three of them have not even signed the treaty, namely India, Pakistan and North Korea. All the other countries participate actively in the work of the PTS, including payment of contributions. India and Pakistan are waiting for each other before they sign and ratify the treaty. India said that it would sign the treaty if the US indicates when it will eliminate its nuclear stockpile, but the US rejected that condition.

At the biennial conference of foreign ministers at the margin of the UNGA to promote the EIF of the Treaty in

New York, I watched the Zimbabwean counsellor delivering the statement while both the Foreign Minister and Ambassador Jokonya, the Permanent Representative, were sitting watching. Since I knew the Ambassador very well in my previous posts at Addis Ababa and Geneva, I went to their desk and asked why they had done so. Ambassador Jokonya told me that it was part of the training for young officers who would take over the mantle of leadership in the future when they left the scene. I wondered if President Robert Mugabe was also doing the same to groom his successors ready for when he leaves the scene.

The Committee for The Peaceful Uses of Outer Space

Due to a myriad activity at the Vienna Embassy and Permanent Mission, I decided to prioritize my involvement in meetings and organisations based in Vienna and left the other less important ones to my officers to cover. But one of those obscure organisations, hitherto neglected, became almost my Waterloo and was the most difficult assignment for me to solve. It was the UN Committee for the Peaceful Uses of Outer Space (COPUOS). The problem was the election of the Chairperson of COPUOS in 2003. Because of its obscurity and technical nature, many member countries as well as their ambassadors showed little interest in its activities. Ambassador Raymundo Gonzalez of Chile remained its Chairperson for many years, as no one showed interest in the post. The Moroccan delegation from the capital, who had chaired the Committee in the past, indicated interest and rallied the African group to support him by claiming the rotational principle, whereby the elections at the UN are rotated among the regional groups. The African group endorsed his request and presented Morocco as the sole candidate, since there was no African candidate who indicated interest. This decision was conveyed to Abuja. One month before the election I received a directive from headquarters to present Adigun Abiodun, the special assistant to President Obasanjo on Outer Space, as a candidate. Prior to his retirement from the organisation and subsequent appointment as special assistant, Abiodun had been the former director on Space Application at COPUOS, so he knew what the position was all about.

The UN Committee on the Peaceful Uses of Outer Space was established by UN resolution in 1959 with the mandate to "review the scope of international cooperation in the peaceful uses of out space, to encourage research and dissemination of information on outer space matters, and study legal problems arising from the exploration of outer space" among other activities.

Before this time, I had never bothered to follow developments at COPUOS because of its technical nature and because it was devoid of political headlines. In any case, we had good expertise from the capital on both of its Legal and Scientific Sub-Committees, led by Robert Ajayi Boroffice, the Director-General of NASRDA (later a member of the Nigerian Senate).

Adigun Abiodun recalled that the Moroccan candidate in question had occupied the position of Chairmanship before and questioned why they should vie for it again. I was placed in a very difficult position since we were bound by the African Groups' consensus by endorsing the Moroccan candidate. I decided to inform Abuja, pointing out that it was too late as we could not stand the humiliation and criticisms from member countries. But my view was not taken lightly by Headquarters and I received a heavily worded message from my very good friend Ambassador Enny Onobu, who directed me to present our candidate. He said that it was a headquarters decision and an instruction which I was expected to carry out without reservation. As expected, there was a wide outcry from many delegations who questioned why Nigeria was always putting them in a difficult position at the last minute, since they would consult with their capitals on how to vote. They recalled a similar situation with the Chairmanship of the IAEA Board of Governors between Nigeria and Algeria.

Faced with this dilemma, I decided to leave all other more pressing issues; I concentrated my energy to ensure victory for our candidate. Since there were fewer African countries south of the Sahara with missions in Vienna, I pitched my campaign with Western Europe and Other Group (WEOG), Asian Group and selected countries in Central and Eastern Europe. My colleagues at headquarters also visited Vienna to lend support. A day before the election, the US Ambassador invited us for a reception, and that occasion also gave an insight as to the importance of the chairmanship of the COPUOS. It was basically a money-making business, as there were many insurance companies from all over the world attending the meeting as observers. They told me that it was big business and mentioned NASA in the US and agencies in many countries doing exploration in outer space. They already knew Abiodun, who was on the staff of the Committee.

Despite our last-minute entry into the race, we had

goodwill support and our campaign paid off, as our candidate was elected with wide margin. I received a commendation letter from headquarters for the successful campaign and the election of our candidate. I left Vienna soon after, so I never knew or saw the benefits we gained from the COPUOS with our chairmanship, apart from the SAT I or II project launched with the help of the Chinese which collapsed soon after it was launched.

UN Convention Against Corruption

At the time I arrived in Vienna in January 2000, the ad hoc committee negotiating the UN Convention against Transnational Organized Crime (TOC) had reached an advanced stage. The Convention deals with trans-border crime such as traffic in human beings, especially women and children, child prostitution and child pornography. The Convention is supplemented by three protocols containing additional specific provisions, namely: The Protocol against Trafficking in Persons, especially women and children; the Protocol against the Smuggling of Migrants; and the Protocol against the Illicit Manufacturing of and Trafficking of Firearms. Abel Ayoko (later Ambassador) was the desk officer on this subject and did an excellent work in articulating the Nigerian position. The negotiations of the Convention and the Protocols (except the last one) was concluded and the signing ceremony was held in Palermo, Italy, in November 2000. Foreign minister Sule Lamido (later Governor of Jigawa state) and Ibrahim Lame, special adviser on Organized Crime, attended the conference. I was thrilled at the signing conference when a ranking minister remarked to me that he wished he was an ambassador instead of a minister, because according to him since his appointment he had never had a good night's sleep due to the numerous visitors to his office and home and in his village, and there was nothing he could do about it. He claimed that an ambassador stays abroad with all the privileges and prestige of his position and lives a good life, dresses well, with wining and dining in addition to fat bank accounts in foreign currencies and no one disturbs him. It was not the case with me or other colleagues in the Nigerian Foreign Service, who hardly got paid for their services at the end of the month. It was on record that some of those political appointees made ambassadors in 1999 by President Obasanjo abandoned their posts and returned to Nigeria due to poor conditions of service.

In the following year the political signing ceremony of the Convention on Transnational Organised Crime was devoted to the Convention against Corruption, and I was appointed as one of the Vice-Chairmen from the African region. There was also the negotiation to conclude the Protocol on Firearms, which was delayed due to serious disagreements on the definition of "firearms", "markings" and "time and place of manufacture". The Chinese held up the negotiations by insisting that in the Chinese language the phrase "firearms" meant a different thing and was not covered by the scope and definition of the protocol in English. After prolonged negotiations, the Protocol on Firearms was adopted and opened for signature.

As Vice-Chairman of the Ad Hoc Committee to negotiate the UN Convention against Corruption, I was charged with the negotiations on the "Return of assets to their countries of origin". That was one of the most contentious and difficult aspects of the negotiations. The problem was to define the "country of origin", for instance if funds were transferred from Nigeria to Lebanon and later transferred to Switzerland, then the country of origin was Lebanon. It was also while I was chairing the Ad Hoc Committee that the Swiss delegation approached us to discuss issues concerning the funds held by General Sani Abacha allegedly stashed in Swiss banks. During the first informal meetings the Swiss delegation held with us, it was clear to me that they were not fully prepared to release the funds to Nigeria. They were making excuses, saying there was no way 100% of the funds would be sent to Nigeria because they had traced them as coming from other countries. Also, since the funds had been "acclimatized in Swiss banks", they would only release a portion, conditionally. The first condition was to tie the funds to the removal of illegal immigrants; the second was to determine the legitimacy of the ownership of the funds; and thirdly, the usage of the funds to prevent them falling into corrupt hands. According to their calculations it appeared that only a fraction of the funds would be released to Nigeria. As we had no mandate for negotiating these issues, we informed them that our capital would contact them through diplomatic channels and preferably through our Mission in Bern or Geneva. All attempts by the Swiss delegation to infuse these concepts into the general content of the Convention were rejected by our delegation, supported by the African Group and the G77 and China.

The Committee recommended that countries should seek mutual legal assistance in tracing, freezing, forfeiting and returning illicit assets to their countries of origin. The

Convention itself is a legal instrument that could be used by contracting parties in the prevention of corruption. The return of looted assets to their countries of origin was the main instrument in the fight against corruption. The Convention also covered bribery as well as trading in influence, concealment and laundering assets linked to corruption. Good governance, the rule of law and international cooperation were needed in the fight against corruption. Preventive measures were also needed to tackle the problems of corruption and illicit transfer of assets through institutional instruments. Although the Convention was not the main reason for the establishment of the Economic and Financial Crime Commission (EFCC) and the Independent Corrupt Practices and Other Related Offences (ICPC) in 2003, it was part of the reason for the establishment of these institutions to fight corruption and money laundering. The EFCC was set up in response to the demand by the Financial Action Task Force on Money Laundering (FATF), while the ICPC was influenced, among other things, by the recommendations of the UN Convention against Corruption. The former deals with all aspects of corruption and money laundering in both the public and private sectors, while the latter deals with public sector corruption and bribery. But the effectiveness of these agencies to curb corruption and money laundering had been questioned over the years. Since their establishment in 2003 corruption seemed to have exacerbated in Nigeria so their establishment has not achieved the desired objectives, to a large extent, in curbing corruption.

The Nigerian delegation to meetings and conferences was always large but often squeezed into one corner without space, which impaired our effective contributions to the debates. As a result, I tabled a proposal that at the beginning of each session of the negotiations or major conferences in Vienna, we should conduct a ballot or lottery for choosing the seating arrangements, as was the case during the UNGA in New York. That proposal was accepted without a vote and after that Vienna adopted this method of balloting for seating arrangements during major conferences. Many delegations applauded our initiative.

By April 2003, circulars went out recalling all ambassadors back to Nigeria to coincide with the end of the first term of the Obasanjo administration on May 29. Curiously, no such letter or telegram was addressed to me; I learned of it from my former boss, Ambassador Pius Ayewoh in Geneva. Since there was no letter sent to me I continued to chair the meetings on the Convention against Corruption, which was concluded on 30 August 2003. But I was well prepared to leave at very short notice, going by the well-known practice at headquarters where someone would walk up and shift blame onto others. I took leave of the Austrian President in early August and during the farewell reception organized for me by the Austrian Foreign Ministry, they remarked that the attendance was remarkable as it attracted many ambassadors from notable countries, both bilateral and multilateral ambassadors as well as the representative of the National Association of Nigerian Community in Austria (NANCA).

On 28 August 2003, I received a phone call from Ambassador Olugbenga Ashiru, the Undersecretary, Regions and International Organisations directing me to report to headquarters as soon as possible. Since it was a weekend I made all arrangements to leave and I reported on Monday the following week. Without any formal letter of deployment, I was directed to report to the director of the International Organisations department, Olusegun Akinsanya (later Ambassador to Ethiopia). He told me that I was to take over the First UN division in place of Ambassador Enny Onobu, who had been appointed Ambassador to Liberia. The decision to send Enny to Liberia really baffled me, because I strongly believed that it was a wrong decision. Similar misplaced postings became the rule, not the exception, with subsequent posting of some of the best brains of the Service to places like Guinea Bissau, Burkina Faso and Chad with the aim of wasting and making nonsense of their expertise in the Foreign Service.

The political signing ceremony of the Convention against Corruption was held at Merida, Mexico. Justice Mustapha Akanbi, Chairman of the Independent Corrupt Practice and Allied Commission (ICPC) led the Nigerian delegation. At the end of the conference I made time as usual to visit the city and savour their food, souvenir, arts and crafts. I went into the market and bought a very colourful woven travelling bag. This attracted Justice Akanbi, who indicated an interest in buying one himself. We walked to the shop, but an ugly incident happened to us. A group of people poured black coffee on us from above the store and three young men and a lady, pretending to help clean up our clothes, descended on us. In the process they stole my wallet with my credit card, but I did not realize this until we returned to the hotel. As we were checking out that evening I discovered that my credit card was missing and did not have any money on me to settle my hotel bills. I didn't even know the numbers on the card, but luckily, I had made my reservation with it and made calls to block and cancel the card. I became a consular case until my colleagues came to my rescue. Within one hour over $3,000 had been spent on the card. Luckily for me the money was refunded after three months of investigation into the signature used during the transactions, which was found to be different from my own.

The Nigerian Community in Austria

During my time in Vienna, I made it a duty to closely relate with the large number of Nigerians in the country. They were not organized into one group but formed mushroom organisations based on ethnic lines. I was enlisted into the Bini and Edo community, called the Enyi-Edo Community of Austria. I was also very close to the Igbos and Omo-Oduduwa groups. I did this intentionally to bring them together into an umbrella organisation which metamorphosed into the National Association of Nigerian Community in Austria (NANCA). Under its first President, Dr. Aganga Williams, it became very strong and they even organized seminars in which notable Nigerians attended. including Prof. Omo Omoruyi, who was the first Director-General of the Nigerian Institute for Democracy, members of the National Assembly and private Nigerians. The Enyi-Edo, Omo-Oduduwa and Igbos organized send-off receptions for me separately, as well as NANCA, which was witnessed by George Akume, the Governor of Benue State, and his entourage. I was also crowned with several of their ethnic titles, clothing and artefacts.

CHAPTER 10

INCIDENTS AT THE INTERNATIONAL ORGANISATIONS DEPARTMENT IN ABUJA

"Diplomats were invented simply to waste time"
David Lloyd George (1863-1945)

"There are few ironclad rules of diplomacy, but to one there is no exception. When an official report that talks were useful it can safely be concluded that nothing was accomplished"
John Kenneth Galbraith (1908-2006)

I returned to headquarters and was deployed to the First United Nations division, which deals with disarmament and arms control issues at the United Nations. It also deals with legal issues, the UN Security Council and decolonization. These are matters of the First, Fourth and Sixth UNGA Committees and related international organisations like the International Atomic Energy Agency (IAEA), Comprehensive Nuclear Test Ban Treaty Organisation and Chemical Weapon Convention. That was my second time in the International Organisations department (IOD); the first time I was in the Second United Nations division, where I was preoccupied with human rights questions, crime prevention, women's issues and humanitarian assistance. I was soon nominated to attend the National Institute for Policy and Strategic Studies (NIPSS) at Kuru near Jos, my home state, but it was withdrawn to enable me to handle the IOD as my boss, Olusegun Akinsanya was appointed Ambassador to Ethiopia.

Located in Block 'C' of the Ministry at Maputo Road, Wuse, Zone 3, it was often referred to as "Siberia" because it was cut off from the main building and utterly neglected by the Ministry in terms of maintenance. The building was never visited by any minister nor permanent secretary. Worried by the neglect and the degeneration of the building, I went to Hakeem Baba-Ahmed, the Permanent Secretary, and asked him to visit. He was accompanied by some directors, and since my office was located on the first floor of the five-storey building, the Permanent Secretary visited only my office and refused to go further due to the smell and odour of the whole complex. He wondered how we operated without lifts, water and generator while the other two blocks 'A' and 'B' had these facilities. And my office was one of the most visited by ambassadors and the staff of foreign embassies accredited to Nigeria and soliciting for Nigeria's support for resolutions and decisions at the United Nations.

I was supported by two versatile and effective directors of FUND and SUND, in the persons of ambassadors Chike Anigbo and Kunle Adeyanju respectively. They were equally supported by many effective and intelligent officers and staff. My first main action was the preparation for the UNGA, which was closely followed by the UN Human Rights Commission the following year. Then there was an outstanding issue of preparation and presentation of periodic reports to many human rights Treaty Bodies. The periodic reports on the Convention on the Elimination of Racial Discrimination (CERD) were pertinent, as the last time we presented the report was the one Uche Gwam and I did in Geneva in 1993, when I was the chargé d'affaires ad interim. That was one of the main preoccupations I embarked upon with Alhassan Hussein, the desk officer on human rights, and it was a huge responsibility upon us to handle effectively. However, with difficulty we made a lot of progress and defended it in Geneva with the assistance of my good friend Ambassador Joseph Ayalogu and Mike Omotosho, our Ambassador and the desk officer on human rights in the Permanent Mission to the United Nations, respectively.

Nigeria and the Organisation Of Islamic Conference (OIC)

One morning, Chike Anigbo came in with a file titled "Organisation of Islamic Conference (OIC)" and told me that he had taken time to study it and even consider its potential benefits and wondered why Nigeria was not taking advantage of the Organisation. He said that whatever we thought he believed that Nigeria should take full advantage of her membership, albeit the decision to attend its meetings at low level. He enumerated its benefits to include supporting our candidates at international organisations, zero interest loans from the Islamic Development Bank and the employment of Nigerians, among other things. He concluded that even if people thought it was only for Muslims, Nigeria did not have a large Muslim population. He followed it up with a memo to the Minister of Foreign Affairs with a view to our active participation as well as to pay all our outstanding contributions, which had been held up since 1999.

The memo went up and was returned with a note that Nigeria had "observer" status in the organisation. But that was a wrong decision, because what we had, which was still standing without a contrary decision by the Federal Executive Council, was that Nigeria should maintain full membership but attend its meetings at low level.

Less than one month from that decision by the MFA, it was announced that Nigeria was joining the Islamic Development Bank and had bought shares in it order to benefit from the provisions of the Organisation. Ngozi Okonjo-Iweala, Minister of Finance, took time to elaborate the potential benefits Nigeria would gain from that decision. That was one of the elements mentioned by Chike in his memo, which was erroneously turned down by the Minister of Foreign Affairs. That showed the lack of coordination in the functioning of MDAs in Nigeria due to their various backgrounds, cultures and religions.

Following from that confused position Ambassador Lawal Munir, who last served in Ankara Turkey, came to see me and said that during a meeting of the OIC in Jeddah which he participated he knew that a vacancy existed for the Assistant Secretary-General zoned to Africa and wanted to present his nomination. We submitted his request for nomination, but it was rejected because Nigeria had observer status, and the position was given to a Cameroonian candidate. But three years later, the position became vacant again and the Nigerian ambassador to Lebanon, Hameed Opeloyeru, was nominated and elected to the post. That was a clear case of inconsistency in the conduct of Nigeria's foreign policy machinery.

Because of worries over these inconsistencies in policy, an ad-hoc committee was set up by President Obasanjo to examine and streamline Nigeria's membership in international organisations. The three-man committee was chaired by Ambassador Oluyemi Adeniji, minister of foreign affairs, and comprised Professor Jerry Gana, Minister of Information, and Ambassador Lawan Gana Guba, minister of the Ministry of Cooperation and Integration in Africa, while I acted as the secretary of the committee. I prepared the initial draft by listing the international organisations for which Nigeria had membership, including the OIC. The committee recommended that in view of the political interest and implications of our work, particularly on the OIC, the report and recommendations should be sent to the Federal Executive Council for decision. There were two conflicting views regarding the OIC, one said Nigeria was a full member while the other indicated that Nigeria was an observer. It was because of these conflicting views that Professor Jerry Ghana called for it to be referred to the FEC for a decision because of its political implications. I accompanied the Minister of State, Buhari Bala, to the FEC meeting and President Obasanjo, sensing the problems it would generate, decided that the memo should stand down and stated that the "status quo" in regard to the OIC should remain. I asked the Minister about the meaning and the implications of that decision in practical terms and he told me that it meant continued full membership. As such all outstanding contributions of over two million US dollars had to be paid and were promptly paid.

However, our memo triggered several comments by many home ministries and organisations, which led to another ad hoc committee chaired by Chief Ufot Ekaette, Secretary to the Government of the Federal (SGF), while I represented the Minister of Foreign Affairs. I recalled that Chief Ekaete was unhappy with the level of participation from MDAs, as low-level officers were representing their chief executives and he directed that only ministers or permanent secretaries were allowed at the meeting. But he made an exception for me due to the invaluable information I was bringing to the meeting. The committee sat for two months and the outcome was surprising to me, as some of the international organisations of which Nigeria had membership were not in our record in the MFA. It showed the lack of coordination and clear policy by government on which organisation we should belong to, as well as the cost benefits associated with membership of such organisations. Worse still, most of the organisations were being owed huge sums of money for unpaid contributions, with negative image consequences for the country.

The Committee decided on which MDAs were responsible for which organisation(s) as well as for paying the contributions, which should be included in their annual budgets. But for the year 2005, and due to the Nigerian quest for a permanent seat on the UN Security Council, it was decided that the Office of the Secretary of the Government of the Federation (OSGF) should collate these outstanding contributions in conjunction with the MFA and send them to the Federal Ministry of Finance to settle them, whether they were budgeted for or not.

It was during such an exercise that a terrible error on payments to the International Seabed Authority in Jamaica was committed by my department during my absence to New York for the UNGA in September 2005. The urgency to settle our outstanding contributions to the UN and all international organisations was also recommended by the committee set up by President Obasanjo to sensitize Nigerians on our quest for a UNSC seat. Time was of the essence as we wanted a clean bill to buttress our bid, and a decision was expected to be made by the end of the year.

Problems at the International Seabed Authority

Before I left for the UNGA in New York with the Foreign Minister and President Obasanjo, I had sent up a memo with a list of all the organisations and the amount outstanding against each of them to the Permanent Secretary, Ambassador Nkem Wadibia-Anyanwu. But there was one obscure organisation, the International Sea Bed Authority (ISBA), based in Jamaica, that almost ruined my career and reputation in the service. Nigeria's outstanding bill was only $ 9,700 for two years, and I clearly pointed this out in my memo to the Permanent Secretary, but for some reason, and due to new additions or comments, the memo returned for amendment, but the file was never passed to me again as I was away in New York. Subsequent minutes on this matter erroneously changed the $9,700 to $4.5million, and it was forwarded to the Office of the Secretary of the Government of the Federation (OSGF) and the Federal Ministry of Finance and was paid along with all other international organisations we submitted. Iliya Fachano, a very hard-working officer, did not check the re-typed memo due to the urgency of the matter, nor did his immediate boss, Emmanuel Ogunnaike, so the error was not spotted. Iliya briefed me on my return from New York and mentioned that there were some errors in some of the payments made by the Federal Ministry of Finance, and since I did not know the magnitude of the errors I told him that they could be credited to Nigeria and carried over into the following year. When he later brought the file to me for other developments I decided to study it and I saw the payment of $4.5 million instead of $9,700 to the ISBA, which made me raise the alarm. I sent a memo to the Foreign Minister and a telegram to our High Commission in Kingston, Jamaica with a view to retrieving the money, a huge amount for an organisation where our annual contribution was less than $5,000.

A week later I received an urgent call from Alhaji Abubakar Tanko, the Minister of State for Foreign Affairs, to see him quite late in the day. When I got to his office, there were four strange-looking people wearing dark glasses and I was told they came from the Economic and Financial Crime Commission (EFCC). I had no idea about their mission and who had invited them. Was that because of my memo or from our High Commission in Kingston, a political appointee who saw my telegram and concluded that foul play was intended?

The Minister of State raised the issue and I confirmed to him what had happened, but the EFCC were not satisfied until I went to search for the file, which was still in the Minister's office and became an exhibit. They were even following me in search of the file in the Registry and the Minister's office until I found it and brought to the Minister of State. They insisted that I should be arrested and taken to their office that night, but the Minister assured them that he would take charge and make me available to them the following day.

The EFCC came back the following morning, took me to their office in Asokoro and interrogated me for the whole day, asking me all sorts of questions about such a huge error, which had been committed without my knowledge since I was the director. There were other problems linked to the promotion of the deputy directors in FUND and SUND to directors, making them the same level as me, and at times they did not send their memos through me. But in that case, I was not in the country; the error was made during my absence.

What saved me from detention was my earlier memo, my passport showing that I was away from the country in the interval when the payment was made, my query about why the payment was made without a "demand note" from the organisation, my telegram and the recent memo to the Minister alerting them to the mistake. I took time to educate the EFCC about the "demand note", which was the letter or bills sent from the organisations showing clearly what sums we were owed and usually attached to the payment voucher. I told them that without that note the payment would not be made. That was what saved me and my career, or the affair would have eroded all my achievements in the service.

Regrettably the EFCC detained Iliya Fachano, one of my able and hardworking officers, who suffered for that error of commission as he was detained in EFCC detention Centre in Lagos for months and even lost out in an ambassadorial appointment for which he was ably qualified. Other officials from the Ministry of Finance and the Central Bank of Nigeria were also detained and interrogated by the EFCC, showing how seriously this matter was viewed by the government. Iliya was later released and pardoned after the EFCC found no attempt to defraud the federal government other than a genuine error made due to the rush to pay all outstanding debts the country owed to international organisations in our run up to the UN Security Council permanent seat. I would have suffered the same fate if I had been implicated in committing such an error of commission or omission.

The format of my memo was different from the amended one that led to the error. While I listed all the organisations and the amount owed by each one of them in the body of the memo, as well as the prayer to the Minister through the Permanent Secretary, the one they subsequently sent was a listing that was attached to the memo, so it was overlooked by whoever approved it and this led to the problem. The investigations by the EFCC exonerated the MFA and the other agencies of government as they found that no one was attempting to defraud the Federal

Government and they were all released and pardoned. Our High Commission in Kingston, Jamaica, was directed to retrieve the money erroneously paid to ISBA and return it to the Central Bank, and the case was closed.

Nigeria and the UN Counter-Terrorism Committee

The UN Counter-Terrorism Committee (CTC) was established by UNSC resolution 1373 (2001) on September 28, 2001 in the wake of the terrorist attacks in New York and the Pentagon on September 11. The Committee comprised all the 15 members of the UN Security Council. The mandates of the CTC were to criminalize the financing of terrorism; freeze funds linked to terrorism; deny financial support for terrorists; share information with other UN member countries on groups planning terrorist acts; cooperate in the investigation of acts of terrorism; arrest, extradite and prosecute those involved in terrorism; and criminalize assistance for terrorism in domestic laws. In 2004, the UNSC further established the office of Executive Directorate of CTC with a mandate to assist the work of the CTC in monitoring the implementation of the resolutions on counter-terrorism. All UN member countries, including Nigeria, were expected to report periodically their implementation of the resolution. Due to the security nature of the CTC and the inability of Nigeria to designate a focal point as to which ministerial department and agency (MDA) was responsible for this task, the EFCC took up the responsibility for coordinating other agencies of government, including MFA, to implement the resolution.

The CTC members visited Nigeria in July 2006 as part

of its mandate to monitor the implementation of the resolution, more so because an expatriate businessman with extensive businesses in Jos was implicated by the CTC and listed on its travel ban on financial terrorism. Ahmed Idris Nasreddin, the owner of NASCO Group Ltd, Jos, whose businesses covered the manufacture of jute bags, biscuits, tea and other consumer food items and detergents, started modestly in 1962 but has emerged a big conglomerate in Nigeria. He has businesses in Malaysia, Turkey, Italy and the Middle East with a residence in Lugano, Switzerland, and was a well-known philanthropist worldwide, but he was wrongly listed by the CTC as a financier of terrorist groups.

Through the intrusive investigative actions by the EFCC and our interactive meetings and verification of Ahmed Nasreddin, the owner of NASCO Group was delisted from CTC terrorist list as a financier of terrorist groups and given a clean bill of health on November 14, 2007. The CTC stated: "Mr. Ahmed Nasreddin is no longer subjected to the travel ban imposed by the UNSC." Unfortunately, the fortunes of his businesses in Nigeria and elsewhere still suffered, albeit temporarily. Those in Jos have not fully recovered due to a combination of factors such as the crisis in Jos and the influx of cheap Chinese products onto the Nigerian market, among other factors. Ironically, as early as 2004, there was an indication that there were terrorist cells in Nigeria linked to Al-Qaeda in the Maghreb, but the government did not take the early warning signs which had since been exacerbated by socio-economic factors.

Emmanuel Akumayo, secretary of the EFCC, invited me to attend a meeting at their office in Wuse II with the visiting CTC delegation from New York, since the issue fell on my desk in the MFA. I was half way into the meeting when my mobile phone started ringing; it was friends and family members inquiring about my safety, as it had been rumoured that I was under arrest and detention by the EFCC. I could not contend with the number of calls I was receiving. Even my family in Jos were already preparing to come to Abuja to arrange a bail. It took me a while to assure them that I was there to attend a meeting. Incidentally, it was one of my friends coming to Abuja who was told that I was at the EFCC and he started calling and sending messages to friends to come to Abuja to rescue me! That was how dreadfully EFCC was seen. Their name implied terror and intimidation instead of fighting corruption. I narrowly escaped them through the ISBA affair, which I mentioned earlier. In that case it was humiliating, as I was interrogated in their office at Asokoro.

One thing which I could not come to terms with was the warnings of the existence of terrorism or possible terrorists' cells in Nigeria; we consistently denied that they existed. These warnings were coming from the United States and the CTC. They were not specific, but the events that unfolded involving the Boko Haram insurgents in the north-eastern part of Nigeria made me wonder if there were connections to these early warnings that we could not manage promptly.

In addition to my schedules on UN issues, I was also representing the Ministry of Foreign Affairs at seminars or meetings organized by MDAs. Professor Shamsideen Elegba, a highly efficient, hard-working and committed Director General of the National Nuclear Regulatory Authority (NNRA), called on me for my views on holding a national conference on Nigeria's nuclear programme for peaceful uses in accordance with our commitments to the IAEA safeguard mechanisms. He intimated me that within one week of the proposal being made public, he had been inundated by inquiries from Western diplomats accredited to Nigeria about the venue of the seminar and the real intention of Nigeria. He was contemplating holding the seminar at an Abuja hotel or the International Conference Centre, but I advised him to contact the NIA, which had good conference facilities for such a seminar. If it was not properly handled it could easily be misunderstood, as with the Iranian nuclear facilities.

One morning I was invited to solve a land dispute between the French Embassy and the FCDA minister at Wuse II in Abuja. The piece of land was allocated to the Embassy to build a French school and had already been launched by Presidents Jacques Chirac and Obasanjo. Ambassador Yves Gaudeul, the French Ambassador, picked me up at the office and took me to see the land. As we got to the place, we found bulldozers levelling the land, including trees that would be regarded as treasured items and monuments to be preserved, adored, cherished and admired. Yves screamed loudly, calling for help to stop them cutting down the exotic traditional trees. The driver of the bulldozer and the labourers burst out laughing, wondering why he was more interested on the trees than the land.

The issue of environmental protection in the new federal capital was amply addressed by the French Ambassador, as many traditional trees in Abuja needed to be preserved in addition to the new brands. That land was mentioned by Ahmed El-Rufai in his book titled 'The Accidental Public

Servant', in which he claimed that the plot had been reallocated to an industrialist to build a school as part of the development of Abuja, since the French Embassy was not ready, and they were trying to convert it to a French Cultural Centre instead of a school.

Benin-Nigeria-Togo Co-Prosperity Alliance Zone

Hakeem Baba-Ahmed, the permanent secretary, directed me to represent him and to also chair the meeting of senior officials from Benin, Nigeria and Togo which was held at Aguda House, Abuja from 6-8 February 2007. The meeting was followed by that of the Foreign Affairs Ministers and the summit of heads of state. The meeting was aimed at bringing these three countries closer together in terms of economic cooperation and markets for goods and services. The main objective, as spelled out in the final memorandum of understanding, was "to strengthen the mutually beneficial traditional links of friendship and economic cooperation existing between the three countries and peoples". It was named the Benin-Nigeria-Togo Co-Prosperity Alliance-Zone (COPAZ). The concept of COPAZ was, inter alia, to:

a) Integrate their national economies based on a common platform that seeks to promote interests in dealing with shared visions and concerns arising from the imperatives of global competitiveness and interdependence;

b) Share mutual aspirations as to committing themselves to political leadership and followers to achieve this endeavour;

c) Admit, in due course, other like-minded neighbours desirous of participating in the Alliance.

But the idea was marred in controversy, as questions were raised about the real intention in relation to ECOWAS. Was it to weaken ECOWAS or a territorial expansion to make these countries puppets of Nigeria? All these questions were discussed, and confidence-building measures were assured and agreed upon. In the communiqué read after the summit by Professor Joy Ogwu, the Minister of Foreign Affairs, the three countries expressed their commitment and willingness to continue to work for the maintenance of peace, security, stability and socio-economic development of the West African sub-region and by contributing to the strengthening of ECOWAS, the African Union and NEPAD programmes. The three countries also agreed to work closely in the international fora on matters of joint interest through enhanced cooperation and dialogue. The communiqué further stated that COPAZ would serve as complementary efforts for achieving the objectives of ECOWAS. COPAZ further agreed that membership would be open to other ECOWAS member countries and those of the Gulf of Guinea Commission. These were Utopian ideas and I sensed that it would never be sustainable unless Nigeria continued to pump resources into its secretariat, which was soon established at Badagry after the summit and headed by Ambassador Rauf Aderele of Nigeria.

Africa-South America Summit

Another major conference which I was actively involved in

was the Africa-South American summit (ASAS), which was held in Abuja in 2006. It was one of the largest gatherings of heads of state and government in Abuja and accommodation and security were a big challenge. I oversaw accommodation, but it was one of my most difficult assignments due to the large number of guests and shortage of hotel accommodation.

The most difficult guest to manage was the Libyan leader, Muammar Gaddafi. We decided to book him into the military guest house in Abuja, but he refused and went to the residence of his Ambassador, which also compounded security challenges as he arrived two days before the others with a large entourage. ASAS also presented accreditation problems for the Sahrawi Arab Democratic Republic (SADR) delegation. The Moroccan delegation threatened to withdraw if SADR was attending, but since Nigeria and most African states recognized SADR as an AU member it was difficult to stop SADR from attending and participating. However, a compromise was reached with the two delegations. Both attended but SADR was not seated, since it was argued that it was not an AU summit and we did not want a situation where some South American countries would withdraw their participation. There was an indication that Morocco had campaigned hard and even persuaded some South American countries to withdraw their recognition of SADR.

The objectives of ASAS were to strengthen cooperation between the countries of the two regions and to forge strategic partnership and promote South-South cooperation. The Summit agreed on many issues ranging from cooperation on UN reforms, human rights, democracy and good governance, peace and security, education and health to transnational organized crime, money laundering, environment, gender mainstreaming, rural development, poverty alleviation, energy and minerals. The summit decided to meet every two years. Because of the active role played by my former boss, Olusegun Akinsanya, it was decided that he would head the secretariat of ASAS, but I do not know what happened after I left for posting to Berlin as ambassador and Ms. Christy Mbonu was accredited to its secretariat in Caracas, Venezuela.

Official Visit to Israel

A selected group of four of us led by Ambassador Tunde Sodipo, director of the Legal and Consular Department of MFA, was invited to visit Israel by the Israeli government. Others were Sani S. Bala (later Ambassador and Permanent Secretary), Aliyu Mohammed Gubuchi and me. The purpose of the visit was to hold bilateral discussions on issues of mutual interest and concern to both countries. The Israeli ambassador to Nigeria, Noam Katz, accompanied us and served as our guide to important historical and holy sites in Jerusalem. As we left Abuja it happened that the Israelis had organized protocol arrangements for us wherever we transited, including Frankfurt airport, where we connected with our flight to Tel Aviv. Concerns on security were part of their challenges to ensure safe entry and exit from their country. It was my first visit to Israel as I had missed the opportunity in an earlier effort to enter from Amman, Jordan in 1996.

We held meetings at the Israeli Foreign Ministry with

officials dealing with disarmament, human rights questions, legal and consular matters and later with the Minister for Tourism, who hosted a dinner for us. Joseph Moustagu, Deputy Director for Non-Proliferation and Counter-Terrorism, whom I had met before in Vienna, was part of the Israeli delegation. They informed us that the State of Israel had not signed the NPT regime, even though they had signed the CTBT but did not ratify it due to the security situation in their region. They also mentioned the capture of two Israeli soldiers by Hezbollah guerrillas in southern Lebanon, saying they were making all efforts to get them released. According to them that incident was an "act of war" that forced them to move their troops to the border with Lebanon, which had already created tension and shaken regional stability.

Mention was made of the nuclear ambitions of Iran with the direct threat to Israel as the justification for the non-ratification of the NPT and CTBT. On human rights questions, the Israelis solicited Nigeria's understanding on the voting pattern at the UNGA and the Human Rights Council and requested that Nigeria should not continue supporting the Palestinians against Israel. The issue of Nigerian pilgrims absconding in Israel was of great concern to them and they called upon Nigeria to devise a screening method to ensure that only genuine pilgrims could enter Israel. They gave us statistics to show that Nigeria was one of the largest non-European or American visitors to Israel, which was welcomed, but those absconding were creating a major problem that could tarnish the good relations between our two countries. Some of these issues were replicated during the dinner hosted by the Israeli Minister for Tourism (not religious matter). That is a subject on its own as visitors coming for pilgrimages were referred to as tourists.

We assured the Israelis that Nigeria believed in the peaceful resolution of the conflict between Israel and Palestine as well as all her neighbours, and it was a misconception that Nigeria supported the Palestinians against the State of Israel. We told them that our policy was for a two-state solution allowing Israel and Palestine to live side by side with secured borders and in peaceful co-existence. Nigeria's position was based on the issue of decolonization and self-determination for peoples all over the world. About disarmament, we reiterated our well-known and consistent position, saying we believed in the NPT regime as a veritable Treaty that would secure the world free of nuclear weapons. That was why Nigeria signed and ratified the NPT as well as the CTBT. On those absconding during the annual Christian pilgrimages, we assured them that the Nigerian Pilgrims Commission had been established and all the problems expressed would be addressed by the newly-established Commission. My visit to Jerusalem as part of the delegation was due to my duties as the director of International Organisations department dealing with disarmament and human rights questions and the voting pattern at UNGA and HRC, which were some of their major concerns.

After the official engagements, we used the afternoon and the evening for visiting historical and holy sites of the major world religions, namely Christianity, Judaism and Islam. Both the Arabs and the Jews were friendly and welcoming as well as the Christians, who were eager to explain to us the history and spiritual importance of the holy places we visited. We visited the Mount of Olives, the Holy Church of the Sepulchre, the Al-Aqsa Mosque and lastly the Western Wall, all nearby or in the same vicinity. It was only at the Al Aqsa mosque that identification was required. They attempted to stop Sani Bala from entering the mosque because his name was unfamiliar to them as a Muslim name until he recited the Al Fatiha, the first Chapter of the Holy Qur'an. The Israeli ambassador, who was Jewish, stopped by the gate and we requested two hours in the mosque to do Asar and Magrib prayers and visit the holy places within. We met a Palestinian boy who guided us through the mosque, but during prayer times he was not praying himself, and Sani Bala asked him why. He told us that he was not a Muslim. It was really a fascinating journey to me and fulfilled my desire to visit Jerusalem, as we had missed that opportunity with Mrs. Maryam Abacha when we visited Jordan in 1996. But we came close to Jerusalem when we bathed in the river Jordan and visited the holiest Christian sites in Jordan.

The problems in Israel are about land and control of the river Jordan, which is basically political and not religious. The Dead Sea, which we visited with Maryam Abacha from Jordan in 1996, shares borders with Israel, Jordan and the West Bank. The Israeli Minister for Tourism awarded each of us a certificate for visiting Israel, which still reminds me with nostalgia of Jerusalem. The Minister also told us that he was responsible for the pilgrims (he referred to them as "tourists") who visit Israel yearly and that Nigeria was among the largest visitors for this purpose outside Europe and the United States.

Because of international and domestic pressure, the two Israelis soldiers who were captured by Hezbollah in Lebanon mentioned earlier were later exchanged with the release of about 430 Palestinians and Lebanese held in Israeli jails.

As a matter of interest to me I decided to look back at the historical background to the crisis between the Israelis and Palestinians, which dates to biblical times. It came in very handy that we were in the King David Hotel on King David Street. It was built in the 1920s and within walking distance of the holy sites in the old city. The history of Israeli-Palestinian conflict was a long one, some of it mentioned in the Holy Bible. The modern history of the State of Israel started with the Balfour Declaration of November 2, 1917, in which the Jewish Zionist movement was promised a Jewish homeland to be carved out of Palestine. Arthur James Balfour was the British Foreign Secretary. This was in response to the WWI efforts and was supported by the British Prime Minister David Lloyd George, who was elected in 1916. The Allied powers needed the support of the influential Jews in the US and Russia in the war against Germany. Palestine was a province of the Ottoman Empire and was under the mandate of the British to work for the interests of both the Jews and the Arab population. As the mandate would expire in May 1948, Britain was under pressure to turn over the territory to the United Nations or fulfil its promise to the Jews for a homeland in Palestine as postulated by the Balfour Declaration of 1917 on the condition which clearly stated, "nothing shall be done which may prejudice the civil and religious rights of existing non-Jewish communities in

Palestine, or the rights and political status enjoyed by Jews in any other country".

It was under this pressure that a UN plan was hurriedly drawn up to partition Palestine into Jewish and Arab states. But there was strong opposition to this decision by influential people in the US as well as in Britain. Even George Marshall (the father of the Marshall Plan after WWII) opposed it, as it would jeopardise the efforts to rebuild in Europe after World War Two with Arab oil resources. The Jews were elated, but the Arabs rejected it and warned of war. Some in Britain argued that it was a "Jewish homeland" in Palestine and not a "Jewish State" as was envisaged by the Balfour Declaration. But in the US, after much debate, President Truman endorsed the UN Plan and even changed the wording in the UNSC resolution of November 1947 from "Jewish State" to "State of Israel", which lives with us today. He was facing re-election and needed the Jewish vote in the November presidential election of that year. Thus, the doctrine of necessity to win re-election overrode any other consideration by Truman in the support for the creation of the State of Israel in 1948.

After that the US presidential candidates continue to lobby the Jewish community for their valuable votes based on the Truman era. There were several other reasons for the British to support the partition of Palestine, such as the need to safeguard the Suez Canal and easy passage to India; it would influence US and Russian Jews in support for the war effort and many other reasons. The Balfour Declaration was the main foundation for the partition of Palestine which resulted to the present crisis in the region. The crisis went on unabated and as I wrapped up this memoir, the US

President Donald Trump opened another flank to the crisis by declaring on December 6, 2017 that Jerusalem is the eternal capital of the State of Israel and planning to move the US Embassy from Tel Aviv there. That decision has attracted condemnation from the United Nations and many cities around the world. The OIC has also declared that East Jerusalem would be the capital of the State of Palestine. So the crisis is still far from solution and only time will tell when it would be solved through negotiations in good faith by both parties.

Reforms of the Ministry of Foreign Affairs

During the second term of President Obasanjo from 2003-2007, there were three changes of foreign ministers and permanent secretaries in the MFA. We were very fortunate in the IOD that Ambassador Oluyemi Adeniji was appointed Minister, while my former boss Ambassador Nkem Wadibia-Anyanwu was the Permanent Secretary. Both were career foreign service officers and had been ambassadors in key capitals as well as important departments at headquarters. Regarded as the specialist on UN matters, Oluyemi Adeniji was also the UN Secretary General's special representative in war-torn Sierra Leone and influenced the appointments of many officers to join the UN. He was highly respected, intelligent and hard working. He was an inspiration to me in the department and he encouraged us to make effective contributions in the debates and participation at international conferences. He motivated us to be successful and credible. That motivation led us to live up to expectations as we redoubled our efforts by involving relevant home ministries, ministerial departments (MDAs), stakeholders, national assembly committees on issues handled by the UN such as human rights questions, environment, crime and justice and women's issues.

Sunday Ehindero, the Inspector General of Police (IGP), was also very helpful as he was already familiar with the issues concerning human rights having been the Commissioner of Police (CP) and served with us in the Ad-Hoc Committee on human rights questions set up by Auwalu Yadudu. Due to my insistence he assigned a Commissioner of Police, Colombus Okaro, as our contact person, who was also to join Nigerian delegation to human rights conferences. Because of the involvement of the Nigerian police at our meetings both at home and abroad, Sunday Ehindero decided to set up human rights desks at all the police facilities in the country. Human rights questions were also included in the police training course manual to promote and protect human rights and the rule of law in Nigeria.

The office of the Attorney-General and Minister of Justice was also actively involved with us, especially in the preparation of the periodic reports to the Convention on the Elimination of Racial Discrimination (CERD) and that of the Human Rights Committee as well as the Economic, Social and Cultural Rights Committee. I never worked under Ambassador Michael Ononaiye, but he inspired me at one of our meetings by telling me that I should rely on the Federal Ministry of Justice for legal advice on all issues of an international nature, because it was only that ministry that had the statutory responsibility to stand up and defend Nigeria's national interests in the legal fields. He said that even though ministries and MDAs had legal advisers, I should not rely on them but deal directly with the office of the Attorney-General and Minister of Justice. I abided by his advice and our efforts paid off in this regard. The Federal Ministry of Justice was overwhelmed with requests from us and I ended up knowing most of the staff of the Ministry of Justice personally, including all their Directors, especially those at the International Law division. Ambassador Adeniji also started the inclusion of retired ambassadors and national assembly members to the UNGA, a practice which had been adopted by subsequent Foreign Ministers.

However, the slow pace of reforms or reduction of staff demanded by President Obasanjo at the Ministry of Foreign Affairs was said to be Adeniji's major weakness. Because of this perception, he was deployed to the Ministry of the Interior and Ngozi Okonjo-Iweala was appointed the new Minister of Foreign Affairs. Ambassador Wadibia-Anyanwu, the Permanent Secretary, was also deployed to the Office of the Head of Service of the federation. Hakeem Baba-Ahmed was deployed as Permanent Secretary. I happened to be on the same flight from London to Abuja with both the new Minister and the Permanent Secretary, so I went to greet both and from the discussion, it appeared they were already aware of their assignment once they got to the MFA. From all indications I sensed that their deployment to the MFA was to carry out mass retrenchment in the name of reforms, especially the senior staff who were regarded as "top heavy". I did not know what that meant, because at that time there were less than 20 officers in that category in the MFA including ambassadors abroad, and some were already about to retire based on service rules of 60 years or 35 years' service. An example was made of the Federal Ministry of Education, where the Minister, Oby Ezekwesili, retrenched over 2,000 workers on assuming duties. But MFA did not have such a number in total, including junior staff.

The new Minister lived up to expectations in her maiden address to the staff and stated that reform was urgent and may be painful to some officers. In that regard a consultant was appointed to work with senior officers on the modality for the reforms. I smelt a problem if I sat on the fence as I was not involved in the reforms exercise due to my busy schedules on UN matter. I decided to act swiftly to prevent mass removals of senior staff, which would be detrimental to the Service. I worked late at night on my laptop checking the websites of Ministries of Foreign Affairs of middle-level countries that were on the same level as Nigeria, namely Brazil, Mexico, India, Indonesia, Egypt, South Africa, and Pakistan.

The study became very interesting and produced the outcome I wanted, so I waited for the meeting of the Policy Planning Committee, chaired by the Minister, to discuss the reform agenda. In the study I found out that MFA had only 2,151 officers and staff both at headquarters and abroad, including clerks, messengers, drivers, cooks and butlers according to the recurrent budget of 2006. I also compiled the number of diplomatic posts and the number of capital-based officers in the various missions mentioned in comparison to Nigeria. To my great surprise, Egypt had 156 missions abroad and Nigeria had 97, but Egypt had fewer staff in most of the missions than Nigeria at an average of 3-5 officers. Egypt also had a Foreign Trade Ministry with officers manned by Trade Officers in addition to tourism offices. South Africa, which had recently emerged from apartheid, also had large diplomatic representations worldwide and this was increasing.

I recalled the meeting between Ambassador Adeniji and his Egyptian counterpart in New York at the margin of UNGA in 2005 during the heat generated by the UNSC reform in which the Egyptian minister gave reasons why Egypt was well qualified to be one of the two African states to clinch the UNSC permanent seat. He said that Egypt had the largest diplomatic representation and the largest military in Africa, as well as a strong economy that should not be ignored in the criteria for the permanent UN Security Council seat. But Nigeria, which had only 97 missions, was closing at the crucial time.

An opportunity came for me to present my findings to the committee on reforms and when I did, Ngozi Okonjo-Iweala could not believe that there were only 2,151 staff in the MFA nominal roll both at home and abroad. She then directed me to widen my studies to include Australia, Japan, Sweden, Canada and the UK, but she resigned before I could present my findings, which was also revealing. Sweden had only four officers in Abuja, but they had 35 in Washington DC alone, apart from Consulates in five US cities besides the Permanent Mission in New York. Canada had three officers in Abuja but more than 500 in the US and over 300 in Washington alone. The UK had over 8,500 staff in the Foreign and Commonwealth Office, with 5,000 staff scattered all over the world.

I concluded that the number of missions and staff a country had abroad depended on the bilateral relations subsisting between the countries concerned and their national interests. It appeared President Obasanjo was unaware of the categorization of missions where a category A mission like the UK, Washington, New York, Paris, Berlin, China or Addis Ababa should have more staff than category B missions with fewer staff. In order to abide by the Presidential directive to reform, some officers and executive cadres were removed, mostly those with disciplinary cases, either pending or resolved. But their removal was done without due process and they took the matter to the Industrial Court, which ruled in their favour and they were reinstated back into the MFA.

As I mentioned earlier, although I was not a member of the MFA reform management team nor any of the Committees set up for that purpose, nevertheless I was actively involved in the reforms processes of 2006-2007. The reforms and recommendations were based on the guidelines provided by the Bureau for Public Service Reforms (BPSR). The aims and objectives of the reforms were said to be as follows:

a) To reposition foreign policy to achieve the goal of placing Nigeria among the 25 most advanced countries by 2025.

b) To reposition the MFA to achieve the objectives of Nigeria's foreign policy.

c) To achieve improvements in the standards of professionalism, commitment and integrity among officers responsible for conducting Nigeria's foreign policy.

d) To improve the image of Nigeria and Nigerians as well as mobilizing the Nigerians in the Diaspora to make greater impact at home.

e) To improve liaison with the other MDAs to maximize the gains made by Nigeria at international for a.

f) To restore professionalism among Foreign Service Officers.

g) To improve the working environment and living conditions of the staff at home and abroad.

These objectives were encapsulated in the main functions of the MFA, namely service to the Nigerian public, service to the Nigerians in diaspora, and service to foreigners, especially the foreign diplomatic missions in Nigeria. The forms and structures of departments were also reformed to make them more effective in-service delivery. But the policy of reducing staff was completely reversed in 2006 by the decision to merge the Ministry of Integration and Cooperation in Africa (MICA) with the MFA, in which I participated actively. The merger created problems because it violated the foreign service regulations of transferring officers beyond the level of counsellor (SGL 12) into the MFA from other arms of government due to training requirements. But we managed to provide vacancies for only those below the level of deputy directors and those above were referred to the office of the head of service for further action.

Even with that arrangement, there was strong opposition to regarding these officers as Foreign Service Officers. They were initially called 'administrative officers' until they attended and passed the examination at the Foreign Service Academy. The merger of staff of MICA with

MFA, coupled with the mass recruitment of staff in 1983/84, resulted in there being more than 200 directors in the MFA by 2010. This inconsistency of policy was the bane of MFA, and I experienced it myself during over 30 years in the Service. It is referred to as the only consistency in the Nigerian foreign service, together with its twin, the closure and reopening of missions.

The reforms did not address the main problems of staff shortage both in quantity and quality. It did not provide remedy for the long-term needs of the Ministry in terms of recruitment and training.

The only time when there was a semblance of high morale creeping back into the service was during the short period when Professor Joy Ogwu, a scholar of high intelligence and international repute, was the Director General of the Institute of International Affairs (NIIA) before she was appointed Foreign Minister. She raised the morale and hopes of the foreign service, and under her foreign service officers were appointed as ambassadors abroad and in situ. That pro-active action was sustained by President Goodluck Jonathan, to the admiration of FSOs. I also benefited from that morale boosting appointment as Ambassador to the Federal Republic of Germany, making it the third time in my career, which was unprecedented in recent times.

CHAPTER 11

THE NIGERIAN QUEST FOR A UNITED NATIONS SECURITY COUNCIL PERMANENT SEAT

"The principle of give and take is the principle of diplomacy – give one and take ten".

Mark Twain (1835-1910)

"Diplomacy is more than saying or doing the right things at the right time, it is avoiding saying or doing the wrong things at any time."

Bo Bennett (1972-)

With the appointment of Ambassador Olusegun Akinsanya to Ethiopia I was deployed to take over his functions as the Director of IOD while Chike Anigbo took over from me in the First UN Division. Kunle Adeyanju was deployed to the Second UN division and both were my deputies. The two directors were efficient, intelligent and hardworking and made my work very easy. Ambassador Oluyemi Adeniji, the

Foreign Minister, provided efficient leadership in addition to the motivation of Olugbenga Ashiru, the Under-Secretary for Regions and International Organisations (RIO) and Nkem Wadibia-Anyanwu, the Permanent Secretary, whom I had worked under in my first sojourn in IOD in charge of the Third UNGA Committee.

The UNGA adopted resolution 48/26 in 1993 that established an open-ended working group to consider the questions of increase in the membership of the Security Council. The last time such an increase in the non-permanent membership from six to ten had happened was in 1965, with no changes to the permanent seat category which remained at five, making the total to fifteen. The UN Secretary-General, Kofi Annan, established a Committee of Eminent Persons to advise him about the way forward on UN reforms in all its organs. The Committee of 16 included three Africans, namely Amre Moussa (Egypt), Salim Ahmed Salim (Tanzania) and Mary Chinery-Hesse (Ghana). The High-Level Panel recommended two options for the reform of UNSC. Option 'A' recommended six new permanent seats to be added to the existing five and to be distributed as follows, two seats each for Africa and Asia, one seat for Europe, and one seat for the Americas and the Caribbean countries.

It was on this basis that Nigeria indicated an interest in clinching one of the two seats recommended for Africa. Option 'A' also provided for three additional two-year non-permanent seats to be shared among regional groups, namely Africa, Asia and Pacific, Europe and the Americas. It provided criteria for membership as follows: those countries that contribute most to the UN assessed contributions financially, militarily and diplomatically as well as voluntary contributions to UN activities; those developed countries that had achieved or were making progress towards achieving the 0.7 percent GNP for Overseas Development Assistance (ODA); countries most representative among developing countries in the decision-making process; those that would not inhibit the effectiveness of the Council; those that would increase the democratic and accountable nature of the Council.

Option 'B', however, provided no new permanent seats but created an eight more four- year renewable term seats and one new two-year non-renewal non-permanent seat to be shared equally among regional groups. Kofi Annan appealed to member states to take urgent action on the proposals by consensus if need be. But that was not the case, as it turned out to be an opportunity for delegates to gird their loins against the reform of the Security Council. The supporters of both options A and B were not negotiating in good faith. In fact, they were bent on killing the process altogether, going by their body language.

In Nigeria the Presidential Advisory Council (PAC), Chaired by Chief Emeka Anyaoku, was very pro-active as it initiated urgent action to mobilize support for Nigeria to clinch one of the two seats allocated to Africa under option A for the permanent seat. The Presidential Advisory Council (PAC) constituted an ad hoc committee to raise national awareness and sensitize Nigerians and the world to actualize Nigeria's quest. Members of the Committee chaired by Chief Emeka Anyaoku were ambassadors Blessing Akporode Clark, Nkem Wadibia-Anyanwu, Oladele Akadiri, Lamin Metteden and Segun Apata. The supporting staff were Professor P.T. Ahire, Mark Egbe (later Ambassador to Burkina Faso) as well as Chudi Okafor (later Ambassador to Thailand) and me. The Committee met on 18 and 19 February 2005 but after two meetings it was decided to widen its scope and a Presidential Committee was established. General Abdulsalami Abubakar chaired the new Committee, which involved state governors, captains of industry, NGOs and civil society. Thus, the membership increased to twenty-two with ten others forming the secretariat, mostly my staff at the International Organisations Department (IOD).

Prior to this development there was a flurry of diplomatic activity soon after the report of the High-Level Panel was published. The Panel made recommendations for the reform of many UN organs and institutions as well as working methods in the economic and social fields, management, the Secretariat, terrorism, disarmament and non-proliferation. It had a responsibility to protect, but the Security Council was the focus of all UN members due to its importance, and overshadowed the other aspects of reform. Sensing that the Security Council debates could delay or truncate the other noble aspects of the Panel recommendations, Kofi Annan issued his own recommendation, titled "In Larger Freedoms", and called for the reforms to be made on a case-by-case basis instead of a package. By so doing he made changes that weakened some of the recommendations made by the Panel, as with the Peacebuilding Commission and the criteria for aspirants to Security Council permanent seats.

The President of UNGA, Jan Ping, also issued another document called the "Outcome Document" based on Kofi

Annan's recommendations for the Summit of Heads of State and Government scheduled for 14-16 September 2005. Similarly, Professor Jeffrey Sachs presented a complementary report on millennium development goals (MDGs) to be achieved by developing countries from 2000 to 2015. The 1,000-page plus report on MDGs and its executive summary were a difficult read, but we picked out the most important recommendation, which was the call for developed countries to contribute 0.7 percent of their gross national income (GNI) for development assistance if the developing countries were to achieve the MDGs by 2015. Kofi Annan pulled a fast one to ensure that the proposed Peacebuilding Commission and the Human Rights Council were approved and implemented before the debates on UN Security Council were conducted. Nigeria supported both the proposed Commission and the Council and was elected into both as pioneer member. But the amendment to the Higher-Level Panel's recommendation on Peacebuilding Commission that diminished its importance or limited its scope rendered the Commission ineffective. The amendment confined its mandate to cover only post-conflict Peacebuilding, whereas the Panel recommended that its mandate should also include conflict prevention and not necessarily post-conflict Peacebuilding. The latter recommendation, if approved, would have helped states to stop crises before they occur. This recommendation was not included in what was approved and implemented due to pressure from some developing countries which insisted that so doing would violate the UN Charter on matters of the internal affairs of member states.

With this method of choosing and picking the

recommendations and implementing them, developing countries, including Nigeria, started to call for the implementation of the other recommendations, particularly the most important organ of the UN, the Security Council. Our stand was that no reform was complete without the reform of the Security Council. That was the focus of our attention, both at national and regional level. The African Groups in New York and Addis Ababa were meeting and reporting on the steps taken within Africa as well as all other aspects of the reforms of those jockeying for the UNSC permanent seats. From Africa the countries that registered their candidacy were Egypt, Nigeria, South Africa, Gambia, Libya and Kenya. But going by the criteria stipulated only three countries were eligible, namely Nigeria, Egypt and South Africa, which were the serious contenders. But the potential losers ganged up to spoil the chances of the serious contenders, not only in Africa but also in the other regional groups. In Asia, the serious contenders were India and Japan. In the Americas, it was Brazil, while in Europe it was Germany. And they faced stiff opposition from their neighbours as Pakistan opposed India, while Italy, Spain and Turkey opposed Germany and Mexico and Argentina opposed Brazil. The serious contenders from outside Africa, namely Brazil, Japan, India and Germany, formed a group of four (G-4) to work together to actualize their dream for the UNSC permanent seat. But since Africa was allocated two seats it could not agree on which countries to represent them, and they could not work with the G-4. Instead they established a ministerial committee of ten plus three (10+3) to address the African common position on UN reforms. The ten were chosen from each of the five zones of the African

Union mechanism, namely West Africa, Central Africa, North Africa, East Africa and Southern Africa. The ten countries were Chad, Botswana, Djibouti, Benin, Congo Brazzaville, Algeria, Libya, Senegal, Ethiopia, South Africa and the core group of three Nana Akufo-Addo (later President of Ghana), Oluyemi Adeniji of Nigeria and Alpha Omar Konare, the Chairperson of African Union Commission.

The Ezulwini Consensus on United Nations Reform

The AU Ministerial Committee on UN Reforms met in Ezulwini in Swaziland from 20-22 February 2005 with a view to fashioning an African common position to recommend to heads of state and government. Due to the interest shown, many Ministers from other African countries attended the meeting as well as the delegations of the G-4 countries. The two-day meeting could not reach any meaningful agreement on which options they would recommend to the African Union Commission as the African candidates. Libya and Algeria, with the tacit support of many African delegations, insisted on a rotation in line with option B claiming that the two seats were allocated to Africa, not a country, and should rotate among African countries based on a formula to be derived and adopted by the AU. But the South African and Nigerian Ministers argued that rotational seats could not at the same time be permanent. They pointed out that Africa would get the worst of it by losing the golden opportunity of getting two permanent seats at the UNSC.

Ambassador Oluyemi Adeniji recounted the benefits to Africa if two of its members were elected into the UNSC permanent seats, because most of the issues before the Council were in Africa. He said that Nigeria, if elected into the Council, would never use her position against any African states, but would instead use it to defend the interests of African countries. As the meeting was almost reaching agreement on this matter, the issue of veto power was raised, but the spoilers of the move, who were in favour of option 'B', namely Libya, Algeria, Senegal and others, cashed in on this to insist that Africa must have permanent seats with veto power. The agreement on veto power became the Waterloo of the reform of the UNSC. It became the double-edge sword to pursue the quest for Africa to get two permanent seats, as well as the sword to kill it.

After a long discussion, it was agreed that Africa should support option 'A' with veto power. That was agreed upon as a bargaining tactic to get concessions from the developed WEOG on ECOSOC, Peacebuilding and humanitarian assistance to Africa. We thought that after negotiating with the other groups, Africa would drop the insistence that the new members must have veto power. Alas we were wrong, as the spoilers found a loophole to nail the UNSC reform by insisting that that was the African common position, to have permanent seats with veto power, and nobody would change it even though the G4 had indicated that they would accept membership of the Council without veto power.

As the debates became acrimonious, Ambassador Adeniji whispered to me and inquired if I had any information about when the Council was increased from 11 to 15 in 1963. Luckily, I carried the UN Charter all the time during the reform process. The decision to increase the membership of the Council for only non-permanent seats, which was done after 16 years of the establishment of the UN in 1945, was not supported by all the P-5 members. Of the P-5 members only China voted in favour of the expansion of the non-permanent members from 11 to 15 in 1963.The UNGA resolution was rejected by France and the USSR, while the US and the UK abstained. It was on record that only four African countries were among the founding members of the UN at San Francisco in 1945. These were Egypt, Ethiopia, Liberia and South Africa. There were also four Asian countries, namely Iran, India, Philippines and China, who were members of the UN. But since the 1960s more than half of the members of the UN had come from Africa and Asia and most of the issues discussed by the UNSC were from these countries.

The African Union Executive Council met in Addis Ababa from 7-8 March 2005 and endorsed the Ezulwini Consensus. The Executive Council then mandated a further meeting of the Ministerial Committee to hold further meetings before the UNGA. A follow-up meeting of the Core Group of Ten plus three on UN reform was held at the Bolingo Hotel in Abuja on 9 June 2005. The meeting, which was chaired by Nigeria's Foreign Minister, Oluyemi Adeniji, had lengthy deliberations on the draft agenda which was later agreed to cover the draft "Outcome Document" by the President of UNGA; other developments since Ezulwini and programme of action of the Committee. An earlier attempt to refer to the G-4 draft resolution was rejected by Senegal, Algeria and Libya. The G-4 countries were fully represented by their Foreign Ministers as observers. They were invited by Nigeria as the host country, but other African countries misunderstood this as Nigeria's attempt to reap benefit from their presence.

Prior to the Abuja meeting the G-4 countries had issued a draft resolution they intended to negotiate with other countries and thereafter table it for action at the UNGA in July 2005. Those countries uniting for consensus also issued their own draft resolution for action at the UNGA. The contents of these drafts differed remarkably from the position of African countries. The G-4 draft resolution called for the increase of UNSC permanent seats from five to 11 and the non-permanent seats category from 10 to 14, making a total of 25 members. Those Uniting for Consensus comprising Argentina, Canada, Colombia, Costa Rica, Italy, Malta, Mexico, Pakistan, Republic of Korea, San Marino, Spain and Turkey and they co-sponsored a draft resolution calling for the increase of the Council from 15 to 25 members without any increase in the permanent seats category. They were aiming at preventing the G-4 and African countries from achieving permanent membership in the Council.

The position of G-4 and Uniting for Consensus dominated discussion at the Abuja meeting of the African Union Committee. Some of the ministers strongly condemned Nigeria on the invitation of the G-4 countries to negotiate the African position, claiming that it was outside their mandate. Libya, Senegal, Algeria and Ghana opposed any move to negotiate the African common position at Ezulwini and to make any concession or compromise on it. To them the Ezulwini consensus was not negotiable, but they forgot that it was supposed to be a negotiating strategy with other groups to strive out concessions from them on the other aspects of UN reforms, especially in the economic and social fields.

The meeting called for the rejection of the draft resolutions by the G-4 as well as that of Uniting for Consensus until after the AU Committee had presented its reports and they had been considered by the AU Executive Council. which would in turn report to the African Union summit scheduled in Sirte, Libya in July 2005. The delegations of Libya, Algeria and Senegal were vehemently opposed to the intention of G-4 countries to negotiate anything with them. They said that Africa countries should present their own draft resolution based on the Ezulwini consensus with Africa having two permanent seats with veto plus additional seats in the non-permanent seat category.

The AU Committee decided that there was a need for Africa to preserve their common position until after the summit in Sirte, Libya. He said that the G-4 and the Uniting for Consensus, or any group, were free to consult with Africa to find a common ground before the 60th session of UNGA. He announced that only China out of the P-5 countries had indicated support for the African position, and that the G-4 framework resolution should be rejected by Africa as it did not meet their aspirations.

Apart from the reform of the UNSC permanent seat, the "Outcome Document" contained important matters to be resolved in the areas regarded as most critical and controversial, namely management, terrorism, the human rights council, the Peacebuilding Commission, the responsibility to protect, economic development through ECOSOC, non-proliferation and arms control. The definition of "terrorism" was the most controversial, as many developing countries could not agree on what it meant in view of their experiences with the rights to self-determination during the dismantling of the apartheid regimes in southern Africa, the Palestinian issue and Western Sahara and other depending territories. Economic and social development was also very high in the agenda of the developing countries, especially in Africa. The Abuja meeting was dominated by the UNSC reform, with little time for the consideration of other equally important subject matters as contained in the Outcome Document.

On the proposal for 'responsibility to protect' civilians in times of conflict where countries were unwilling or unable to protect their citizens, some delegations rejected the arbitrary use of the intervention under the pretext of protecting lives and property. They claimed that it would violate article 4 of the AU Charter and article 2 of the UN Charter on sovereign equality of member states and non-interference in their internal affairs. They claimed that although the AU Charter authorized the Assembly of Heads of State and Government to intervene in such a situation, the provision is not used arbitrarily to undermine the sovereignty of states to protect the lives and property of their citizens.

The ministers were contradicting themselves contrary to their earlier decisions in Ezulwini. For instance, they agreed at Ezulwini to engage other groups and interested parties on UNSC reform, but at the Abuja meeting they refused even to engage the G-4 countries who were invited by Nigeria as observers, which was a good opportunity to engage them and ask questions as well as sell them the

African common position. More so, the Ezulwini consensus was not sacrosanct, as it was a stopgap for negotiation to strike concessions on MDGs and development assistance. It was clearly demonstrated that Africa was not ready to be in the permanent seat category of the UNSC. It appeared that Senegal wanted the two seats allocated to Africa to be shared between Francophone and Anglophone Africa and on that basis, it could work to get the support of France, which has indicated that she would support Germany for the seat allocated to Western Europe. Due to the war in Iraq, for which both France and Germany had indicated that they would vote against a UN resolution authorising the war, the US withdrew its support for Germany and favoured Japan to be the only country in the UNSC permanent seat. But China was strongly opposed to Japan being elected into the Council.

The day after the meeting, both the German and Japanese ambassadors visited me in my office to review the future of the reforms process. The Japanese Ambassador reported that Libya had indicated its candidacy for a permanent seat on the Security Council. The two envoys told me that they would keep up the momentum to ensure that they presented their draft resolution for action before the summit in September. They told me that they were encouraged by Kofi Annan, who said the only window of opportunity was in July for the decision on enlargement of the Council under option A without the veto. The second stage was another resolution after the September summit, which would name the new members as well as the amendment to the Charter. They were already naming countries that had promised to vote in their favour, those against as well as those that would abstain. They also told me that they would use the carrot and stick to ensure success in their two-stage strategies. The German ambassador was emphatic that they would get their way, as they would use more of the stick than the carrot against any developing country that abstained or voted against their draft resolution by withdrawal of aid and technical assistance. But I told them that the UNSC reform was dead, since Africa had already blocked any progress on the subject matter. It was clear that the "spoilers" never wanted any reforms of the UNSC under option A. Apart from Nigeria, Egypt and South Africa, which spoke openly in support of option A, all others spoke with two voices and mostly leaned towards option B. They only used Ezulwini and the veto power to block progress under the pretext of African consensus.

Some African countries were even postulating that when the chips were down the decision would be Nigeria and South Africa under the notion that Egypt was not truly an African country, but they were wrong. Had they forgotten that Boutros-Boutros Ghali contested for UNSG with Bernard Chidzero of Zimbabwe, but the latter lost, and the former was elected as an African candidate? Had they also forgotten that Egypt also broke diplomatic relations with the United Kingdom in 1965 over the unilateral declaration of independence (UDI) of Ian Smith in Southern Rhodesia, now Zimbabwe? The Egyptian diplomacy was divided almost equally between Africa and the Middle East and stood a good chance of winning the vote if the decision was taken at the UN General Assembly which favoured her if it was decided by the UNGA. According to information available to us, both Egypt and South Africa were fighting Nigeria, alleging corruption and bad governance. The two seats for Africa could have gone to any of the three African countries, Egypt, Nigeria or South Africa, depending on where the final decisions were made. But it was clear that Africa was not ready, and she was responsible for scuttling the reforms.

The Presidential Committee on National Awareness on UN reform continued its activities through shuttle diplomacy to seek for African support as well as dinners and other activities by the organized private sector, NGO s and civil societies to raise national awareness and to sensitize them on the importance of Nigeria's candidacy for permanent membership of the UNSC. I accompanied Chief Emeka Anyaoku to some of the countries he visited, namely Tanzania, Mozambique and Zimbabwe, while my colleagues accompanied General Abdulsalami Abubakar to other countries, namely Namibia, Uganda, Gabon, Mali, Niger, Senegal and Gambia.

At a meeting of the committee on 28 June 2005 at the Presidential banquet hall in Abuja, over 30 members attended, including the secretariat. The briefing on most of the countries was revealing on the level of bilateral relations subsisting between our two countries. Many the countries evaded the Nigerian delegation by travelling abroad and directed their deputies or Foreign Ministers to receive the delegation. That was the case with Zimbabwe and Gabon. Due to the negative signals, the delegation did not travel to Senegal and Gambia, whose presidents travelled out of the country. The other countries visited, however, gave tacit support to Nigeria's bid for a permanent UNSC seat. Some countries, namely Mozambique, Mali, Niger and Namibia, said they would support Nigeria even if there was only one seat allocated to Africa. Apart from Zimbabwe, whose grievance with Nigeria was the fact that Nigeria did not invite them to the 2003 CHOGM, all the countries in Southern Africa paid glowing tribute to Nigeria's support for the liberation of Southern Africa from apartheid. Tanzania, Mozambique and Namibia predicated their support for Nigeria on the track record and credentials as a champion of Africa's cause at the AU and the UN, which was unsurpassed by any other country in the continent.

The Question of Veto Power at the United Nations Security Council

An issue central to the UNSC reform was the question of veto power to new members. We knew that progress could not be made on this by the P-5 countries as such. Nigeria supported the position of G-4 countries that it was better to be inside the Council without veto than to be outside it. We believed that once we had been elected into the Council as a permanent member, then progressively the issue of veto would be resolved. After all, the question of veto had been insignificant as only the US and to a lesser extent Russia had used the veto to block a substantive resolution. But the main problem for Africa was which of its members would be elected into the UNSC permanent seat.

To block the process, the "spoilers" resorted to the Ezulwini consensus on veto power or no reform. The African Union Assembly in Sirte did not make any progress in choosing the two Africa members to represent them at the

UNSC. In fact, the Sirte summit was even more acrimonious, and the spoilers seemed to have prepared to kill the process altogether. Instead of taking a categorical decision, the Summit referred it to their permanent representatives in New York to engage the others interested parties, like the G-4, the Uniting for Consensus and P-5 countries. What an irony that the heads of state and government should fail to take a decision but refer to their permanent representatives to decide. That was an indication that Africa was not interested in which of its members should represent them, and most of them did not want any reform but preferred option B.

The development in the Middle East regarding the Iraq war created further problems as the US was said to favour the increase of the Council only by the addition of Japan. She dropped the earlier support to Germany due to its opposition to the war in Iraq. Germany was one of the countries that openly opposed the war and indicated that she would vote against the US resolution at the UNSC. Germany was a non-permanent member of the Council and with the opposition by France, which threatened to veto the US resolution on the war in Iraq, that changed the chemistry regarding the reform of the UNSC.

The African permanent representatives in New York put a final nail in the UNSC reform in their meeting at the AU office in November 2005, where I was listening to the arguments like a comic drama. The ambassadors were opposed to any shifting of ground on the veto power and insisted that the Ezulwini consensus was the only position they would accept. Only Nigeria and South African ambassadors were conciliatory by calling for negotiation with other groups as mandated by the Heads of State and Government at Sirte. Egypt, which seemed to have lost the battle to bring the choice of African candidates to the UN General Assembly for a vote, seemed to have shifted ground in favour of option B, instead of losing to Nigeria and South Africa. Egypt was speaking from both sides of her mouth, as we say in Nigeria, but was strongly in favour of rotational seats for Africa. All efforts by the Nigerian PR, Aminu Wali, and South Africa to calm the nerves of the others failed and the acrimonious session ended abruptly and with it the end of the UNSC reform process. We could not blame them, because their capitals were not committed to the UNSC reforms. Why should the summit of heads of state and government in Sirte not decide on who among them should represent Africa in the Council but refer it to their representatives in New York?

The Uniting for Consensus movement comprised some powerful countries with equally powerful neighbours in the G-4 whom they did not want elected into the UNSC permanent seats due to the war of attrition between them. These were intractable problems that exacerbated the problems, and this needed confidence-building measures before any progress could be made in the UNSC reforms. But despite these intractable problems we believed that once Africa decided on who should represent them, the Gordian knot would be untied if the P-5 did not create their own problems, as the US publicity pronounced that not more than two countries should be granted permanent seats in the UNSC, namely Japan and probably Germany because of their contributions to the UN budget. It was also feared that even if the UNGA decided on the reform of the UNSC, it would still be a herculean task to implement the resolution by member countries. To do so, article 23 of the UN Charter would have to be amended and approved by a two-thirds majority and ratified by two-thirds of member countries, including the P5 countries.

An attempt was made to keep UNSC reform alive by the UNGA, which held a debate on it on 20 July 2006 to discuss the proposals by various groups. The group of Uniting for Consensus, the African group, G-4 and that of the S-5 countries presented proposals calling for amending the UN charter but with divergent recommendations for doing so. The G-4 proposal presented by Brazil and co-sponsored by Germany, India and Japan called for an increase in the UNSC seats from 15 to 25 by adding six permanent members and four non-permanent members to be elected as follows: two from African states; two from Asian states; one from Latin America and the Caribbean states; and one from WEOG states. The four new non-permanent seats should be elected as follows: one each from African states, Asian states, East European states and Latin American and Caribbean states.

Uniting for Consensus tabled a draft proposal dated 26 July 2005 which was co-sponsored by Argentina, Canada, Colombia, Costa Rica, Italy, Malta, Mexico, Pakistan, Republic of Korea, San Marino, Spain and Turkey and called for the UNSC to consist of 25 members with no new permanent seats to the existing P-5 countries. The 20 non-permanent seats should be elected based on equitable geographical distribution, with due regard to their contributions to the UN in maintenance of international peace and security.

Algeria, on behalf of the African states, submitted their

proposal dated 18 July 2005 and calling on the enlargement of the UNSC by allocating two permanent and five non-permanent seats to raise the Council from 15 to 26. The seats would be distributed as follows: African states should have two permanent and two non-permanent seats; Asian states should have two permanent and one non-permanent seat; Eastern European states should have one non-permanent seat; Latin America and Caribbean states should have one permanent and one non-permanent seat, while Western Europe and other states should have one permanent seat, bringing the total additional seats to eleven. The new permanent members would have the "same prerogatives and privileges as those of the current permanent members, including the right to veto". The representatives of the Small Five (S-5) countries, namely Costa Rica, Jordan, Liechtenstein, Singapore and Switzerland, presented a proposal on the working methods of the Council to be more democratic and inclusive. The debates ended in stalemate as there was no convergence of views and positions and no proposal was tabled for action, as it was clear that no single group was ready to shift ground to the pleasure of the United States, which opposed an expansion of the UNSC and the use of the veto power beyond Japan. It was clear that the stalemate on UNSC could be unblocked, by African countries, because they had 54 votes and could swing that number to their favour once they decided on which of its members would be elected to represent them at the UNSC as a permanent seat. But the reform process was scuttled by the countries that had been making statements calling for the democratization of the Council through an increase in the decision-making process of the Council. The debates in the African Group were not focused, as it was full of contradictions, and one wondered whether they ever wanted to be in the permanent seat category or not.

Despite the decision of the AU Committee at Ezulwini (which had taken into consideration the Harare declaration of 1997) to favour option A with veto power, many delegations were still referring to the Harare declaration as their national position. A close consider the Harare declaration shows that it favoured option B. Article 2(a) states "Africa should be allocated no less than two permanent seats, and that these seats will be allocated to countries by a decision of Africans themselves, in accordance with a system of rotation based on the current establishment intent of the OAU". Article 2(b) says "Africa should be allotted five non-permanent seats." But for African delegations to continue to refer to the Harare declaration and state that the two seats for Africa should be rotated among African states was a fallacy. What is permanent cannot at the same time rotate and become non-permanent. All attempts by Nigeria, supported by S/Africa, to point this out to the delegations were rejected.

The African delegations seemed to have forgotten or wished not to remember how the issue of veto power was decided by the P-5 countries at the Yalta Conference in February 1945 just before the end of the Second World War and the establishment of the UN in 1945. It should be recalled that the right of veto power was a necessity and was called "the principle of unanimity" among the great powers, United States, Britain, Soviet Union, France and China, because the five countries believed that they would continue to be allies as well as continue to bear the burden of maintaining peace and security after the Second World War. The conditions that gave rise to this provision on the veto power and safeguard to the P-5 countries have not dissipated but still exist and are increasing in new forms. So, there is no way the P-5 would relinquish their hold on the veto power to others who were the causes of its application in the first instance. And for African countries to hold on to their demand to extend the veto power to new members was wishful thinking and a clear indication that they were not prepared to allow two members to be elected into the Council's permanent seats. The postulation by Algeria that the seats belonged to Africa and not a country, supported by many countries, also opened a new wound that would not heal and invariably nail the UNSC reform for a much longer time than we envisaged.

Building on this concept of a regional seat, there had been postulation that there should be a regional or geopolitical representation through regional organisations that represent their member countries. In this connection the two seats for Africa should be an African Union seat and not for a specific African country. The same with the French and UK seats, which would become European Union seats. But I do not see any future agreement based on these proposals which would compound the difficulty to reaching agreement on the UNSC reforms.

I agreed with the view of David Hannay in his book "New World Disorder" that the only way forward for an enlargement of the UNSC was through option B as an interim measure or stepping stone towards moving to option A. This option was appealing to many more members of the

UN than that under option A, which had strong opposition from equally powerful countries, including the United States, which could veto the decision by not ratifying the changes to the UN Charter to bring them into effect. Alternatively, I strongly called for the decision to admit new members into the UNSC to be taken through voting at the UNGA and not left to the regional groups to present candidates. This would be the only way of solving the quagmire in Africa and other regional groups.

Diplomatic Anecdotes with ambassadors in Abuja

I became very close to many the G-4 countries' ambassadors, particularly Ambassador Dietmar Kreusel the German Ambassador in Nigeria, and his wife Monika, as well as Ambassador Akio Tanaka of Japan to Nigeria. I learned through them that all their embassies abroad were monitoring developments on this issue daily. My name as the desk officer on this subject in Abuja circulated widely among them. For instance, the Japanese Ambassador to UN offices in Vienna, Yukio Takasu, who later became the Japanese permanent representative in New York, knew me by name even before we met. As the Chairperson of CTBTO, he was instrumental to my election as the Chairperson of CTBTO Working Group A in 2005; I served in that capacity for almost five years. The Germans also rewarded me handsomely as I was the first to receive my agrement within ten days in March 2007 out of a total of 28 nominees as ambassadors to various countries that year, because of the constant contacts I already had with them.

One of my encounters with Dietmar was during the heat

generated by President Obasanjo's third term bid. He called on me and told me that even though he knew I would not have any influence about it he felt he should make his points known to a close confidant in the MFA. He said that President Obasanjo was a highly respected person in Germany and internationally, but the third term bid had eroded that respect and standing, and that the earlier he distanced himself from that ambition the better for him. He cited the position of Nelson Mandela in the world and said President Obasanjo could do the same, but the third term bid was disastrous to him and Nigeria. Dietmar continued to hammer this issue until it was aborted by the National Assembly, presided over by Senator Ken Nnamani. His residence and that of the Japanese Ambassador were frequently visited by me and at times with my wife and family for dinner.

Ambassador Akio Tanaka would always thrill us with his tea-making techniques after a dinner, and it was a wonderful experience for me and my family to learn how tea was made in Japan. He was later transferred to Vienna as his country's bilateral Ambassador to Austria. A simple letter of introduction from Ambassador Tanaka to his former boss who was in Berlin, Ambassador Takano, proved a wonderful asset to me during my tour of duties in Germany. The level of cooperation between our two missions was very close as we always attended our functions at ambassadorial level until he left Germany. That proved the point that in diplomacy, knowledge of each other from previous posts is very important in strengthening bilateral relations between two countries. That is why career officers in general tend to be more intrusive in strengthening and deepening diplomatic relations with their countries of accreditation due to contacts they have made at previous posts.

The failure to achieve one of the most important aspirations of my country under my desk, that is, the election into the UNSC permanent seat category, was frustrating to me. My colleague, Ambassador Chike Anigbo, was even more committed to this issue as he put all his efforts to achieving this seat for Nigeria. Unfortunately, towards the end of the negotiations he was incapacitated by a ghastly accident which he barely survived.

CHAPTER 12

BERLIN: THESE STRANGE GERMAN WAYS

"There are many people in the world who really don't understand or say they don't understand or say they don't know. What is the great issue between the free world and the communist world? Let them come to Berlin. There are some who say that communism is the wave of the future. Let them come to Berlin. And there are some who say in Europe and elsewhere we can work with the communists. Let them come to Berlin.

All free men, wherever they may live are citizens of Berlin and therefore as a freeman, I take pride in the word 'Ich bin ein Berliner.'

Who possesses Berlin possesses Germany and whoever controls Germany controls Europe."

President John Kennedy (1917-1963)

———◆◇◆———

As with other old European countries, the history of the Federal Republic of Germany is difficult to summarise in one paragraph. Therefore, I would start my summary from German unification under the leadership of the Prussian Chancellor Otto von Bismarck in 1871. By that time and as the result of the industrial Revolution, Germany was the dominant Powers, Bulgaria, the Ottoman Empire and Austria-Hungary, in WWI (1914-18) against the Allied Powers, France, the United Kingdom, Serbia, Russia, Italy, Belgium and the United States. Germany lost that war and was compelled to pay reparation in accordance with the Treaty of Versailles. She also lost the colonies and her control of Poland. After her defeat, the Emperor was deposed, and the Weimar Republic was proclaimed. With Adolf Hitler in power, Nazi Germany invaded Poland, which led to WWII. German forces occupied most of Europe except the United Kingdom and Greece. She was in alliance with the fascist regime of Benito Mussolini in Italy. Hitler and Stalin divided Eastern Europe, but the invasion of the Soviet Union in 1941 led to the defeat of Germany at Normandy in 1944 because of the entry of the United States into the war on the side of the Allied powers. At the end of WWII Berlin was divided into two, the Soviet sector and the Western sector controlled by France, US and UK. The former became the capital city of Eastern Germany (German Democratic Republic) and the other half was part of West Germany (Federal Republic of Germany) until the end of the Cold War in 1990, when Berlin became the capital of unified Germany.

The arrivals and departures of ambassadors to take up or leave their posts often follow routine procedures. Armed with the letters of credence and recall of the previous Ambassador, and in my case Professor Tunde Adeniran, a message about my arrival in Berlin was conveyed to the Embassy. A protocol officer from the German Foreign Office would receive the Ambassador-Designate if arrival was during working hours from Monday to Friday. But since my arrival was on a weekend, there was no protocol officer waiting for me except some African ambassadors, staff of the embassy and the leaders of Nigerian community. But at the check-in counter in London my ticket read Brussels instead of Berlin and there was no British Airways flight that evening as the last one had left. However, I changed to Lufthansa, German Airlines, which arrived in Berlin via Frankfurt very late in the night. That was one of the greatest diplomatic blunders I ever encountered due to the last day in the office in Abuja, and my personal assistant bought the tickets for me from the travel agency. That was child's play, as I discovered on arrival that my credentials were addressed to the late former German President, Johannes Rau, who had left office in 2004 and died on January 27, 2006. That was due to improper keeping of records in our Protocol department. I was really surprised by such a blunder, since the Protocol department received the credentials of my counterpart Ambassador, Joachim Schmillen, who had presented them to President Obasanjo some years before my appointment to Germany. It took time before a new one was sent to me for accreditation and presentation to the German President on June 1, 2007.

The Nigerian Embassy in Berlin was in the former East Berlin in a place previously used as a prison yard. Apart from its proximity to the German Foreign Office, it lacked any security as it shared a common entrance with shops and had no reserved parking space for embassy cars. That was my second experience of a chancery building without security. The other one was in Geneva, but the former was Embassy property while the latter was rented, so it could be excusable since it was a temporary location.

I never dreamed that I would be posted to Berlin as I had condemned the chancery during the seminar for Nigerian ambassadors in Europe in 2002 due to its poor location. The residence is in one of the most prestigious parts of Berlin at Dahlem, even though the building itself was collapsing before it was purchased and poorly maintained. Dahlem housed many embassies and residence, large parks and gardens as well as the Frei Universität Berlin, scattered around the area according to specialized faculties.

Before moving to Berlin, the Nigerian residence in Bonn was one of the most splendid buildings in Nigeria's diplomatic residences. It contained about 18 rooms with a lift from the kitchen to the dining room in the upper floor, underground parking garage for 13 cars, a large courtyard and garden. It was in a highly prestigious residential area of Bonn. When the Embassy moved to Bonn it became desolate and abandoned. Attempts to sell it became a problem as it could not be used for a private residence or converted to commercial use due to the town planning regulations. The cost of heating, cleaning and maintenance was huge, and the furnishings were deplorable and unserviceable. That was a classic example of diplomatic vanity and wastage. It was not an isolated case, as there had been many examples of ill-conceived policies made in building or purchasing houses in some missions only to close them soon after. That was the case with the Nigerian Embassy in Belgrade, Yugoslavia, which had been reopened and the country renamed Serbia.

I was armed with a book entitled "These Strange German Ways" by Susan Stern, given to me by Joachim Schmillen. I started to confirm or refute some of the 'strange ways' mentioned in the book, but I did not find anything strange. Maybe it was comparing Germans with other cultures, probably the Americans. Luckily for me I had many friends in the German Foreign Office, people who I knew intimately during their posting to Abuja from 1994-98 and 2004-2007, and several others at the UN conferences in Geneva, Vienna and New York. I had similar intimate contacts with the British, American, French and Japanese diplomats in Abuja and elsewhere, but the Germans were more in number and quality in contacts than the others. So, the "strange German ways" were more to do with their hospitality than otherwise.

Due to the importance of Germany to Nigeria in terms of economic and commercial cooperation, I regarded my appointment as key to pursuing our policy of economic diplomacy. Germany was the third largest economy in the world after the US and Japan until it was overtaken by China in 2008 and the first in Europe, so my appointment was not taken lightly. More to the point, it was my last posting before retirement from the foreign service as I would clock sixty in two and half years' time. It was more than twenty years since a career foreign service officer, Ambassador Asuquo Emenyi, had served as Ambassador in Germany for a very brief period, so I knew the expectation on me to show the differences with non-career officers.

In this last assignment for me abroad before I retired from the Service, I found some highly-trained officers with whom I worked with for the next three years. Notable among them were Ayodeji Lawrence Ayodele, Muntari Kaita, Ladan Sidi, Roddy Nwokeabia, Clement Uwaifo, Salihu Atimah, Austin Ekeanyanwu, Mahmud Lele Mohammed and Kabiru Adamu, some of whom I had worked with at headquarters. In addition to these there were the Administrative and Technical staff who were locally recruited. Patrick Okoye replaced Atimah and Amedu Ahmed replaced Kabiru Adamu one year later.

On the day scheduled for the presentation of credentials to the German President, the French President, Nicolas Sarkozy, made an unscheduled visit to Germany and the presentation was cancelled. A new date of June 1 was fixed for the ceremony. According to German practice, four ambassadors present credentials on the same day in order of their date of arrival in Berlin and without their spouses. The ambassadors who presented the credentials with me were from Gabon, Chile and a non-residence Ambassador of Guinea-Bissau resident in Brussels.

In accordance with diplomatic practice, you cannot fully practise or be recognised as an ambassador in the host country until you present your credentials to the host president or whoever is designated to receive them. In the case of Germany, once the *copie d'usage* had been presented to the Chief of Protocol, you could perform diplomatic functions except addressing the press or making public statements. This silence is the golden rule during the waiting period. President Horst Köhler had a good knowledge of African social and economic problems and he was being referred to as "Mr. African" in the Germany Foreign Office due to his experience in dealing with African affairs when he was the Managing Director of the

International Monetary Fund (IMF). In our short private discussion after the presentation of the credentials, he commended Nigeria for her role in ECOWAS, particularly in Liberia and Sierra Leone. He also confirmed to me that Africa was dear to his heart, and that he had organized the Africa Forum with a few presidents, civil societies and non-governmental organisations to address social, economic and cultural development in Africa in an informal setting. Nigerians President Olusegun Obasanjo attended the Forums held in Berlin and Accra during the previous years.

Six days after the presentation of credentials, President Yar'Adua visited Berlin for the G-8 summit. As he himself had just been sworn in as Nigeria's president on 29 May 2007, he arrived with a delegation, most of whom were later appointed ministers. Thus, his first foreign trip as President of Nigeria was to Germany, a week after his inauguration and six days after I presented credentials as Nigeria's Ambassador. There were minor issues of protocol reception at the airport. My deputy, Ayo Ayodele (later an ambassador), who was familiar with protocol issues, advised against treating the airport reception formalities as a state visit, which was different from official or working visits. He said a bouquet of flowers would not be presented at the reception at the airport, nor other formalities for state visits. But down the line and unknown to both of us, that instruction was not carried out. We arrived at the airport to find all his advice had been ignored.

Then at the Intercontinental Hotel, where we had reserved rooms for the President, a man was making efforts to enter the lift with him but Ambassador Taofeek Oseni, State Chief of Protocol (SCOP), refused to allow him. The man, whom I had not met, protested that he had a message for the President which must be delivered that night as a matter of urgency. He turned out to be Hans Wittmann, Deputy Chairman of Julius Berger/Bilfinger Berger, a construction giant in Nigeria, and a traditional titleholder as *Sarkin Hanya* of Katsina, where Umaru Yar' Adua was governor. I told him to follow protocol, as we had no knowledge of his visiting the President with an urgent message, and we assured him that we would inform the President accordingly.

Hans Wittmann was the CEO of Bilfinger Berger and deputy chairman of Julius Berger, a very intelligent and hardworking chief executive of the company, located at Wiesbaden. He was responsible for all the arrangements for President Yar'Adua's visits to Germany even before Yar'Adua was elected as Nigeria's president. Some of his actions turned out to undermine those of the Embassy through direct contacts with President Yar'Adua, especially those related to the previous and subsequent visits to Germany for medical treatment, forgetting that presidential visits have elements of security and diplomatic protocol with the host authorities that must be respected.

The G-8 Summit was held at Heiligendamm, a secluded northern seaport on the Baltic Sea, to prevent the usual demonstrators against the Summit which had led to deaths in previous years, in Seattle, USA and Genoa, Italy. We were all flown by helicopter to the venue and returned to Berlin late in the evening of 8th June. There were no specific duties for us except that the President held separate meetings with G-8 countries and another meeting among the African heads of state and government, namely Algeria,

Senegal, Ethiopia, South Africa, Nigeria and the AU Commission chairperson, Omar Konare. I found myself with Ojo Maduekwe who was the secretary of the PDP, the ruling party and unknown to me he would be the Nigerian minister of Foreign Affairs. President Hosni Mubarak of Egypt did not turn up for the meeting. I was told that he was angered by the classification of G-8 +5 and the Africa outreach countries. I was also curious about this classification and had difficulty explaining it to our President in the briefs which were prepared and handed to all the participants that came with him. Ayo Ayodele was charged with that responsibility and did a good job, which included talking points and an executive summary which the President found very useful.

The main agenda item with the theme 'Growth and Responsibility' focused on investment, innovation and sustainability, transparency, intellectual property rights, energy efficiency and climate change. There was also an item specifically for Africa, namely good governance, sustainable investment, peace and security, which were of great concern to President Yar'Adua. Good governance included free and fair election. The Nigerian president admitted that his election had not been free and fair, and he must do something about it. Before the President arrived on German soil, there were negative remarks by the German public and government condemning the 2007 presidential election in Nigeria. Apart from that, Germany was the President of the EU countries which had issued a strong condemnation of the 2007 presidential election. As a result, President Yar'Adua was worried that he would be embarrassed by the press, the government and the large

Nigerian community in Germany, but he was surprised that that was not the case throughout his interactions with his colleagues, the business community and the Nigerian community in Germany.

There were also several bilateral meetings with the Presidents of Italy, Japan, Germany, India, Brazil and China. The meeting with the Brazilian president was held in the Brazilian Embassy in Berlin. During that meeting President Lula told Yar'Adua that the four-year period of his presidency would pass like the wind, so he had to make the best of it to provide the basic needs of Nigerians. He said that Brazil was ready to assist Nigeria in energy instead of excessive dependence on petroleum for its energy supply. He said that ethanol, extracted from sugar cane and other plants, was the main sources of energy for Brazil and even exported overseas. He gave our president a dateline of the end of July to send his experts to Brazil to exchange ideas in this aspect.

The meeting with the Chinese President took place at the Intercontinental Hotel. Due to problems caused by one of the President's aides, who decided to pull me out of the car carrying the President, there was a small hitch during the meeting. Even with our well-written briefs, the President called me to say that the Chinese leader was not the "President" but the "Premier". I did not understand how that came about, but since there was no way to argue with him I kept quiet and he conducted the meeting by referring to President Hu Jintao as Premier. At the end of the meeting the Chinese Ambassador, who did not even know that Nigeria had an ambassador in Berlin, as I was yet to circulate a *note verbale* and pay courtesy calls to them, asked for our chargé d'affaires to protest at the reference to their president as Premier, a lower position in the Chinese hierarchy. Dupe Quist-Adebiyi (later Ambassador), the state chief of protocol, saw the problem and she advised the presidential assistants that at posts abroad the President was expected to sit with the Ambassador, who would brief him about that country as well as on the issues for discussion. Because of this, they should not struggle as to who was to sit with the President in the car. In any case, there was no foreign minister appointed to whom the President would refer questions.

The President also had two other engagements; one was with the organized private sector. The Afrika Verein organized a large delegation of businessmen and women with businesses in Nigeria and West Africa. The President enunciated a six-point agenda and said that the first, second and third priorities of his administration would be economy, economy and economy.

The second meeting was with the Nigerian Community in Germany (NCG) at the residence of the Ambassador. During the dinner, the President insisted that his dinner table should be among the people and not secluded from them. That alone endeared him to the Nigerian community and was applauded by them. He spoke for over thirty minutes and won over sceptics who wanted to raise embarrassing questions about the 2007 elections. That meeting ended on a positive note and even saved me from being removed and replaced by a political appointee, as many of them had a high-level lobbyist to remove me from the post, considered a gold mine to the politicians, for medical reasons as well as close contacts with Julius Berger for their personal benefits. I was also labelled "Third-term Ambassador" to lobby for President Obasanjo's aborted third term bid, but President Yar'Adua had full confidence in me and did not change my posting. I was the first career foreign service officer posted to Germany since 1991.

Barely two months after the visit, Frank Walter-Steinmeier, the German Foreign Minister (later President), visited Nigeria, the first foreign visitor to Nigeria during the Yar'Adua presidency. The week of his visit, from 8 August 2007, was the week the Federal Executive Council was constituted and sworn in. Chief Ojo Maduekwe was appointed Foreign Minister two days previously and was representing the President at an equally important function in Cotonou, Benin Republic, and was not available to receive the German Foreign Minister, so Bagudu Hirse, the Minister of State, was to receive him. But the Germans were worried that Nigeria was downgrading the visit as their minister was being received by a junior one. We assured them that Nigeria would hold bilateral talks with their minister at the Aso Rock villa, so the visit was not diminished by the reception at the airport. I also reminded them that according to German practice, it was the chief of protocol that receives dignitaries, including Presidents, at the airport, so they should not complain that we were downgrading the visit of their Minister.

The visit was very fruitful. President Yar'Adua requested German assistance in electricity, power generation and distribution as the most important factor inhibiting industrial development in Nigeria. The German Foreign Minister assured the President that within two months he would assemble a team of German experts to visit Nigeria to assess her needs. Two months later, Georg Boomgaarden, the Foreign State Secretary, led a team of German experts to visit Nigeria. That led to the memorandum of understanding (MOU) on Nigerian-German Energy Partnership which I had the privilege to sign on behalf of Nigeria, while Joachim Schmillen signed it on behalf of Germany in Abuja on 18 August 2008.

The MOU covered three areas, namely gas, the power sector and capacity building. It envisaged the addition of 6,500 megawatts of electricity to the national grid. The project covered solar, hydro, wind, waste, gas and coal as well as renewable energy. To implement the project there was a need for technical audits of existing power plants all over the country. The MUO was to be operational for a period of five years and renewable. The objectives of the partnership agreement were complementary to the benefits of both countries. Whereas Nigeria needed assistance in establishing a reliable electricity supply, Germany could offer innovative assistance, and in return exploit the vast reserves of gas in Nigeria. It was a win-win situation for both countries, if the agreement was fully implemented.

The German-Nigeria Energy Partnership was initiated by President Umaru Yar'Adua during a meeting with the German Foreign Minister, Frank Walter-Steinmeier, when the latter visited Nigeria in August 2007. This issue was erroneously reported as being between President Yar'Adua and Chancellor Angela Merkel at Heiligendamm in June 2007. It was the German Foreign Minister who wanted to know the single most important priority request Nigeria wanted from Germany to foster closer cooperation between the two countries. That was why President Yar'Adua stated that it was electricity and power supply, to which the German minister decided to send Georg Boomgaarden with energy experts to visit Nigeria in October 2007. Several German companies swung into action to cash on this MOU agreement, notably EON Ruhrgas and NAPTIM/GTZ for capacity building and training as well as Bilfinger Berger/Julius Berger for construction.

The Federal Republic of Germany comprises 16 federated states administered by ministers-president (governors) and each state has several opportunities for cooperation activities with Nigeria. An ambassador posted to Berlin has a lot to do to attract investment to Nigeria by deepening and strengthening relations both at the state and federal levels. President Horst Köhler facilitated contacts by organising annual visits to different states in the country for ambassadors and chargés d'affaires. It was on one such visit that I interacted with the BASF chemical company, one of the largest in the world. The company officials told me that they had been in Nigeria but later de-invested in 1979 and with the favourable economic climate they were contemplating returning. I later arranged a meeting with the company in Mannheim and was accompanied by Austin Ekeanyanwu, the desk officer on economic matters. BASF had since returned to Nigeria as the main supplier of chemicals in the country. Hitherto, Nigeria was importing the products from their branches in South Africa.

German-African Forum in Wiesbaden

A summit of four African presidents under the initiative of President Horst Köhler was arranged in Germany for

December 2008 and President Yar'Adua indicated an interest in attending, but the MFA advised against it. Dr. Hakeem Baba-Ahmed told me that we should discourage the President from participating at that summit. So, we rode in his car to meet the President, and Chief Ojo Maduekwe joined us later. At that meeting the issue of his attending that summit was raised and the Permanent Secretary advanced reasons to dissuade him from attendance. But when I noticed that the President wanted to use the occasion for health reasons, I supported him. When we left the villa, the permanent secretary did not hide his anger from me that we should have all spoken with one voice to discourage the President from attending, at least for political reasons, as his absence from the seat of government had negative consequences on his administration. There was a strong desire by the President to go for a medical check-up under the cover of the summit before the dates set for it. The only problem was for us to manage the private visit prior to the summit from the view of protocol arrangements with our German host, as well as the political impact to his presidency in the country.

President Yar'Adua's arrival in Germany a week before the summit in Wiesbaden created protocol problems for our German host. In any case Germany still went ahead to provide protocol for our President. The only problem was the kind of announcement to be made to the Nigerian people as to the reasons for the visit. I did not see this mentioned by Olusegun Adeniyi in his book "Presidency, Government and Death". During this visit, President Yar'Adua was accompanied by Turai, the first lady. It was on that occasion that I considered the history of the President's health.

Halima, my wife, visited the First Lady and offered to assist them with whatever they wanted in the city, like shopping. She was stunned to be told by Turai Yar'Adua that she knew the city better than her and they had been visiting the place for up to twenty years and knew the shops, restaurants, hospitals and clinics in the area. That showed that President Yar'Adua's illness had been present for much longer than we had realised.

The President arrived about a week before the summit and held discussions with the German president, just to fill the gap as well as to attend to his medical condition. At the end of the summit, which was attended by the Presidents of Botswana, Ethiopia, Rwanda and Nigeria, President Horst Köhler hinted to me his desire to hold the next summit in Abuja in the summer of 2008.

Establishment of Renewable Energy Organisation

I was kept busy with other issues of multilateral nature as I was still the Chairperson of CTBTO Working Group A in Vienna which held meetings four times in a year. Also, my attention was occupied by the climate change meetings in Bonn preparatory to the Copenhagen summit in December 2009. In addition to this the stream of visitors to Germany through Frankfurt was unending. Most of them were coming for medical treatment at Wiesbaden and wanted the Embassy's assistance. Some were on transit to other destinations in Europe and still wanted protocol assistance. I found such requests ridiculous and in most cases ignored them, since we were in Berlin about 600 kilometres away and about one hour by air. But this stance of mine almost backfired on me, as when I was attending a CTBTO meeting in Vienna, the wife of the Vice-President, Patience Jonathan (later First Lady), made a stopover with the wives of the senate president, governors and other dignitaries. They arrived in Frankfurt but could not see me nor my deputy but a lower level officer who did not receive them properly, and they had to walk a long distance from one terminal to the other. I received several complaints from my colleagues in Brussels and had to leave what I was doing in Vienna to receive them on their return stopover at Frankfurt Airport. I then realized the reasons for their complaint, as there was no proper arrangement to provide the kind of assistance they needed to connect from one terminal to the other.

It was after that problem that we recommended a consulate in Frankfurt, not only for consular and protocol matters but for economic and commercial purposes in southern Germany. The major businesses with substantial investments in Nigeria in the area were the Lufthansa Airline, Deutsche Bank, Commerz Bank, Julius Berger/Bilfinger, BMW and Mercedes Benz, as well as the DANA company, which built the Defence Industrial Cooperation and Nigerian Air Force hangars in Kaduna and Lagos respectively and have their headquarters in the area.

Apart from the climate change conference preparatory process in Bonn, the German Foreign Office invited all ambassadors in Berlin to brief them on their intention to start negotiations for the establishment of an international organisation to address the subject of renewable energy. I recalled that a similar attempt was made by France, backed by Germany, to establish an international environmental organisation during the 60th session of the UNGA in 2005.

As I was the director of the International Organisation Department (IOD) at headquarters, I kicked against that proposal as it would undermine or diminish the importance of the United Nations Environmental Programme (UNEP) in Nairobi, the only UN organisation in Africa. I thought the new initiative by Germany was reaching the same idea, but after a series of meetings the Germans gave good briefings to assure us that renewable energy, although an environmental matter, was completely different from the mandates of UNEP.

With headquarters approval, we played an active part in the formation of the new organisation. Professor Abubakar Sambo, the Director-General of Energy Commission, and Muntari Kaita, one of my able officers, worked strenuously to ensure the realisation of the new organisation. Unfortunately, the Germans could not muster enough votes to site the new organisation in Bonn as they envisaged. United Arab Emirates (UAE) mounted a campaign, using unconventional means, to woo delegates to its side. At a meeting in Sharm-el-Sheikh, Egypt, the UAE paid for hotels and provided transportation for all delegates coming from developing countries, including Nigeria. They also campaigned in capitals and obtained written support and came to the meeting with over 70% delegates, including Nigeria, supporting them.

Germany, after sensing defeat at the election, decided to back down and asked to site one of the scientific aspects of the organisation in Bonn and another in Vienna, Austria. Thus, the International Organisation for Renewable Energy was sited in Abu Dhabi, UAE and elected a French lady as the interim Director-General pending ratification and entry into force of the organisation.

A Collection of Benin Cultural Artifacts in a Berlin museum

One of the most important assignments of an ambassador is representational duties and the promotion of friendly relations between the receiving and sending states, which were my top priorities. So I made myself available by attending most events organized by the host authorities, captains of industry and commerce, arts and culture, especially those that had some beneficial effects or lessons for Nigeria. One such event was an exhibition by the Ethnological Museum in Berlin. It was a fascinating event with more than 2000 works of arts from Benin, Edo state, Nigeria. The Museum had over 500,000 pieces of art from all over the world, 75,000 from Africa and 580 from Benin, with a few from Ife and other parts of Nigeria. There was also a book on display entitled "Benin" by Frank Willett, which showed that the museum had the largest and probably the most important collections of Benin arts in the world, in terms of quality. Most of the items were in pricey ivory and bronze.

I was curious as to how the museum had acquired the items. Mr Peter-Klaus Schuster, the Director of the museum, told me that the items were bought at an auction from the British Museum in London and had been acquired after a punitive expedition and attack on the Kingdom of Benin in 1897. Probably due to lack of space in London, the items were auctioned to them. Conducting me through the exhibition housing two floors up in the magnificent museum, Mr Schuster remarked, "Mr Ambassador, do you think these beautiful items would have been preserved intact and appreciated as they were now if they were still in Nigeria, instead of in this house?" He continued without waiting for my response and as if he wanted to fuel my anger and pointing to one small piece, he asked, "what value can you guess for this piece of art at auction today?" He told me that it would fetch not less than 3.8 million euros. And there were 80 much bigger ones, showing how much Nigeria had lost to that museum alone. There was one piece called 'Queen Mother Idia' which was said to equal or rival Nefertiti, Queen of Egypt in a sister museum (Altes Museum, Berlin). It was said to be the most expensive and could never be allowed to leave the museum due to the cost of insurance on it.

I responded coolly but angrily that these were stolen items or acquired through violent means and wondered about their moral justification. But it was not the question of morality but business or commercial interest and sharing values which the museum claimed to be doing through the exhibition, to be conducted in four cities, Benin, Vienna, Paris and Toronto, over a period of two years. The Nigerian Minister of Culture and Tourism, Prince Adetokunbo Kayode SAN, led a Nigerian delegation to the exhibition in which he called for the listing and documenting of all Nigerian cultural artefacts in all museums in Germany, so that at least Nigeria would know where these items were located. He said that it would be foolhardy for anybody to call for their return to Nigeria, which was his priority, but that at least reparation through compensation for the loss suffered by Nigeria should be considered.

It was reported that the Oba of Benin attended or sent a representative to the exhibition in Vienna and called for the return of all the items to his kingdom. The Toronto exhibition met with demonstrations by Nigerians in Canada calling for their repatriation. At the end of the visit of the Minister of Culture and Tourism, the museum management presented four catalogues containing 580 pieces of items in heavy books to the Nigerian National Museum and Monuments with a copy for my library, which I appreciated very much.

The list of artefacts which also came from other museums in Germany, for the exhibition, were as follows: 580 in Berlin, 227 in Rushmore, 196 in Hamburg, 182 in Dresden, 167 in Vienna, 98 in Heiden, 87 in Leipzig, 80 in Stuttgart, 76 in Cologne and 51 in Frankfurt, making a total of 1,744 works of arts from Benin and over 600 in the UK. I sent a dispatch to headquarters and requested that Nigeria should make a formal request for the return of these items or pay reparation in accordance with the UNGA resolution of 4 December 2006. The UN resolution in question called for the "restitution and the return of cultural property to their countries of origin". I argued that since the Germans had also asked the Russians and the Poles to return their cultural objects stolen or violently acquired during the two World Wars, she should be compelled to return these items acquired illegally and violently to the Benin Kingdom.

President Köhler's Visit to Nigeria

President Horst Köhler visited Nigeria to attend the fourth

African Forum for selected African leaders, which he initiated from 6-12 November 2008. It was followed by a state visit. During the summit at Ladi Kwali Hall at the Sheraton Hotel, the Abuja 'Leadership Newspaper' reported that President Yar'Adua was too ill to attend the meeting, but the President was inside the hall taking part in the proceedings of the conference. The editor and the reporter of the newspaper were interviewed and charged with false publication. After their apology they were released, and the case withdrawn. My anger was that even if the President's condition was critical, since he was physically present in an event with visiting delegations comprising presidents and foreign ministers, to report that he was incapacitated was an irresponsible act by the news media.

After the summit, the German president undertook a state visit in which bilateral issues were discussed. The energy partnership featured prominently and by that time a pilot project with wind energy had been launched in Katsina state by EON Ruhrgas, a German company as part of the agreement. The German President advised that Nigeria should not embark upon large projects but small ones, which were more effective to cover towns and villages instead of a huge project that would cost more to install and maintain.

Before the commencement of the bilateral talks, and unknown to us, Lufthansa Airlines and Julius Berger had prepared an agreement, awarding themselves the maintenance and civil aviation services at the Nnamdi Azikiwe International Airport at Abuja. The MOU was to be signed between our two countries as part of the outcomes of the visit. As we lined up to receive the visiting German

President, one of President Yar'Adua's aides approached us to know who was signing the MOU on behalf of Nigeria. But neither Enny Onobu, the Under-Secretary for Regions and International Organisations, nor I had any idea about the document and who had prepared and negotiated it. We raised the issue with Chief Ojo Maduekwe, the Foreign Minister, as well as Mrs Diezani Alison Madueke, the Minister for Aviation, who also told us that she had no knowledge of it. The Minister for Aviation told us that she was just being invited to the villa to sign the document. Enny then informed the two ministers that it was imperative for the document to be studied by senior officials before its signature. We therefore recommended that the signing ceremony be postponed until we had closely studied it. We also advised that since Lufthansa was a company it would have been better to find its counterpart in Nigeria, and in the absence of Nigeria Airways a director in the Ministry of Aviation should sign the memorandum of understanding (MOU) on behalf of Nigeria but not a minister.

Our position and recommendation did not go down well with President Yar'Adua, who had seen the text and assured Julius Berger that it would be signed at the bilateral talks. As we entered the Federal Executive Council chamber, the two tables set for the signing ceremony were already set but we had them removed. The CEO of Julius Berger, Hans Wittman, moved to my side and wondered why the MOU was not being signed as the "highlight of President Köhler's state visit to Nigeria". I told him that I had not seen the document and neither did the ministers of the Ministries of Foreign Affairs or Aviation. He then gave me a copy and said that President Yar'Adua had seen it and agreed that it would be signed as part of the visit. I told him that there was a need for us to study the MOU and see that there were benefits to our two countries before it would be signed later. I asked him who had prepared such an important agreement without involving the Nigerian officials so that it went straight to the President and he expected us to sign it. I wondered whether such an action would be acceptable to Germany if we did it to them. He then retorted angrily that the actions by Nigerian bureaucrats tended to delay things that hamper development whereas businesses acted with a speed that facilitated progress. He appeared not to realise that civil servants have their jobs cut out for them by law to be cautious to protect the interests of their country both in Nigeria and in Germany. And that was what Enny and I did, without any fear that it could jeopardise our careers if we were protecting the national interests. Our loyalty was to the nation first and foremost.

The German President, in his concluding statement during the bilateral talks, mentioned the MOU and said he hoped it would be signed at the end of the meeting. President Yar'Adua then turned to Ojo Maduekwe instead of Diezani Madueke and directed that the MOU should be signed before we left the Aso Villa. During the press conference between the two leaders, the MOU became the main issue and President Yar'Adua was furious that the document was not signed. Enny Onobu, who had just glanced through the copy given to him, said "Abdul, don't mind them. We need to work on it and not to succumb to pressure to consider Nigeria's interests." He went to Ojo

Maduekwe and asked why MFA was being blamed instead of the Ministry of Aviation, and Ojo responded to him incoherently and said, "but what do you want me to tell the President?" Enny told him the reasons why the MOU needed to be negotiated because it had nothing beneficial to the Nigerian aviation sector but was one-sided in favour of Lufthansa and Julius Berger.

Consequently, we scheduled a meeting with the special assistant to the President on aviation, Captain Shehu Usman Iyal, and made necessary changes by inserting paragraphs on training facilities and advisory services to the Nigerian aviation sector before it was eventually signed.

This was a classic example of what the MFA always went through in defending the interests of Nigeria and in most cases under pressure by vested interests from the top echelon of our society for personal gain at the expense of the country. The Germans wanted to take advantage of the personal relationship between President Yar'Adua and the Julius Berger CEO, who was conferred with the title of "Sarkin Hanya" (Chief of Roads) of Katsina during the time the President was the Governor of Katsina state. It was assumed that that personal relationship could be exploited and would override Nigerian national interest. But they were wrong, because Enny stood his ground and succeeded in amending the agreement to reflect the overall interests of Nigeria. It also showed that if an officer knows his stuff well and stands by it, no matter the pressure, nothing will happen to him or her.

As if we knew that the MOU would not stand the test of time, it was reported that the Ministry of Aviation terminated the agreement after the demise of President

Yar'Adua and it created a diplomatic row between our two countries. The issue of external forces interfering with the proper functioning and decision-making processes of our external relations was amply demonstrated by this incident.

The German President visited the business community in Lagos and witnessed the Hausa culture in Kano where a special Durbar was staged for him, after which a horse was presented to him by the Emir Ado Bayero. President Köhler presented to the Emir a photograph of Heinrich Barth, the first German and scholar, who spent several years in Kano in the 1850s, and promised technical assistance for the restoration of the old Kano city mud fence as a historical monument. The Germans were also thrilled by a student of German language who spoke the language fluently and was the unofficial translator during the visit to the Emir's Palace. The German Ambassador later told me that they would strengthen their German cultural centre in Kano to encourage such talents in the German language and culture.

After the hurriedly-signed MOU between Nigeria and Lufthansa in Abuja during President Horst Köhler's visit to Nigeria in November 2008, Captain Shehu Iyal, the senior special assistant (SSA) to the President on aviation, visited Germany several times to hold discussions with the German airline. The objectives of the MOU were to assist in the development of Nigeria's aviation industry, while the German carrier was to be given concessional or preferential handling of cargoes and construction at Lagos and Abuja airports. In one of such visits, Lufthansa invited me for an interesting exercise at their training facility at Frankfurt Airport. The facility had training in all areas of aviation, control tower, flight engineers, ground crew, pilot training, security, take-off and landing of aircrafts including the designs of airports. The most interesting was flying one of their Airbus A330-300 simulators. It was fascinating to sit in the captain's seat and take off, piloting the aircraft simulator and zooming off to Bole airport in Addis Ababa, then returning. I encountered simulated bad weather, thick clouds and rain as we approached Addis Ababa, and landed at the airport in heavy rain. Some aircraft were seen parked on the tarmac and the visibility was poor. The plane was telling me the approach distances and what I was expected to do. The return journey was smooth with good weather and clear visibility, only hills and valleys. The take-off and landing, although similar, have different instructions on the distances showing the length of the runway. I learned that pilot training was quite different from car driving in the sense that you cannot change from piloting an A300 to a Boeing or another type of airbus unless you undergo training in that aircraft and hold a licence for it. That training facility was part of what would be available to Nigeria to train ground crew under the MOU agreement, but since Nigeria does not have a national carrier she could not benefit from the agreement.

President Yar'Adua's Visits to Germany, and his Death

Before my arrival in Germany as ambassador, President Yar'Adua had been visiting Germany for several years for medical treatment at the German clinic at Mainz near Wiesbaden for kidney-related complications. As mentioned earlier it was reported that he had been going to Germany for about twenty years for such treatment, even before he was elected governor of Katsina State in 1999. It was widely reported that he collapsed at a campaign rally in the heat of the Presidential campaigns of 2007 and was flown to Germany by Julius Berger in an air ambulance. Rumours circulated widely that he was dead, which prompted President Obasanjo to telephone him on his hospital bed in the same clinic in Germany and ask, "Umaru, the papers said you were dead. Are you dead?"

With my arrival in Berlin there were several rumours that the President was being flown to Germany, so we were always on the alert. Ayo Ayodele was always warning us at our weekly staff meetings that we should be ready always, as President Yar'Adua could arrive in Germany at very short notice, as was the case when he arrived unannounced without the knowledge of the mission and it was rumoured that he had died. Due to this we made sure that the rickety vehicles in the Embassy were boarded and new ones bought to replace them. Chief Ojo Maduekwe and Ambassador Baba Kaigama, the Foreign Minister and the Permanent Secretary respectively, were sympathetic to our request for new vehicles, but when the approval came it was not backed by resources from headquarters. That was strange indeed. Instead we were directed to use our resources, but since Berlin, like all missions abroad, lacked adequate resources, we had to find a solution by using our own initiative. We visited the diplomatic sales division of Daimler-Benz and they offered us between 45% and 55% discount for their cars if they were used within Germany. That was a big relief and because of that discount we bought four brand new Mercedes Benz cars with the meagre resources available to us. They were bigger than those approved by headquarters for missions abroad. Before that, most of the mission's vehicles were used ones with heavy maintenance costs. I advised that our mission in Berlin should continue to build on this initiative and continue to buy new Mercedes Benz cars instead of buying used ones in order to redeem the image of our country and save on maintenance costs. In fact, all the officers that served with me at that time also bought their personal cars at reduced costs that many of us had never known before.

One afternoon, Ambassador Bagudu Hirse, the Minister of State, phoned to say that President Yar'Adua was already airborne and would arrive at Frankfurt Airport soon for medical check-ups. It was four hours by road and one hour by air from Berlin, so I had to dispatch the representational car driver and a back-up car to proceed to Frankfurt and then rushed, without any spare clothes, to the Berlin Tegel Airport to catch any available flight. Luckily for us the President's flight was delayed, and we got to the airport before the Presidential plane touched down. There were several problems with protocol, logistical arrangements and hotel bookings as well as security, such as a police escort. The Julius Berger company had already positioned their cars at the airport and denied access to our vehicles, so it took a fighting match before we could get our cars with Corps Diplomatique (CD) plates to receive the President. The latter humiliated us that our cars often broke down and were therefore not suitable for presidential reception. That was the reason for denying us access at the tarmac.

That was not the only fracas with them. When we got to the hotel which they had reserved for the President and his entourage, there was no advance team to check the rooms, so President Yar'Adua was left seated in the hotel lobby until we arrived a few minutes later. There was no doubt that he was very ill, yet he was left sitting down alone and abandoned to his fate while his aides were checking suitable rooms with security devices. That incident was one of the most embarrassing moments for us, and I wondered who had made the hotel arrangements prior to the President's arrival.

On top of this, he was booked into an unsuitable double room. We later understood that it was Julius Berger that had made the arrangements, and the Embassy was completely cut off. Although Julius Berger had good intentions, the president of a country visiting another country is not purely a private affair as it involves elements of diplomatic protocol. We wondered what would have happened if the President had been kidnapped or attacked without a police escort and security.

Yar'Adua was due to return to Abuja within seven days, but his stay was extended to two weeks and it was becoming embarrassing to handle. There were movements from one clinic to another outside Mainz and I was becoming agitated about what was happening. Nigerian Intelligence Agency (NIA) colleagues were seeking information about the President's health, but nothing was being made available to them due to the confidential nature of the treatment, in accordance with medical ethics worldwide. It was clear that all our telephones were being monitored by the security staff of the President, and I decided to limit my movements and stayed with Ambassador Ghali Umar, the state chief of protocol (SCOP). President Yar'Adua seemed to be very kind, as he was always asking me about the welfare of the staff attached to the delegation and hoped that we were treating them well.

The Nigerian community in Mainz planned a peaceful demonstration at the hotel to protest at poor hospital facilities in Nigeria and wanted to hand over a protest letter to the President to call upon him to improve health facilities at home instead of coming to Germany for medical treatment. While we recognised their rights to peaceful assembly, including demonstration, we had to use all sorts of skills and dissuaded them from their action by asking them to pray for the President's health. I visited the President every other day in the clinic until he was discharged to the hotel. President Yar'Adua was in high spirits, jovial and strong minded and always dishing out orders by receiving and sending out messages to Vice-President Goodluck Jonathan, every day. That was why I was surprised that he was not doing the same thing when he was flown to Saudi Arabia, which confirmed to me that the situation was grave, and the end was near.

There were several goodwill messages sent to him through me and I dutifully relayed them through Major Mustapha Oneveta, the ADC. The Libyan Ambassador in Berlin, with whom I had served in Vienna, sent a bouquet of flowers to the President from Muammar Gaddafi and was duly acknowledged. President Köhler also sent goodwill messages to him through me.

During one of my visits to President Yar'Adua, he thrilled us by telling the story of his older brother, the previously-mentioned Major-General Shehu Musa Yar'Adua, who brought a form seeking a plot of land in

Lagos when their father was the Minister for Lagos Affairs in the first republic. According to him, Shehu Musa Yar'Adua told his son to take the forms to queue up like others at the land registry and never to use him to get a plot of land for himself in Lagos. He considered that a conflict of interests and asked if it could ever happen in the Nigeria of today. He said he wished those good old days could return to the Nigeria of today, but corruption would not allow it.

The President finally left Germany in early June 2009 after about sixteen days. I was not sure of his health was better or worse, as the yellow spots on his face and neck had increased. I believed it was worse; some German surgeons had told me that as the number of spots increased on the surface, they affected the internal organs and were life-threatening as well.

Barely thirty minutes into the flight, the pilot of the presidential plane telephoned me to say that they were having trouble flying over Switzerland and Italy and wanted urgent intervention with the German authorities to help. Luckily, I was still on the airport premises and within ten minutes I had contacted the diplomatic protocol section and launched a request with them for the President's plane to fly through Italy and Switzerland, and our request was promptly granted.

The issue of clearance for aircraft overflying other countries was always a problem with our diplomatic missions because due to security implications, the requests were often made very late and often at weekends when the host foreign offices were closed with only skeleton services, if any. In both Germany and Austria where I served, there was no problem with civilian planes, only military ones. Our presidential planes were classified as civilian planes even though piloted by air force personnel, so they did not require overflight clearance. The countries beyond Germany and Austria were not within our jurisdiction, but nevertheless it was our responsibility to ensure free passage of the President leaving our shores. That experience of staying a little longer at the airport after seeing off departing senior officials or foreign visitors was one of the lessons I learned through the years from my bosses, because if anything went wrong they could return to the airport.

I had the feeling that it was the last time President Yar'Adua would visit Germany for medical treatment. That was proved right, as on 18 August 2009, after a meeting with German officials to sign the MOU on Energy Partnership between Nigeria and Germany at Aso Rock Villa, the President left the country for Umrah in Saudi Arabia and medical check-ups. At first I was told he had left for Germany and I became confused since I was still in Abuja, until it became clear that he was in Saudi Arabia. I concluded that the end was near as there was no way the President, with over twenty years' medical records in Germany, would start all over again in Saudi Arabia, which had poorer medical facilities. The President's aides or close associates cashed in on his health problems by playing the scene in the American movie, "Weekend at Bernie's" where they pretended that a dead rich man was still alive and moved him around like a puppet. What happened thereafter is now history as amply reported by Olusegun Adeniyi, the Presidential adviser on information. President Goodluck Jonathan took over as President in February 2010 and Yar'Adua died at the presidential residence in Abuja on May 5.

The Nigerian Community in Germany

The Nigerian Community Germany (NCG), an umbrella organisation of all Nigerians resident in Germany was moribund just as it had been in Austria when I served there. An attempt was made by my predecessor, Professor Tunde Adeniran, to resuscitate it before my arrival. The Nigeria in Diaspora Organisation (NIDO) as well as the Nigerian professionals' organisation in Germany, were active and both organisations welcomed me with receptions and dinner, but the NCG was not so organised. Instead they were organised on ethnic lines and we had to resuscitate them under one strong umbrella. We encouraged them by attending their functions and vice versa and we found them useful. We made it a duty to host any Nigerian ministers, CEOs of MDAs and National Assembly members on a visit to Berlin at the residence and invited the Nigerian community to interact with them on developments at home. I found such interactions very useful and they were also appreciated by the NCG, as well as our visitors, who used the occasions to inform them of what they were doing at home.

Similarly, the African group of ambassadors was very active as it offered a platform for us to deal with the host country as a group in addressing common problems of Africans in Germany. The Moroccan ambassador, although not a member of the AU, always coordinated the activity of the group and did it very well. African Day on May 25, annually commemorating the founding of the OAU in 1965, was often celebrated with a reception and a football match between African embassies and the German Foreign Office and was always well attended. At the football match in

2010, the visiting Ethiopian minister, the President of Togo and German President were the special guests of honour. It was full of fun and fulfilled the adage that "All work and no play makes Jack a dull boy".

The year 2010 was departure time from Berlin as well as my exit from the Foreign Service. It was also the year my chairmanship of Working Group A of CTBTO would end and be renewed, if I was still available for re-election. Of course, I was still available, as it was a soft landing for me. The delegates were favourably disposed to renewing my tenure by two years, but without assurance for continued funding by Abuja, I decided to decline re-election. I blamed that decision on myself because I had never made a formal request for renewing my re-election as I thought it would not be approved. Unknown to me, Abuja had given approval for me to continue even after retirement with assurance of funding but had mistakenly forwarded the message to the permanent mission of Nigeria in New York. Accordingly, both Vienna and Berlin were unaware of that development until I had relinquished the position to the Brazilian Ambassador in Vienna.

Before I left Berlin and left the Foreign Service, there were developments that still stick to my mind. I had an appointment to bid farewell to the German president (Horst Köhler) on 30 May 2010 and a week before that he invited several ambassadors to a meeting at his official residence at Schloss Bellevue on an issue very dear to his heart, the continuation or otherwise of his African Partnership Forum, which was last held in Abuja on 7-8 November 2008. The meeting deliberated on the outcome of these meetings, two in Africa (Ghana and Nigeria) and two in Germany.

At the end of the meeting he asked me about the health of my president, and recounted his visit to Lagos and Kano. He also asked me about the symbolic gift of a horse presented to him by the Emir of Kano, Ado Bayero. He also made references to the traffic flow in Lagos, how state roads merged into federal roads and created traffic jumps with negative consequences to commercial activities in the city. At the end of the encounter he said he would meet me the following week during my farewell bit to continue that conversation. He had also scheduled a visit to one of the states with ambassadors, to which I was invited, a day after. It was an annual ritual for him to tour a state with all the ambassadors accredited to Germany once a year. But surprisingly, that evening he resigned his presidency over a remark he made while visiting German troops in Afghanistan. President Köhler was only one year into his second four-year term and was very popular both in Germany and abroad, particularly in Africa. But the "people's president" came under fire for comments in which he linked military involvement in Afghanistan with German economic interests. Since the German involvement in Afghanistan was very unpopular, any justification, however misquoted, proved embarrassing to the centre right government. He was succeeded by Christian Wulff, governor of Lower Saxony who later resigned over corruption charges involving a dubious home loan as well as attempt to stop the story from being published.

These resignations showed that transparency in governance is a virtue worth emulating by African leaders. They were service to the people and country and not for personal gain.

I was one of the first ambassadors to meet and bid farewell to Christian Wulff, who assured me that he would continue to pay attention to African affairs issues like his predecessor. But he did not have the time to do so as he resigned abruptly because of corruption allegations against him when he was the Minister President (Governor) of Lower Saxony.

The Significance of Diplomatic Gifts

Before departing from Berlin, the German Foreign Office gave a farewell luncheon for me and some of my colleagues and chief executives of many German companies with business links to Nigeria. As usual with such occasions, the luncheon was rounded off with a gift from the Foreign Secretary which was well wrapped. Due to previous experiences I never opened gifts until I got back to my private room, in case they were not amenable to me. Ayo Ayodele, (later Ambassador to Greece) signalled to me to open it, but I declined. As we got back to the office, I thought that it would be something worth keeping, but it turned out to be disappointing. It was a beautifully modelled ornamental porcelain pig with an equally beautiful supporting base. I am sure it cost them a fortune, but a pig in any form or symbol is not acceptable to me and there was no way I could display it anywhere in my house due to my faith. I was in a dilemma wondering what to do with it. I could not return it to them as it could be misunderstood, so I decided to take it home and Halima advised me to put it in a trunk rather than display it. Instead we ordered a good painting of the "Brandenburger Tor" (Berlin gate) to replace the gift and displayed it along the ones given to me from other posts.

I wish to make references to King Abdullah II of Jordan's lessons in diplomacy and gift giving during his visit to North Korea in his book "Our Last Best Chance". When he arrived in North Korea before he became king, during a formal dinner, one of the North Korean generals leaned over to him and asked, "what gifts are you going to give the great leader?" The future king said, "I have brought a clock, a traditional Jordanian dagger and a gift box from my wedding". The general nodded his approval, but not long after midnight there were twenty officers returning to ask for more detail on each of the gift items. "What is the meaning of the clock?" asked one of them. The future king said that he remembered the basic rules of diplomacy, which was to make up some incoherent explanation, and he told them "the clock signifies the precious time my father and the Great Leader spent together at Tito's funeral and the time that had passed since then". The North Korean generals nodded and were scribbling notes. He further told them, "The dagger is a gift from one warrior to another". The generals further asked, "and the wedding box was for what?" He explained, "I look at the Great Leader as a father and so this gift from my recent wedding is from a grateful son", and the generals nodded and left him. This routine was played back again during the exchange of the gifts with the Great Leader and the future King of Jordan said he barely remembered what he had earlier told the generals for fear of contradiction.

I believe that gifts are an important ingredient of diplomatic relations which should take into consideration the sensitivity of all the parties involved if they are to be appreciated and to be used for good effects. The porcelain pig given to me by Berlin has never seen the light of day since it was presented to me with such fanfare by the German State Foreign Secretary. I did not ask them the significance of giving me the pig. I believe that the protocol department could have done a better job as they do with meals or food allergies at diplomatic functions to avoid disappointment of this sort.

President Olusegun Obasanjo's Private Visit to Berlin

Former President Olusegun Obasanjo visited Berlin on a private visit at the invitation of Peter Aigin, the founder of Transparency International, less than a month before I left Berlin. Although I had met President Obasanjo and even dined with him several times, I never had close contact with him, nor liked him. However the visit became very important to me as it changed my perception of the former President. Although he appointed me Ambassador in two key diplomatic posts, Vienna and Berlin, without knowing me in person, I never had a personal liking for him. This was because I had read his first book entitled "My Command".

Chief Obasanjo compounded this dislike for during the ill-fated third-term saga. When the Nigerian senate threw out the bill on a third term bid, my office erupted in jubilation, including clerks, secretaries and messengers who were watching the debate live on television. On his arrival at the Berlin Tegel airport, his special assistant told President Obasanjo, "This is the Ambassador who condemned the use of 'Keke-Napep' as reported in the This Day Newspaper". I granted an interview to Juliana Taiwo, a reporter from 'This Day' newspaper, in which I condemned the policy of using 'Keke Napep' for transportation because they were being faced out in Pakistan and India, which restricted them to a few urban centres, but it was being introduced in Nigeria with a fanfare during his administration. The Keke-Napep was launched by President Obasanjo before he left office. I condemned the scheme due to my experience with it in Karachi, Pakistan when I was the consulate-general. It was called "Rickshaw" in Karachi or "Maruwa" in Lagos and was being phased out and confined to regional capitals and banned in the capital city of Islamabad, yet Nigeria was introducing it as a means of transportation, even in the twenty-first century.

In a chat with me before he left Berlin, President Obasanjo said that although he recycled some of his friends or their families into government during his time, he believes that there were many talents all over the country to be hunted and exploited for the benefit of the country. He condemned the excessive reliance on those people who were well known, forgetting that there were more qualified Nigerians that were not known either at home or abroad. Those remarks and many others endeared him to me and changed my negative perception of him. I was also surprised by a letter of commendation signed by him to me after the visit, making a total of seven such letters hanging on the wall of my living room.

Diplomatic service to me was full of challenges, risks, opportunities, benefits and rewards, and I never regretted enlisting in the Nigerian Foreign Service. I was one of the few in recent years to be appointed as Ambassador at different times in three very important capitals, Lusaka, Vienna and Berlin as well as in Karachi as head of the consular post.

A British former Ambassador remarked that diplomatic service to him was like Christmas every day; and so to me it was like Sallah or Eid every day.

CHAPTER 13

AN OVERVIEW OF THE NIGERIAN FOREIGN SERVICE

"Diplomats are just as essential to starting a war as soldiers are to finish it. You take diplomacy out of war and the thing would fall flat in a week."
Will Rogers, 1879-1935.

"Our experience is not just our own property, it must be shared."
Ela Ramesh Bhatt (born September 1933)

"Once the Xerox copier was invented, diplomacy died."
Andrew Young (born 1932)

"I was never the diplomatic diplomat."
Adolfo Aguilar Zinser (1949-2005)

———∞———

The conduct of foreign policy must be done by an efficient and strong Ministry of Foreign Affairs. Before I delve into the functions of the Ministry, there is the need to examine the concept of the Nigerian foreign policy. Basically, a country's foreign policy is the interests the country seeks to promote and protect in the international arena. According to the 1999 Constitution of the Federal Republic of Nigeria (as amended), there are five main foreign policy objectives which the country had been pursuing with minimal changes since independence from Britain in 1960. These were as follows:

a) Promotion and protection of the national interest
b) Promotion of African integration and support for African unity
c) Promotion of international cooperation, consolidation of universal peace, and elimination of discrimination in all forms
d) Respect for international law and treaty obligations
e) Promotion of a just world economic order.

In the pursuit of these objectives, our domestic policy has overriding influence on our foreign policy in accordance with the maxim that a country's foreign policy reflects her domestic policy. This had been reflected on the contributions of Nigeria to the debates and treaties the country signed with other countries bilaterally and multilaterally, especially at the OAU (now AU), ECOWAS and the United Nations. Consequently, there had been cases of the "Boomerang Effect" in which the international arena had influenced our domestic policy in the fields of economic, environment, human rights, women and children matters.

To implement these objectives, there was a need to put in place efficient machinery to implement and pursue our foreign policy to the benefit of the country. In this connection, the Ministry of Foreign Affairs should be well-focused and well-funded with clear functions that are implementable. But what are the functions of the Nigerian Foreign Ministry? According to the handover notes by General Ike Nwachukwu for the incoming Minister, Ambassador Matthew T. Mbu (now late) in January 1993, as well as by the final report of the reforms process of the MFA in 2007, the MFA was said to have the following functions, among other things:

a) Conduct government business relating to the operation and the management of international affairs.

b) Offer advice to government on issues relating to foreign affairs and international matters of specific and general interest to the government and peoples of Nigeria.

c) Collect and collate information about other countries in areas of interest to Nigeria with the aim of enhancing better understanding between Nigeria and other countries.

d) Represent and protect Nigeria's national interests at international and regional organisations such as the UN, OAU (now AU), Commonwealth, and NAM.

e) Handle consular matters, including protection of the interests of Nigerians abroad as well as taking a conciliatory role between our nationals and their hosts in economic, social and cultural fields.

f) Coordinate arrangements for international conferences, workshops and seminars on bilateral issues.

g) Collect and disseminate information on Nigeria's economic potentials for prospective foreign investors.

h) Take responsibility for the cooperation of Joint Economic Commissions and negotiate together with relevant ministries and departments terms of agreements with other countries.

i) Cater for diplomatic mails between Nigeria and missions abroad.

j) Establish and service Nigeria's diplomatic and consular missions abroad.

k) Coordinate and render consular and other logistical support services with MDAs on pilgrimage matters.

l) Arrange receptions and programmes for foreign official visitors to Nigeria.

m) Handle relations with diplomatic corps and international organisations in Nigeria.

n) Be responsible for the repatriation of destitute Nigerians abroad.

o) Train Nigerian officials for diplomatic and consular duties at home and abroad.

p) Offer technical assistance under the Technical Aid Corps Scheme.

q) Negotiate technical assistance from other countries and international agencies to Nigeria.

r) Maintain relations with the Commonwealth and its Agencies.

s) Handle and offer advice on refugees and humanitarian assistance in line with the United Nations Guidelines.

t) Mobilize and utilize Nigeria's human resources in the Diaspora.

u) Facilitate the acquisition and the use of technology for the rapid development of Nigeria.

I never kept a diary of the events reported in these memoirs. They have all been described from recollections, although I had a few copies of reports on important issues which I prepared alone or in consultation with others as well as using the internet facilities for reality checks for names of people, events and their dates. It is on record that there had been several policy reversals or changes that either improved or enhanced the Nigerian foreign service while others were inimical to it.

When I transferred from the Plateau State service to the MEA in 1982 there was a report of the panel on the reforms of the foreign service by Patrick Bolokor. The panel made recommendations which were approved by President Shagari in Council with enhanced conditions and remunerations with different rates of allowances for married and unmarried officers. The report also provided allowances for children of officers up to four and under the age of 18 years old. Health and educational supplements were also limited to this category of children. This policy posed problems and some officers tended to use unconventional methods to escape or circumvent the regulations. Some unmarried officers registered themselves as married, and those without children adopted some. Those with children 18 years and above had difficulties caring for them in colleges and universities. I had an experience in taking unilateral action as the head of mission in Berlin to assist a senior officer whose child was over 18 years old but was facing a life-threatening mishap due to the exorbitant bills for hospitalization. With a good explanation on humanitarian reasons, headquarters approved my action and continued to render assistance to the officer, whose child later died from the accident.

With the increase in the number of female officers in the Service, strong arguments were made for equal pay for equal work of equal value to improve the allowances of officers, whether they were single or married, men or women. That was done through the consolidated salary and allowances of all officers in the Federal Civil Service, which also applied to foreign service officers. That was part of the reform programme of the Obasanjo administration, in which I played a partial role.

There was also the difficulty of interpretation of headquarters circulars in different missions. I recall that while serving in Geneva there were different applications on the shipment of personal effects compared with that of our mission in Berne in the same country. Those in Berne were better remunerated than those of us in Geneva in the allocation of resources for the shipment of personal effects. There was also a discrepancy in the currency used in the payment of allowances for some missions. While the directive was to make payments in US dollars to officers in all missions, some missions continued to make payments in local currencies to better their earnings due to the differential rates of currency exchanges. I was one of those who wrote to defend payments in local currencies in those countries with convertible currencies, especially in Europe, but it was rejected. The decision to make payments in US dollars in all countries adversely affected our missions in Europe, which saw earnings eroded or fluctuated by the falling rate of the US dollar. I visited my former boss in Berne, Ambassador Ola Moshood Abiola (now late) who was the brain behind the new decision to pay allowances in US dollars. He lamented to me about his allowances, which were much lower than those of his predecessor, Ambassador Saad Abubakar, a non-career appointee who was receiving his allowances in Swiss francs. I reminded him that some of us advised against paying allowances to officers in US dollars instead of local currencies, especially in Europe, but he rejected our advice. With the introduction of the euros in EU countries, we further advised that officers in Eurozone countries should receive their allowances in Euros, but that too was not acceptable to MFA. While I was in Vienna and Berlin I was informed that some missions were receiving their allowances in euros, but there was no approval for us to do the same.

One other crucial matter was the ceiling for educational supplements for children under the age of 18 in non-English speaking countries. Apart from a stint of few months in Zambia, all my postings were in non-English-speaking countries, so I had wide experience in the application of this directive, parts of which were conflicting. In Brussels, my boss (the late Joshua Iroha) agreed that since there was no school in Brussels that conformed to the ceiling, our children should attend schools without recourse to the ceiling on educational supplements and he even added an item (transportation) that sent the school fees much higher than the approved ceiling. I had the same experience in Geneva, Vienna and Berlin. But that decision was not complied with by some missions, depending on how the Head of Chancery and heads of mission interpreted the circular.

I recall an incident on or before 28 August 2003 on the eve of my departure from Vienna, when I ran into stormy waters with my officers when I discovered that some of them had decided to register their children in the most expensive schools in Vienna instead of Danube International School or Vienna International School, where most UN and missions staff in Vienna send their children, including me. Their arguments were that their children had US nationality, so they should attend the American International School, which was very expensive compared to comparable schools in Vienna. There were other officers who did not have school-age children and could not accept that the meagre resources available to the mission should be used for paying fees at their own expense. The fallout from that encounter resulted in a further stringent circular from headquarters compelling the officers to withdraw their children and conform to the directive, which was still difficult for them.

Ratifications of Treaties, and Voting Patterns

Due to my relatively long sojourn in the International Organisations department (IOD) and multilateral diplomacy I witnessed some embarrassing incidents, some of them due to the manner Nigeria ratified international instruments without considering their binding obligations and responsibilities. Nigeria is a signatory to several international human rights instruments without reservations to their application in conformity to her national legal instruments. But most UN member countries tended to ratify these instruments with reservations on those articles or paragraphs that were incompatible with their domestic legal instruments. My view is that before a treaty is signed and/or ratified, it should be examined side by side with our relevant domestic legal instruments. That is the only safeguard allowing us to wriggle or escape from international instruments when there are conflicts of interest.

Nigerian voting patterns at UN resolutions seemed to have been very consistent over the years, especially at the UNGA and the UN Commission on Human Rights, even though there were a few cases which were handled by junior officers without clear directives from headquarters. Some of our decisions were made in solidarity with the African group or G77 and China and at times the Non-Aligned Movement (NAM), such as the resolution on the US embargo against Cuba. But on Palestinian resolutions we were guided by the well-known position of Nigeria on decolonization and the rights of peoples to self-determination. Although we called for a two-state solution between Israel and Palestine to exist side by side in peace and secured borders, we believed that the State of Israel already existed. But the Palestinians were still struggling to have their own state, even though they rejected it in 1948, so we always voted in favour of their resolutions claiming their right to self-determination. Nigeria always voted in favour of the Palestinian resolutions, including those on human right questions. This consistent policy was well known and acknowledged, and it was also taken for granted. But for reasons unknown to us in the IOD, the Nigerian delegation at the Third Committee abstained in the resolution in 2005. The reaction from the Arab delegation was dramatic. The Ambassador of Egypt called on me at my office in Abuja wanting to know if there was a shift of policy by Nigeria in supporting the fight of the

Palestinians for self-determination.

I could not understand what had happened in New York and I believed that if urgent steps were not taken the same thing would be repeated at the UNGA when the report of the Committees was presented for action, with negative consequences for Nigeria within the G77 and China. Our preliminary investigation indicated that it was someone from the presidency who was attending the UNGA who had cast the vote, saying that Nigeria should show neutrality in accordance with the "secular" nature of our constitution. But the Palestinian issue was not religious; it was the issue of their right to self-determination and against human rights violations. I decided to get a presidential directive to send a telegram to all our missions as well as New York and Geneva that our policy had not shifted. I drafted a memo for President Obasanjo, which the HMFA took by hand, and it was promptly approved with a directive that Nigeria should reverse the damage already done at the Third Committee of the UNGA and that in future Nigeria should stand by the Palestinians in their struggle for self-determination. This incident brought to light the kind of confusion often made in assuming that all Palestinians were Muslims while the Jewish state of Israel were Christians. In fact, the Israelis are not Christians but Jewish, while there are as many Christians as Muslims among the Palestinians. The first Palestinian Liberation Organisation leader was George Abbas, who was a Christian. So the issue of religion was immaterial in our support for the Palestinian quest for self-determination.

As Nigeria signed and ratified UN treaties, conventions and protocols, I wondered whether the instruments of ratification considered their provisions vis-à-vis the Nigerian Constitution and Nigeria national interest. All the UN treaties, conventions and protocols we ratified were without reservation on any article to exempt their application to some of our peculiarity as a Federal Republic. These issues manifested during the military regime as the actions of government seemed to have violated the provisions of the International Covenant on Civil and Political Rights. It also violated the African Charter on Human and People's Rights as well as the International Covenant on Economic, Social and Cultural Rights. The Treaties have obligatory periodic reporting on their implementation, but Nigeria always reneged on or delayed such reporting as it was getting more burdensome with the increasing number of treaties, conventions and protocols she was signing and ratification as a matter of prestige without recourse to their consequences. The periodic report to the CERD which we presented with Uchenna Gwam in 1993 was never reported until 2006, after I returned to the IOD. As Nigeria ratifies so many treaties, she should also plan properly to get her nationals elected into their Treaty bodies as independent experts, as was the case with many countries.

What Do Diplomats Do, and is it a Worthwhile Career?

Was diplomatic service worthwhile as compared to other services, I was often asked? My answer would be yes of course, but there are risks as well as opportunities. It is an elitist service, full of protocol, and hierarchical in form and content or practice. Some of my colleagues died during their service. Some died during the Lebanon wars, and a close friend of mine from Plateau State perished in Somalia; others got dismissed or removed from the service for very trivial offences of commission or omission, as almost happened to me with the wrong payment to ISBA, Jamaica which I mentioned earlier.

But what do these ambassadors do that attracts more headline news than any other service, even more than military services? I asked this as my concluding question because during the period when Nigeria was under sanctions and suffering pariah status, a politician very close to the military regime invited me to his hotel suite in Abuja. The man, from all indications, did not sound as if he had been educated beyond secondary school. The man stunned me when he asked what ambassadors do at missions abroad, as he wanted to tell the head of state, General Sani Abacha, to appoint him as an ambassador. He said he liked the title very much to add to his chieftaincy titles, honorary doctorate degrees, Alhaji etc to enhance his status in the society. I told him that the work of an ambassador is like that of military commanders in a war zone. While the military use force to achieve their objectives of defending their country's national interest, the Ambassador is also the commander in the field in defending Nigerian national interests but using negotiation, conciliation and arbitration to achieve the same or even better results. I told him that apart from the glamour, wining and dining, there were also risks and obligations he must abide by in accordance with the laws of both the sending and receiving states. I said he must protect and defend the interests of his country but with due respect to the laws of the receiving states. As ambassadors extraordinary and plenipotentiary protecting the interests of their countries, they were expected to represent their countries in the receiving states. I told him that it was the most important job he could do, and to notify his host whenever he was travelling out of that country through a *note verbal* with copies sent to all his colleagues in that country specifying the dates of his departure and return to post. I said an ambassador was also expected to foster and deepen the good relationship subsisting between the two countries through his actions. He or she was also expected to explore trade, commercial, cultural and investment opportunities between the two countries. Apart from these he should deal with the welfare of Nigerians living or passing through the country of his accreditation, particularly issuing assistance, consular help, visas and passports. The ambassador was also to engage in the negotiation of bilateral treaties between the two countries, considering the interests of his country. He was also expected to render periodic reports on political, economic and cultural developments in his country of accreditation to headquarters in the form of dispatches.

The High Chief, who also doubled as Alhaji and Dr, which were prefixed to his name on his business card, asked me if he would be assisted by officers in the Embassy with "all this long list of responsibility considering my old age". I assured him that there would be career officers to work with him and that if he chose less taxing missions he would not have difficulty in discharging these functions. I then cautioned him that if he was sent to a crisis-prone country he might find his life cut short, as this had happened with some of my colleagues. The High Chief interrupted me to say that he would choose London, Paris or Washington and nowhere else. I asked him if he spoke a foreign language such as French and he looked at me with amazement as if I did not come from this planet, being a Nigerian. We joked over this matter when I told him that these countries must accept his nomination in the form of an agremént before he would be posted, as they could reject his appointment. I left him bemused by his ambition, which was not accomplished, as General Sani Abacha died, and he could not realize his dreams.

I was not surprised that when President Olusegun Obasanjo appointed ambassadors in 1999 and 2003 there were more non-career officers, mostly politicians to give jobs to party supporters, than career officers, and only a few of them did the real job of promoting and protecting Nigerian interests abroad. I almost lost my well-deserved appointment in 1999 due to the struggle by politicians to grab the title regardless of what they would do with it. Interestingly, I was saved from that ordeal by Bagudu Hirse, who was the person who encouraged and facilitated my entry into the Foreign Service in the first place. He was assisted by Ambassador Magdiel Geno Supo Samaki, then the Chief of Protocol to Vice President Atiku Abubakar, or else I would have lost my appointment to a politician from my state. It is gratifying to note that the administration of Goodluck Jonathan has swung the pendulum in favour of career Foreign Service officers over non-career. It was hoped that this would be sustained, but unfortunately that changed during the administration of President Muhammadu Buhari, where there were more non-career ambassadors.

The most common questions I was asked as I was about to retire from the Foreign Service were as follows: Would you choose to be a diplomat, if you were given another chance to do so? Is diplomacy still relevant today in the face of globalization and improved technology? Which post(s) gave you the greatest challenges and job satisfaction? What will you do after retirement? These were the weighty questions most of us face after thirty-five years globe-trotting around the world wearing well-tailored designer suits and ties and riding in luxurious Mercedes Benz cars. If you were lucky you would retire with a Mercedes or two, or the equivalent, as I did at reduced prices in Berlin, thanks to the Diplomatic Sales Department of the Daimler-Benz company. That often gave the wrong impression of the Diplomatic Service and its worth in the larger society. I will briefly say that diplomacy is still as relevant today as it was practised in the traditional way, despite the advent of globalization. The subjects of diplomacy have invariably changed, such as climate change, terrorism, drugs and crime, globalization and technology and faster communication through the internet, but they have not replaced traditional diplomacy. They only enhanced or compounded the practice of diplomacy by enabling decisions to be made much faster, more easily, or more difficult, than hitherto.

I have also noticed that morals in the Nigerian foreign service have fallen very low due ostensibly to the continuing multiplicity of non-career appointees as ambassadors. It was better under the Goodluck Jonathan administration, where career foreign service officers were more numerous than non-career appointees as ambassadors. That improvement had been put asunder under the Muhammadu Buhari administration, when it was 50-50 between career and non-career appointees. I strongly believe that such a scenario would lower the quality of our diplomatic practice. There was no doubt that there have been many non-career appointees who have brought value to the practice of Nigeria's diplomacy, but their number should be curtailed and limited to key posts to get the best out of their expertise and not just to fulfil some political permutation and combination.

I wish to end by remarking and sharing a view like that of the US army officer who said that "if I had to do it again, I would do it the same way. I would just put more time and resources into getting the public diplomacy part much stronger than I was able to." If I had the chance to do it again, I would do the same thing.

The following are letters of commendation to the author

MINISTRY OF FOREIGN AFFAIRS
OFFICE OF THE PERMANENT SECRETARY
ABUJA

P.M.B. 130, Garki
Telephone: 5230210
Telefax: 5230394

Ref. No: PSO/C. 353/127

Date: 29 Dec. 2006

Amb. A. B. Rimdap,
Director (IOD)
MFA,
Abuja.

COMMENDATION

I wish to convey the appreciation and gratitude of the Honourable Minister and Honourable Minister (State), Foreign Affairs for your invaluable contribution towards the organisation of the Africa-South America Summit, as well as the meeting of the Peace and Security Council of the African Union which held from 26 – 30 November, 2006.

2. In spite of some initial hitches, your contribution and those of other colleagues helped to ensure the success of the two Summits. I hope that future demands on your time and energy by the nation will be taken up by you with equal level of enthusiasm, zeal and commitment.

3. This letter is copied to be treated officially as a commendation.

4. Please accept my sincere thanks.

Amb. (Dr) Hakeem Baba-Ahmed, OON
Permanent Secretary

MINISTRY OF FOREIGN AFFAIRS
FIRST UNITED NATIONS DEPARTMENT
ABUJA

P.M.B. 130, Garki – Abuja
Tel. No. (09) 5230582
Fax: (09) 5230582
Telegram: External Abuja

Ref: Fa 61
Date: 17th July, 200?

His Excellency
Mr Abdul Bin Rimdap
Embassy of Nigeria
Vienna
Austria

LETTER OF COMMENDATION: ELECTION OF DR ADIGUN ADE ABIODUN AS COPUOS CHAIRMAN

As may be recalled the UN Committee for the Peaceful Uses of Outer Space (COPUOS) at its 46th Session which ended in Vienna on 20 June, 2003 unanimously elected our candidate, Dr Adigun Ade Abiodun, its Chairman for the biennium 2004-2005. Needless to say that the event was of immense historic proportion as this was the first time in 45 years of existence that the Committee had elected an African as Chairman.

2. The development is surely one more feather in the cap of our diplomacy at a time when our country seeks to project a viable profile in world affairs. The Honourable Minister is pleased at the positive and contributory role that the Ministry is playing in this regard. In particular, he has asked that his appreciation be conveyed for the commitment, diligence and active role that Your Excellency personally and your Mission played in ensuring the success of Dr Abiodun's candidature.

3. Very warm regards.

(Enny E Onobu)
for the Honourable Minister

CONFIDENCE IN DIPLOMACY

Olusegun Obasanjo

Agbe L'oba House, Quarry Road, Ibara
P. O. Box 2286, Abeokuta, Ogun State, Nigeria.

May 19, 2010

His Excellency,
Amb. Abdul Bin Rimdap,
Nigerian Ambassador to Germany,
Embassy of the Federal Republic of Nigeria,
NEbE JakobstraBe 4,
10179, Berlin,
Germany.
Email: abrimdap49@yahoo.com

Dear Ambassador,

LETTER OF APPRECIATION

On returning home, I hasten to write to thank you and your staff for the wonderful reception and hospitality accorded me during my last visit to Berlin, Germany, to attend the meeting organised by the Africa Progress Panel.

I congratulate you and your staff for the good work you are doing at the Embassy. More grease to your elbow.

Please, convey my thanks and appreciation to all your staff who made our visit so pleasantly memorable.

Once again, many thanks.

Yours Sincerely,

OObasanjo

OLUSEGUN OBASANJO

Tel: 234-39-722419, 2417731, 242005, 243547, 722741
e-mail: obasanjomg@yahoo.com

BIBLIOGRAPHY

Barber, Brian; *What Diplomats Do: The Life and Work of Diplomats Rowman and Littlefield,* 2014

Carrick, Sir Roger; *Diplomatic Anecdotage: Around the World in 40 years,* Elliots & Thompson 2012

Brigid, Keenan; *Diplomatic Baggage: The Adventure of a Trailing Spouse,* John Murray 2006.

Burney, Derek H; *Getting it done: A memoir*, McGill-Queen's University Press 2005

Cowper-Coles, Sherard; *Ever the Diplomat: Confessions of a Foreign Office Mandarin,* Harper Press 2012

Dobrynin, Anatoly; *In Confidence: Moscow's Ambassador to America's six Cold War presidents (1962-1995)*

Hannay, David; *New World Disorder,* Ibtauris & Co 2008

Levy, Gregory; *Shut up, I'm talking and other Diplomacy lessons I learned in the Israeli Government, A Memoir*, Free Press 2008

Marker, Jamsheed; *Quiet Diplomacy: Memoir of an Ambassador of Pakistan,* Oxford 2010

Murray, Craig; *Dirty Diplomacy*, Scribner 2006

Mumo, Alan; *Keep the Flag flying: A Diplomatic Memoir,* Gilgamesh Publishing 2012

INDEX

Abacha, Maryam, 161, 162, 165, 168, 170, 171, 175, 262

Abacha, Sani (Gen), 113, 127, 140, 142, 145, 146, 150, 153, 166, 168, 169, 170, 171, 172, 175, 236, 350

Abdulai, Yusuf, 9, 10

Abiodun, Adigun, 232

Abiola , Chief Moshood, 74, 76, 82, 85, 127, 138, 163, 173, 344

Abiola, Kudirat, 153

Abuah, Ejoh (Amb), 29, 36, 37, 127

Abubakar, Abdulsalami (Gen), 173, 191, 192, 215, 276, 287

Abubakar, Alhaji Ahmed, 96, 249

Abubakar, Atiku (Vice-P), 219, 352

Abubakar, Dahiru M, 139

Abubakar, Fate (male), 5

Abubakar, Fati (female), 168, 178

Abubakar, Mohammed Lamino, 3

ACP, 51, 52, 53, 55, 67, 68, 107, 109, 130

Adams, Aret, 13

Adamu, Dahiru, 204, 206, 207

Adedeji, Adebayo (Prof), 33

Adekeye, Olabode, 6, 17, 19, 74, 92

Adekuoye, Ade-, 6, 7, 11, 161

Adeniji, Oluyemi, 246, 265, 267, 269, 273, 279-281

Adeniran, Tunde (Prof), 299, 331
Adeniyi, Olusegun, 312, 330
Adeyanju, Kunle, 244, 273
Adiwu, Adamu, 2
Adwa, Battle of, 15, 43
Afolabi, Peter (Amb), 46
AFRC, 4, 77, 78, 146
African First Ladies Peace Mission, 162, 168, 175
African Partnership Forum, 332
Africa-South America Summit, 257-9
Agbamuche, Michael, 151
Aga Khan University Teaching Hospital, 188-9
Ahire, P. T., 276
Ahmadu Bello University, introduction, 4, 11
Ahmadu, Hamzat, 122
Ahmed, Kabir, 138
Ahmed, Ramatu, 139, 156, 160
Aigin, Peter, 336
Akadiri, Oladele, 275
Akanbi, Mustapha, 239, 243
Akinsanya, Olusegun, 239, 243, 259, 273
Akinyemi, Bolaji, 9, 82,
Akufo-Addo, Nana, 279,
Akumayo, Emmanuel, 253
Akume, George, 241
Al-Aqsa Mosque, 165, 262
Al-Arabi, Jalal, 149
Amnesty International, 140, 147, 149, 153

Ani, Olufemi, 6

Anigbo, Chike, 135, 244, 273, 297

Annan, Kofi Boutrous, 274-7, 285

Anne, Princess, 54

Anyanwu, Christina, 141

Anyaoku, Chief Emeka, 275, 287

Apata, Segun, 74, 114, 119, 130, 138, 139, 159, 163, 275

Araque, Ali Rodriguez, 219

Ashiru, Olugbenga, 160, 238, 274

Attah, Judith Sefi, (Ambassador), 74, 76, 86, 112, 117, 119, 120, 128, 136, 159, 161

Auta, Ibrahim, 142

Awani, Charles, 81

Ayewoh, Pius, 11, 143, 168, 171, 238

Ayodele, Ayo Lawrence, 303, 304, 306, 325, 334

Ayoko, Abel A, 206, 234

Azikiwe, Emeka Ayo (Ambassador), 92, 93, 105, 108, 138, 139

B

Baba-Ahmed, Hakeem, 243, 256, 267, 312,

Babangida, General Ibrahim, 59, 67, 71, 75, 77, 84, 86, 87, 96, 97, 119, 124, 127, 140

Bakassi Peninsula, 75, 80-83

Bala, Buhari, 247

Bala, Sani S, 259, 262

Barkin-do, Mohammed, 218

Bashir, Alhaji Mohammed, 57-59

Bell-Gam, Eric, 92
Bello, Buharo, 109, 149
Benibo, K W, 16, 20-21, 25, 59
Benti, Teferi, 16
Bilfinger Berger, 305, 311, 314
Blankson, Ampim Jim (Ambassador), 17, 24, 25, 27, 93
Boomgaarden, Georg, 310, 311
Boroffice, Robert Ajayi, 232,
Boyede, Adeboyega I., 46, 64, 175
Brill, Kenneth, 225
Buhari, Muhammadu (Gen), 4, 19, 37, 46, 66, 70, 352

C

Camara (Ambassador), 36
Cartagena des Indias, 95, 98-101
CD (Conference on Disarmament), 124, 228
CERD (Convention on Elimination of Racial Discrimination), 116, 122, 244, 266, 349
Chiluba, Frederick Jacob, 191, 193, 195, 196, 200
Chinade, Jibrin (Ambassador), 73, 88, 89, 138
Chinery-Hesse, Mary, 274
Chipare, Godfrey, 100
Chirac, Jacques, 255
Chissano, Joaquim, 31-32
CHOGM (Commonwealth Heads of Government Meeting), 145-147, 150, 154, 163, 167, 288
CHRI (Commonwealth Human Rights Initiative), 145, 149

Clark, Blessing Akporode, 4, 275
Cole, Dele, 194, 211, 212
Commonwealth Eminent Persons Group, 193
Comprehensive Safeguard Mechanism, 221, 223, 225
Congress of Vienna, 44, 203, 206, 215
COPUOS, 217, 231-234
Cowper-Coles, Sherard, 7, 371
CTBTO, Foreword, 98, 131, 217, 227-229, 295, 313-314, 332
CTC, 252-254
CWC, 123

D

Dahiru, Suleiman (Ambassador), 5, 71
Dalman, Ola, 229
De Klerk, Frederick F.W., 84
Defence Housing Authority, 169, 179, 187
Deme, Joseph Chuwang, 3
Dibie, Anthony, 46
Dikko, Umaru (Alh.) 37-41
Dimka, Ezekiel, 3
Diya, Oladipo, 140
Doe, Samuel (President), 77, 79
Dogonyaro, Laila, 160
Dombin, Danjuma, 3
Durlong, Ignatius, 1

E

ECA, 18, 2, 21, 24, 27, 29, 30-32, 36
EFCC, 237, 249, 250-254
Efretei, Kevin, 46, 72
Efreiti, Arit, 47
Egbe, Mark, 276
Egwa, Emmanuel, 139, 144, 151
Ehindero, Sunday, 149, 266
Ekaette, Ufot, 247
Elabor, Habeeb, 173
Elbaradei, Mohammed, 221, 222
Elegba, Shamsideen, 223, 254
Elias, Teslim O., 82
Elizabeth, Queen, 54
Ella, Akatu "Washington", 5
Emir of Kano, 323, 333
Emuchay, Okey, 207
Enikonlaiye, Sola, 74, 81
Ennaceur, Mohammed, 132, 133
Equatorial Guinea, 81
Esan, Remi, 159, 163, 189, 228
Eze, Mark (Ambassador), 72
Ezulwini, 56, 279, 284, 286, 288, 289, 293

F

Fabiola, Queen, 163
Fachano, Iliya, 249, 251

Falana, Femi, 143

Falase, Gabriel (Ambassador), 8, 73

Falashas, Ethiopian Jews, 41, 42, 48

Fall, Ibrahima, 115

Fernandez, Antonio Dehinde, 56

Ferrero-Waldner, Benito, 210, 213, 215,

Fourth World Conference on Women, Beijing, 156-162

G

G77, 95-96, 98, 102, 103, 107, 114, 115, 222, 225, 229, 236, 347, 348

G-8 Summit 304, 305, 306

Gambari, Ibrahim Agboola (Prof.), 27, 29, 30, 40

Gana, Jerry, 246

Gana, Lawal, 207, 246

Gaudeul, Yves, 255

Garba, Joseph Nanven, 4

Garba, Kabiru (Ambassador), 92

GATT, 92, 95, 105, 106-114

George, Femi (Amb.), 7, 74, 97

Germany, 203, 205, 225, 229, 272, 278, 285, 289, 290, 291, 296, 298-338

Ghali, Boutros-Boutros, 286

Gotip, Agwom G., 3

Guba, Lawan Gana, 246

Gubuchi, Aliyu Mohammed, 259

Gulf of Guinea Commission, 75, 81, 82, 257

Gwam, Cyril Uchenna (Uche), intro 1, 6, 105, 113, 117, 118, 119, 121, 123, 128, 150, 244, 349

H

Haider, Jorg, 213
Haak, Hein, 230
Hananiya, Haladu (Gen), 37, 38
Hannay, David, 294, 371
Hashemite, Kingdom of Jordan, 164
Hirse, Bagudu (Ambassador), 3, 309, 326, 352
Hussein, King, 164
Human Rights Council, 260, 277, 283
Hussein, Alhassan, 244
Hussein, Saddam (President), 90, 213

I

IAEA, 204, 216, 221-225, 233, 243, 255
ICCPR, 127, 140, 141, 144, 145, 146, 150, 151, 152
ICESCR, 140, 144
Ige, Bola, 166, 206
Ihim, Chukudi, 92, 94, 95
Ikimi, Tom, 97, 145, 146, 156, 160
Interim Govt. of National Unity, 126
IPU, 127
Iroha, Dorothy, 47

Iroha, Joshua (Ambassador), 46, 47, 49, 50, 53, 58, 61, 66, 345

Ironsi, Johnson Thomas (Junior), 178, 187

ISBA, 248, 249, 252

ISS, 2, 18, 47

Iyal, Shehu Usman, 322, 323

J

Jokonya, Tichaona (Ambassador), 34, 131, 231

Jenkins, Peter, 216

Jintao, Hu, 209

Jehangir, Soli, 149

Johnson, Prince Yormie, 78, 79

Jonathan, Goodluck (President), 182, 272, 328, 330, 352, 353

Jonathan, Patience, 314

Julius Berger, 305, 308, 311, 314, 319, 320, 322, 325, 326, 327

K

Kabiru, Muhammed, 149

Kadiri, Audu, 74, 163

Kaita, Muntari, 303, 315

Kangai, John, 194

Katz, Noam, 259

Kaunda, Kenneth, 193, 194, 195, 196, 201

Kaunda, Wezi, 193

Kayode, Adetokunbo (Prince), 317
Keshi, Joseph, 60, 62, 84
Keshi, Stephen, 62
Keynesian Theory, 6
Kida, Mustapha Musa, 109, 140
Kingibe, Baba Gana, Foreword, 127, 136, 138, 142, 177
Klitgaard, Robert, 9
Kodjo, Edem, 33, 34
Köhler, Horst, 303, 311, 313, 318-324, 328, 332, 333
Kolo, H.B., 2
Konare, Alpha Omar, 279, 306
Koroye, Philip Binye (Ambassador), 74, 76, 82
Kreusel, Dietmar, 295, 296
Kromah, Alhaji, 124

L

Lame, Ibrahim, 234
Lamido, Sule, 212, 215, 216, 234
Laose, Maria, 229
League of Nations, 92, 123, 215
Leopold II, King, 45, 63
Livingstone, David, 190, 197, 198
LNTG, 126
Lome Convention, 50-57, 67, 68, 107, 109, 130
Longjang, Ignatius, 3
Lukman, Rilwanu (Dr), 89, 217, 218, 219

M

Machel, Samora, 31, 32
Maduekwe, Chief Ojo, 306, 309, 312, 320, 321, 322, 325
Madueke, Diezani, 320, 321
Maina, Zainab, 160
Manzo, Ahmed Dauro, 12
Major, John, 147
Mamven, Jefferson Sindir, 3
Mandela, Nelson, 83, 85, 128, 129, 147, 296
Mariam, Mengistu Haile, 16
Merkel, Angela, 310
Marker, Jamsheed (Ambassador), 114, 371
Mbonu, Christy, 120, 168, 259
Mbu, Matthew T., 117, 127, 135
Metteden, Lamin, 275
Metternich, Klemens Wenzel von, 203, 205, 215
Military expenditures, 102
Mitee, Ledum, 151
Mohammed, Abdullahi Kaoje, 92, 95, 96, 106, 108, 109, 129
Mohammed, Ismael B. (Ambassador), 40, 42, 43, 71
Mohammed, Sani L., 206
MOSOP, 123, 133, 142, 151, 152
Moussa, Amre, 274
Muhammed, Safia, 172
Mukhtar, Ambassador, 221, 222
Munir, Lawal, 245

N

NADECO, 140, 148, 154, 163, 173
NANCA, 238, 240
Nanjira, Don, 132
NASCO Group Ltd, 253
Nasreddin, Ahmed Idris, 253
National Human Rights Commission, 111, 120, 154
NCG, 308, 331
N'diaye, Bacre Waly, 148
Nene, George (Ambassador), 71
NIDO, 331
Nigeria-Benin-Togo Co-Prosperity Alliance Zone, 256-157
Nigerian-German Energy Partnership, 310
NNPC, 7, 13
NNRA, 223, 254
Noor, Queen, 164
NPT, 102, 103, 223, 224, 225, 228, 260, 261
Nwachukwu, Ike Omar Sanda (General), 69, 75, 77, 80, 89, 97, 127, 144, 341
Nwokeabia, Roddy, 303
Nwokedi, Ogbuefi, 13
Nwosu, A.B.C., 209

O

Obasa, Daniel (Ambassador), 74, 81
Obasanjo, President Olusegun, 82, 140, 142, 191, 193, 201,

205, 211, 217, 218, 219, 232, 235, 246, 247, 248, 255, 265, 267, 270, 296, 300, 304, 309, 325, 336-338, 348, 352

Obasanjo, Stella, 205

Obodozie, Jonikull Onuorah, 138

Offor, Marius, 118, 119

Ogoni Four, 142

Ogoni Nine, 145, 148

Ogoni People, 121-123

Ogundele, Samuel (Ambassador), 71

Ogunnaike, Emmanuel Ademola (Ambassador), 72, 191, 200, 202, 249

Okafor, Chudi, 276

Okar, Godwin (Major), 142

Okaro, Columbus, 266

Okon, Bassey, 145

Okonjo-Iweala, Ngozi, 176, 245, 267, 269

Okwuaka, Godwin, 17, 19

Oladeji, B.D., 123, 124

Olisemeka, Ignatius (Ambassador), 4, 78, 80, 85, 165, 174

Ologun, Moses, 45

Olurin, Olatunji (Major-General), 124, 125

Oumaru, Ide 35

Omene, Scott (Ambassador), 60, 86, 92, 105

Omojokun, Solomon Kikiowo (Major-General), 31

Omoruyi, Omo, 240

Onemola, Rauf Bukun, 206, 221, 223

Oneveta, Mustapha (Major), 328

Ononaiye, Michael (Ambassador), 119, 266

Onobu, Enny (Ambassador), Introduction, 5, 30, 223, 233, 239, 320, 321,

Onu, Peter (Ambassador), 33, 34, 35

Opaleye-Majekodunmi, Jumoke J (Ms), 50

OPEC, 9, 10, 104, 204, 206, 217, 218, 219, 220

OPEC Fund, 10, 217

Opeloyeru, Hameed, 246

Operation Moses, 42

Organisation for African Unity, 19

Osakwe, Chiedu, 65, 105, 106, 128, 134

Oseni, Taofik, 304

Otuokon, Emmanuel, 74, 76, 80, 82

Otuyelu, Samuel, 150, 155, 160

P

Pam, John Wash, 2

Parasini, Christoph (Ambassador), 199, 211, 212

Peacebuilding Commission, 276, 277, 280, 283

Pelindaba Treaty, 228

Petra, 164-165

Philip, Prince, 54

Porbeni, Festus (Capt. N.N.), 8

PRC, 141, 143, 144, 145, 146, 150, 151

Preware, Godfrey B. (Ambassador), 212

Q

Quist, Dupe Adebiyi (Ambassador), 308

R

Rice, Susan, 113
Rights to development, 120, 132-136, 215
Rimdap, Abdallah, Introduction,
Rimdap, Halima Hajiya, Introduction, 92, 170, 185, 187, 313, 334
Rimdap, Ibrahim, Dedication, Introduction, 92,
Rimdap, Ishaq, 92, Introduction,
Rimdap, Yusuf, 45, 92, Introduction,
Rimdap, Ramallan, Introduction,
Rimi, Abubakar, 215

S

Sachs, Jeffrey, 277
Sahrawi Arab Democratic Republic (SADR), 33, 258
Salim, Ahmed Salim, 274
Sambo, Abubakar, 315
Sani, Hajo, 171
Sarkozy, Nicolas, 303
Saro-Wiwa, Ken, Foreword, 121-123, 134, 142-155
Sata, Michael, 195
Schmillen, Joachim, 300, 302, 310

Selassie, Emperor Haile, 15
Selchum, Binfa, 3, 128
Shagari, Shehu, 12, 19, 37, 71, 343
Samaki, M.G.S. (Ambassador), 352
Sharif, Nawaz, 187, 188
Sheni, Decent (Prof), 23
Sidi, Ladan, 139, 160, 303
Smith, Ian, 286
Sodipo, Tunde, 259
Starr, Richard, 229
Sulaiman, Oluwale, 119, 139

T

Tabi'u, Muhammad, 149
Takasu, Yukio, 295
Tanaka, Ambassador Akio, 295, 296
Tanko, Abubakar, 249
Tanzam Railways, 190, 196
Taylor, Charles, 77, 78, 79, 124
Thot, Tibor, 229
Touré, Sekou, 11, 12
Transparency International (TI), 184, 336

U

Udoh, Okon (Ambassador), 92, 95, 105
Uhomoibhi, Martin (Dr), 156

Ukaeje, Ngozi, 139, 160
Ukonga, Adenike, 160
Umar, Ghali (Ambassador), 327
Umar, Ibrahim, 222
Umar, Jonathan Kabo, 10, 204
UNCHR, 148, 153, 154, 201
UNCTAD, 92, 94, 95, 96, 98, 101, 102, 103, 107, 110, 114
UNCITRAL, 217
UNODC, 216
UNSC, 93, 95, 131, 225, 226, 248, 252, 253, 264, 269, 274, 278-292, 294, 295, 297
Usman, Bukar, 149, 152
Uwais, Mohammed, 158

V

VAMED, 210
Vatsa, Mamman (Gen), 142, 151, 152
Victoria Falls, 190, 197, 198

W

Wadibia-Anyanwu, Nkem, 139, 156, 168, 174, 248, 265, 267, 274, 275
Wahid, Abdurrahman, 220
Wali, Aminu, 290
Walibuta, Ken, 192
Walter-Steinmeier, Frank, 309, 310

Wase, Sulaiman Yero, 2
Wittmann, Hans, 305, 320
Williams, Aganga, 240
Willoughby, Korode (Ambassador), 60
Wolde, Goshu (Col), 29, 48
World Bank, 9, 34, 158
World Conference on Human Rights, 110, 114-118, 127, 132, 155, 167
World Conference on Women, 156-162
WTO, 51, 52, 92, 108, 109, 135
Wulff, Christian, 333, 334

Y

Yadudu, Auwalu Hamisu, 149, 150, 153, 154, 155, 266
Yalta Conference, 293
Yar'Adua, Shehu Musa, 140, 141, 142, 182, 304, 305, 306, 307, 309
Yar'Adua, Turai, 312, 313
Yar'Adua, Umaru Musa, 310, 312, 319-322, 324-334
Yom Kippur War, 33
Yudhoyono, Susilo Bambang, 220
Yumkela, Kamdeh, 227
Yunusa, A. Razaq (Ambassador), 89, 178

Z

Zuma, Nakasone Dhalamini, 35

www.ingramcontent.com/pod-product-compliance
Lightning Source LLC
Chambersburg PA
CBHW062040080426
42734CB00012B/2514